# loslogos™

# THE LOGO:
# TAKING STOCK.

by Roland Müller

How does logo design react to the sociological, cultural, economic and technological changes that define our time? This is an exciting question, as there is scarcely another expressive media tool better suited to measure the current climate than the trade mark. Omnipresent multinational brands versus local names. The ups and downs of the internet economy. Globalisation versus anti-globalisation. Widening credibility gaps in corporate America. Start-up euphoria and start-up crashes. Multi-ethnic cultural fusion versus national delimitation.

Post-modern and post-post-modern cultural trends. Patchwork technology, the assimilation and transformation of foreign materials. "The death of the author". Mechanical reproduction of artworks and thus the end of their authenticity in a classical sense. New viewing and perception habits. Virtuality versus reality. Hedonism versus fundamentalism. Life-style, the fun society and 'anything goes' versus the new seriousness. These are just some of the phenomena defining the current climate. Not a bad time to assess the state of the logo.

The LosLogos project.

" I can't understand why people are frightened of new ideas. I'm frightened of old ones," confessed John Cage – and thereby points out LosLogos' basic approach: curious about new ideas, new forms of expression and new approaches in the design world in general and, pertaining to the project, in logo design. That's why we initiated the LosLogos project.

LosLogos was conceived as a representative cross-section of contemporary logo design. It deliberately intends to be a platform for young global designers, focusing on aesthetic innovation in alternative fields: we want to find new trends and directions and lend them visibility. We want to record current trends and communicate them via images. We want to provide a kind of compendium – an orientation aid, reference work and source of inspiration, aimed not only at graphic designers, but anyone interested in contemporary cultural tendencies. This concept reflects our attitude to design and also plugs a gap in current design literature.

A book finds its authors.

Now the parameters are set. And what about the content? In this case the conventional approach, where an author looks for and finds a publisher who wedges the material between two covers, would of course not work. The opposite approach was the right one: we invited young designers from all over the world to submit their own trademark creations for the LosLogos project. And the response to our invitation was overwhelming.

And what did the feedback look like? What filled our mailboxes to the brim, 24 hours a day? Pictograms, typograms, lettering and entire thematic productions for all types of brands, companies, service-providers, non-profit-making organisations, own brands and clubs – from the local hairdressing salon via hip music labels to industrial multinationals. Trade marks of all shapes and forms, some conforming to CD rules, some not, provocative, hip-hoppy, retro, ironic, poetic, aggressive and fanciful; courting interest in restrained tones or 'shouting' for attention – in a word, a multivocal logo panorama for our times.

3500 pictographic signs of the times from 4 continents.

If we had included all submissions LosLogos would have become a weighty logo bible – an unrealistic project. And so we had to reduce, evaluate and structure. A difficult process (compulsive elimination can be painful!). At the end of the process LosLogos, with its 3,500 creations, was structured according to the following criteria:

Logos:
Pages 020 – 077

Pictographic logos
Iconographic logos
Ideographic logos
Illustrative logos

Lettering:
Pages 078 – 203

Type as type
Type as a brand
Pictorial type
Type as pictures

Typograms:
Pages 204 – 243

Type as type.
Type as a brand
Pictorial type
Type as pictures

Combinations:
Pages 244 – 329

Pictograms in which a new sign is created by combining logo and lettering with additional graphic elements.

Collected themes:
Pages 330 – 391

Thematic productions that cannot be allotted to one of the three previous, clearly defined categories.

Statistics:
Pages 392 – 403

Uses graphics to show the distribution of designers and studios across various geographical regions and their preference for the possible approaches.

The local hero.

Scene of crime: Shanghai, Nanjing Dong Lu, 2002: countless pennants in the characteristic blue-red combination of the 'for a new generation' brand of cola are fluttering on the Broadway of the Far East. A typical development: decades of being hermetically sealed against Western influence and the short, wild period of counter-revolution were followed by gradual demolition of the anti-capitalist Wall of China. The 'Paris of the Far East' slowly remembered its ambivalent past. And the Global Giants were the first to take over the newly opened spaces. But the more the big boys thrust ahead, the more difficult it becomes for the small fry – the local brands that give a cityscape its unmistakable character, making it identifiable, something you can experience. A lot of big cities tell the same story – especially in developing countries striving for progress.

We feel that a radical No Corporate Logo approach would be the wrong response to this development. All the more so as the local brands, as this book shows, are alive and kicking, and anyway it is entirely legitimate for multinational brands to conquer new markets, and consumers respond well to this, too.

Nevertheless, the "Local Hero" needs support. LosLogos, as a publication reflecting local trade marks, has launched a parallel initiative alongside this book: together with the Destruct office in Bern we set up a web portal for people from all over the world to post their favourite logos, making them accessible to anyone who is interested. This web portal is structured like a virtual LogoTown. You can walk around as long as you like and it is changing all the time.

Visitors are more than welcome at: www.loslogos.org

"Symbols are the doors we have to stride through."
Naomi Klein, "No Logo".

Faces in the crowd.

Everywhere we go, we are faced by brand symbols: in the street, in supermarkets and restaurants, reading the paper, watching television, visiting websites, on our mobile phone display, in the cinema, on sports fields and even in the theatre or concert hall, where the sponsor leaves us in no doubt about who we should thank for helping us to see the great actor or famous opera singer. Estimates suggest that every day 6,000 logos pass across our field of vision, trying to communicate their messages and tell us their stories.

Listen to me!

In Marcel Proust's main work "A la recherche du temps perdu", the repeat encounter of a sensual impression – like the fragrance of freshly-baked madeleines – triggers off memories of experiences linked with these impressions.

This example illustrates the way Corporate Communications managers and designers would like logos to work: they are intended to tell the stories the trade marks are built upon, in a greatly reduced form. The more positive the story, the more positively its recipients will anticipate it. Thus the value of a brand is shaped by the appraisal of its target group. The logo reproduces these ideas and reinforces the brand value. But the reverse also applies: if the public finds a story lacking in credibility, because of actual or alleged "Bad Corporate Behaviour", the entire brand may collapse, as some distinguished recent examples have proven.

But reactions of this kind – positive or negative – require one vital ingredient: perception! An author wastes his time if his story isn't read by anyone. A trade make that does not register on the scale of perception will struggle to survive. In the early days of industrialism the entrepreneurs simply put a picture of their factory on their letterheads as a company emblem, a sign easily identified by their clients and suppliers! And it conveyed a positive image, too: the captain of industry with the most chimneys belching out smoke had to be successful, and therefore a valuable business partner. Those were the days. Nowadays, the situation has become infinitely more complex: given the constant flood of signs and symbols at home in our real and media worlds, a brand symbol based on conventional ideas will do nothing to make its company stand out. But, on the other hand, creating an "ego-construct", a brand personality, has become essential for a brand's success, indeed for its survival.

There can be no argument about the value and significance of logos as part of the contemporary visual vocabulary. But it is possible to argue about their quality: you need a logo that is quickly identified because of its strikingly individual and above all positive qualities, and one that is correct in every particular way (colour, typeface, media presence). Only such a logo can truly tell its story and make people pay attention to it.

A short trip back to the beginning.

Signs are as old what they stand for. Ancient, in other words, if you think of cave paintings, smoke signals, markings, tribal signs, seals, coats of arms, branded signs, talismans, magic signs etc.

So what about the sign we focus on: the logo. Etymologically, in other words in terms of the origin of the word, logo must be related to logos, Greek for speech, work and language, defining the meaning

enshrined in the concept. An interesting analogy can be derived from this relationship: Heraclitus, the philosopher who worked in Ephesus around 500 BC, regarded logos as a force that creates an order and a structure in the flow of nature – in other words, something that helps us to make sense of nature. So we could say that 'our' logo lends meaning and form to the content it symbolises, thus structuring the world it represents: the logo helps us to make sense of things as well!

A cultural leap to Australia: in "The Songlines" Bruce Chatwin vividly describes how the Aborigines' ancestors explored virgin country by singing songs, and staked out the territory with their song lines. And there's a parallel here, too: logos mark out the pathways of commercial society! And while on the subject of audio signs: a branding expert recently had church bells rung to accompany a lecture, as a universal aural logo of Catholicism as a world-wide brand.

The Swoosh and Hungry Jack.

In 1971 Caroline Davidson, allegedly for the 'proud' fee of $ 35, came up with a stylised version of the Greek victory goddess Nike's wing for the eponymous new sports brand: "the Swoosh" was born, the beginning of an exemplary brand success. Exemplary because a successful logo will take on a life of its own, and sometimes this can turn into a negative factor. Of course kids everywhere bought and buy Nike products to feel strong and invincible – as the brand myth suggests. Products for real winners. Quite a number of them had "the Swoosh" tattooed on their skins (which is slightly reminiscent of branding). But by now Nike is so well known that the brand is much more vulnerable in a variety of fields than companies which act more 'discreetly': even though sweatshops in developing countries are a general – and rightly pilloried – concern, it was mainly Nike which had to bear the brunt of the protest. In the beginning, many other perpetrators were more or less left out. And why? Their 'brand story' is not, or not yet, part of our popular culture! Nike is perfect for many great wordplays, too: the motivating "just do it" is easily twisted into "don't do it".

To sum it all up: brands, especially successful ones, develop characteristics that are uniquely theirs – which is exactly the strategic approach of a brand personality. A lot of Corporate Identity strategists might prefer a logo that conveys its message as neutrally as possible, to avoid being misinterpreted from the outset. Unfortunately this leads to a certain uniformity, a stereotypical image of urban spaces that isn't aesthetically appealing and doesn't generate the desired impact.

One entirely typical feature of the Corporate World is a high degree of sensitivity and care when it comes to communicating its brands. A newcomer to Australia who wants eat a burger but not a Big Mac will not be able to find a Burger King. The parent company in the States does have a presence 'down under' with the same products, house colours and even logos as everywhere else in the world, but it does not use the same name. Burger King is called Hungry Jack in Australia, to rule out possible anti-monarchist reactions from the start.

Logo design and responsibility.

And how does a designer who has to create these logos, those artefacts of the mass media age, fit in with all this? He needs to be aware that aesthetics represent values, that logo design also has a social dimension which cannot be addressed by stylistic measures alone. In other words: responsibility is an essential part of the logo designer's tool kit. The function of his sign is paramount. Obviously, while a logo for a freaky TV soap can be crazy and weird, the logo of

a financial institution needs to tell a serious story that inspires confidence. But between these two extremes remains a great deal of uncharted territory that may well conceal the odd pitfall. Permanently questioning your own work is part of the job as well: is the logo design on your screen really 'the bee's knees', or does it say more about the identity of the designer than the identity of the brand?

Sometimes the most sensible reaction to a logo commission is to turn it down. When the designer Dirk Rudolph was asked whether he would like to redesign Bayern Munich's logo, he said no: he was sure that the present version was working perfectly well and that a more up-to-date substitute would be counter-productive and wouldn't convey the 'spirit' of the team. A logo like the Shell shell, which has become an icon – even the film "Some like it Hot" draws on it – has undergone only miniscule changes over the decades: the company is built to last! And the utterly abstract version of four car tyres that makes up the Audi logo follows a similar philosophy. But the opposite can also be the case: a lot of familiar international brands disappear, and with them their gradually built-up confidence, when a big company buys up their producers and foists a multinational, anonymous image onto the brand. In such cases, building 'old', well-known brand images into the new company is the more constructive approach: does anyone other than stock exchange specialists and financial consultants know that the world-famous Toblerone chocolate has been part of a company selling more than just sweets for some time now?

Acknowledgements.

A number of experts have been kind enough to help me with my fact-finding for this essay, and I would like to thank them here: Elke Schulz, Richard Feurer, Dr. Martin Fritsche, Robert Krügel and Daniel Zehntner.

# EINE BESTANDS-AUFNAHME.

von Roland Müller

Wie reagiert das Logo-Design auf die unsere Zeit prägenden gesellschaftlichen, kulturellen, ökonomischen und technologischen Wandlungsprozesse? Eine spannende Frage, denn: Kaum ein anderes mediales Ausdrucksmittel eignet sich besser als Sensor zum Messen des aktuellen Klimas als das Markenzeichen. Omnipräsenz multinationaler Brands versus lokale Marken. Die Ups & Downs der Internet-Wirtschaft. Globalisierung versus Antiglobalisierungs-Bewegung. Wachsende Glaubwürdigkeits-Defizite in Corporate America.

Start-up-Euphorien und Start-up-Crashs. Multi-ethnische Kulturverschmelzung versus nationale Abschottungstendenzen. Postmoderne und post-postmoderne Strömungen in der Kultur. Patchworktechnik, Aneignung und Transformation fremden Materials. „Tod des Autors". Mechanische Reproduzierbarkeit von Kunstwerken und damit das Ende ihrer Authentizität im klassischen Sinne. Neue Sehweisen und neues Rezeptionsverhalten. Virtualität versus Realität. Hedonismus versus Fundamentalismus. Lifestyle, Spaßgesellschaft und ‚anything goes' versus neue Ernsthaftigkeit. Das sind einige der Phänomene, die das aktuelle Klima bestimmen. Kein schlechter Zeitpunkt also für eine Standortbestimmung des Logos.

Das Projekt LosLogos.

„I can't understand why people are frightened by new ideas. I'm frightened of old ones", bekennt John Cage – und gibt damit die Richtung an, in der sich das Projekt LosLogos bewegt: Wir sind neugierig auf neue Ideen, neue Ausdrucksformen, neue Denkansätze in der Welt des Designs im allgemeinen und, auf's Projekt bezogen, im Logodesign im besonderen. Deshalb haben wir das Projekt LosLogos initiiert.

Das Buch LosLogos ist als repräsentativer Querschnitt durch das zeitgenössische Logo-Design konzipiert. Es ist ganz bewusst als Plattform für die junge Designerszene der Welt angelegt, wobei der Schwerpunkt auf ästhetischen Innovationen in alternativen Bereichen liegt: Das Werk will neue Trends und Richtungen aufspüren und sichtbar machen. Es will aktuelle Tendenzen registrieren und diese bildhaft kommunizieren. Es will eine Art Kompendium sein – als Orientierungshilfe, Nachschlagewerk und Inspirationsquelle nicht nur für den Grafikdesigner, sondern für den an kulturellen Zeitströmen Interessierten ganz allgemein. Mit diesem Konzept, das unsere Haltung gegenüber dem Design reflektiert, schließt LosLogos nicht zuletzt auch eine Lücke in der aktuellen Designliteratur.

Ein Buch findet seine Autoren.

Damit war der Rahmen abgesteckt. Und die Inhalte? Die konventionelle Vorgehensweise – Autor sucht und findet Verleger und der befördert den Stoff zwischen zwei Buchdeckel – konnte in diesem Fall naturgemäß nicht funktionieren. Der umgekehrte Weg war der Richtige: Wir haben junge Designer aus aller Welt eingeladen, sich mit ihren eigenen Markenzeichen-Kreationen am Projekt LosLogos zu beteiligen. Das Echo auf unsere Einladung war überwältigend.

Und wie sah das Feedback aus? Was füllte im 24-Stunden-Rhythmus unsere Mailboxen? Piktogramme, Typogramme, Schriftzüge und ganze thematische Inszenierungen: für sämtliche Kategorien von Marken, Unternehmungen, Dienstleister, non-profit-Organisationen, Self-made-Brands und Clubs – vom Frisörsalon um die Ecke über das szenige Musiklabel bis zum Industrieunternehmen. Markenzeichen in den unterschiedlichsten Ausformungen und Stilrichtungen: CD-regel-konform und nicht-regelkonform, provokativ, hiphoppig, retro, ironisch, poetisch, aggressiv und verspielt; mit verhaltenen Tönen um Aufmerksamkeit werbend oder mit ‚lauter Stimme' Interesse einfordernd – mit einem Wort: ein vielstimmiges Logo-Panorama unserer Zeit.

3.500 piktografische Zeitzeichen von vier Kontinenten.

Bei Aufnahme sämtlicher Einsendungen wäre LosLogos zu einer voluminösen Logo-Bibel geworden – ein unrealistisches Vorhaben. Also mussten wir reduzieren, evaluieren und strukturieren. Ein schwieriger Prozess (der Zwang zum Eliminieren kann gelegentlich auch schmerzhaft sein!). Ziel war eine Struktur, die das ‚Navigieren' durch das Buch einfach macht, die Vergleichsmöglichkeiten innerhalb der einzelnen Kategorien ermöglicht (nicht „Äpfel mit Birnen vergleichen!") und daneben interessante Parallelitäten und wechselseitige Beeinflussungen innerhalb der Designerszene aufzeigt.

Am Ende dieses Prozesses stand die folgende Struktur des Buches LosLogos, das 3.500 Kreationen präsentiert:

Logos:                 Pictografische Logos
Seiten 020 – 077       Ikonografische Logos
                       Ideografische Logos
                       Illustrative Logos

Schriftzüge:           Schrift als Schrift
Seiten 078 – 203       Schrift als Wortmarke
                       Bildliche Schrift
                       Schrift als Bild

Typogramme:            Schrift als Schrift
Seiten 204 – 243       Schrift als Wortmarke
                       Bildliche Schrift
                       Schrift als Bild

Kombinationen:         Piktogramme, bei denen durch die Kombi-
Seiten 244 – 329       nation von Logo und Schriftzug mit zusätz-
                       lichen grafischen Elementen ein neues
                       Zeichen entsteht.

Themen-                Thematische Inszenierungen, die sich der
sammlungen:            Zuordnung zu einer der drei klar definierten
Seiten 330 – 391       Typologien entziehen.

Statistiken:           Stellt über Grafiken dar, wie sich die
Seiten 392 – 403       Designer und Studios auf verschiedene geo-
                       grafische Regionen verteilen und welches
                       ihre Präferenzen bezüglich der unterschied-
                       lichen Umsetzungsarten sind.

The Local Hero.

Tatort: Shanghai, Nanjing Dong Lu, 2002: Auf dem fernöstlichen Broadway flattern unzählige Wimpel im Blaurot der Colamarke ‚for a new generation'. Eine typische Entwicklung: Nach Jahrzehnten hermetischer Abgrenzung gegenüber westlichen Einflüssen und der kurzen wilden Zeit der Kulturrevolution folgte ein allmählicher Abbau der antikapitalistischen chinesischen Mauer. Langsam besann sich das ‚Paris des Fernen Ostens' auf seine schillernde Vergangenheit. Und es waren die Global Giants, die die neuen Freiräume als erste besetzten. Doch je mehr die Großen powern, umso schwerer haben es die Kleinen – die lokalen Marken, die einem Stadtbild seinen unverwechselbaren Charakter verleihen und es identifizierbar und erlebbar machen. Eine ähnliche Tendenz lässt sich in zahlreichen Metropolen beobachten – besonders in solchen aufstrebender Entwicklungsländer. Eine radikale No Corporate Logo-Haltung wäre nach unserer Meinung die falsche Antwort auf diese Entwicklung. Um so mehr, als die lokalen Brands, wie dieses Buch zeigt, trotz allem quicklebendig sind und im Übrigen das Erobern neuer Märkte durch multinationale Marken nicht nur völlig legitim ist, sondern von den Konsumenten auch honoriert wird.

Trotzdem: „The Local Hero" verdient Support. LosLogos, als Reflektor der Anliegen lokaler Markenzeichen, hat deshalb neben dem vorliegenden Buch eine Parallel-Initiative gestartet: In Kooperation mit dem Büro Destruct, Bern, wurde ein Webportal aufgeschaltet, das es Menschen aus aller Welt ermöglicht, ihre Lieblingslogos allen Interessierten zugänglich zu machen. Dieses Webportal ist als ein virtuelles LogoTown angelegt, der unendlich lang begehbar ist und sich permanent verändert.

Besucher sind herzlich willkommen unter: www.loslogos.org

„Symbole sind die Türen, die man durchschreiten muss."
Naomi Klein, „No Logo".

Faces in the crowd.

Überall blicken uns Markensymbole an: auf der Straße, im Supermarkt und Restaurant, beim Zeitung lesen, fernsehen, Websites ansteuern, auf dem Handy-Display, im Kino, auf dem Sportplatz und selbst im Theater oder Konzertsaal, wo uns der Sponsor nicht im Unklaren darüber lässt, wen wir den Auftritt des großen Mimen oder der berühmten Diva mit zu verdanken haben. Laut Schätzungen bekommen wir täglich 6.000 Logos ins Blickfeld, die uns ihre Botschaften vermitteln und ihre Geschichten erzählen wollen.

Listen to me!

In Marcel Prousts Hauptwerk „A la recherche du temps perdu" löst die Wiederbegegnung mit sinnlichen Eindrücken – wie beispielsweise dem Duft frischgebackener Madeleines – die Erinnerung an Geschichten aus, die sich mit diesen Eindrücken verbinden.

Dieses Beispiel illustriert die von Corporate Communications Managern und Designern angestrebte Funktionalität von Logos: Sie sollen, in stark reduzierter Form, die Geschichten erzählen, auf denen die Markenzeichen aufgebaut sind. Je positiver eine solche Geschichte ist, desto positiver wird sie von den Rezipienten antizipiert. Der Wert einer Marke bildet sich also aus den Vorstellungen, welche die Zielgruppen von ihr haben. Das Logo reproduziert diese Vorstellungen und bestärkt den Markenwert. Dies gilt jedoch auch im umgekehrten Fall: Wird eine Geschichte vom Publikum als unglaubwürdig empfunden, etwa wegen tatsächlichem oder angeblichem „Bad Corporate Behaviour", dann kann die ganze Marke in Schieflage geraten, wie einige prominente Beispiele aus letzter Zeit zeigen.

Nur setzen solche Reaktionen – positive wie negative – eines voraus: Wahrnehmung! Eine Geschichte, die kein Mensch liest, ist vergebliche Liebesmühe ihres Autors. Ein Markensymbol, das durch das Wahrnehmungsraster fällt, fristet ein unbeachtetes Mauerblümchendasein. In den Anfängen des Industriezeitalters setzten die Unternehmer einfach das Bild ihrer Fabrik als Firmensymbol auf den Briefkopf. Ein leicht identifizierbares Symbol für Kunden und Lieferanten! Und auch schon eines mit positiver Imagewirkung: Der Industriebaron, bei dem die meisten Schornsteine rauchten, musste ja erfolgreich und somit ein interessanter Partner sein.

Gute alte Zeiten. Heute ist die Situation unendlich viel komplexer: Angesichts der Überflutung mit Zeichen und Symbolen, die für unsere reale und mediale Umwelt typisch sind, kann ein nach konventionellen Vorstellungen gebautes Markensymbol überhaupt keine Differenzierungsleistung mehr erbringen. Anderseits jedoch ist das Herstellen einer „Ich-Konstruktion", einer Markenpersönlichkeit, unabdingbare Voraussetzung für den Erfolg, ja für das Überleben einer Marke überhaupt.

Über Wert und Bedeutung von Logos als visuelle Vokabulare der Gegenwart kann es also keine Diskussion geben. Wohl aber über ihre Qualität: Nur ein durch seine Eigenständigkeit rasch identifizierbares Logo, dem der Rezipient positive Eigenschaften zuordnet und bei dem auch das Umfeld stimmt (Farbe, Schrift, mediale Umsetzung), kann seine Geschichte erzählen, der man gerne zuhört.

Kurzer Ausflug zu den Ursprüngen.

Zeichen sind so alt wie die Dinge, für die sie stehen. Also uralt, wenn wir an Höhlenzeichen, Rauchzeichen, Markierungen, Stam-

meszeichen, Siegel, Wappen, Brandzeichen, Talismane, magische Zeichen und andere denken.

Stellt sich die Frage nach jenem Zeichen, das unser Thema ist: das Logo. Etymologisch, also vom Wortursprung her betrachtet, muss das Logo mit dem Logos verwandt sein, das im Griechischen Rede, Wort und Sprache meint und einen durch den Begriff aufgehobenen Sinn bezeichnet. Eine Verwandtschaft, aus der sich eine interessante Analogie ableiten lässt: Für Heraklit, den um 500 v. Chr. in Ephesos wirkenden Philosophen, galt der Logos als eine Kraft, die eine im Fluss der Natur wahrnehmbare Ordnung und Struktur herstellt – mit anderen Worten: sinnlich erfahrbar macht. Also könnte man sagen, ‚unser‘ Logo verleiht einem von ihm symbolisierten Inhalt Sinn und Form und strukturiert damit die von ihm repräsentierte Welt: Auch das Logo macht seinen Inhalt sinnlich erfahrbar!

Kultursprung nach Australien: Die Urahnen der Aborigines erschlossen, wie Bruce Chatwin in seinem Roman „The Songlines" anschaulich schildert, das Land durch das Singen von Liedern und steckten mit ihren Songlines das Territorium ab. Auch hierzu bietet sich eine Parallele an: Logos als Wegmarken unserer Wirtschaftsgesellschaft! Apropos tönende Zeichen: Ein Branding-Fachmann liess kürzlich anlässlich eines Vortrags Kirchenglocken als universelles Audio-Logo des Weltkonzerns Katholizismus erklingen.

Der Swoosh und Hungry Jack.
Als Caroline Davidson, angeblich für das ‚stolze‘ Honorar von 35 $, im Jahr 1971 den Flügel der griechischen Siegesgöttin Nike zum Symbol für die neue Sportmarke stilisierte, war „The Swoosh" geboren, und eine exemplarische Markenstory begann. Exemplarisch deshalb, weil ein erfolgreiches Logo eine Eigendynamik entwickelt, die unter

Umständen manchmal auch ins Negative kippen kann. Natürlich kauften und kaufen fast alle Kids Nike-Produkte und halten sich – ganz im Sinne des Markenmythos – für stark und unbesiegbar. Für echte Winnertypen eben. Nicht wenige applizierten den Swoosh gar als Tattoo auf ihre Haut (was ein bisschen an Brandzeichen erinnert). Doch gerade weil Nike einen so enormen Bekanntheitsgrad hat, bietet die Marke auch mehr Angriffsflächen als ‚diskreter‘ agierende Firmen: Obwohl die Sweatshops in Entwicklungsländern ein allgemeines – und mit Recht an den Pranger gestelltes – Problem sind, war es vor allem Nike, das die volle Wucht der Protestszene zu spüren bekam. Zahlreiche andere blieben erstmal mehr oder weniger verschont. Der Grund: Ihre Markengeschichte ist kein oder noch kein Bestandteil unserer Populärkultur! Es lassen sich ja auch schöne Wortspiele mit Nike machen, und aus dem motivierenden „just do it" wird im Handumdrehen ein „don't do it".

Fazit: Marken, vor allem sehr erfolgreiche, entwickeln ihre ureigenen Befindlichkeiten – was auch ganz der strategischen Zielsetzung entspricht, die eine Markenpersönlichkeit anstrebt. Vielleicht wünschen sich deshalb manche Corporate Identity-Strategen ein Logo, das seine Botschaft möglichst neutral kommuniziert, um Missinterpretationen von vornherein auszuschließen. Leider resultiert daraus eine gewisse Uniformität, ein stereotypes Bild urbaner Räume, das weder ästhetisch anspricht noch den gewünschten Impact hat.

Überhaupt ist ein typisches Merkmal der Corporate World ein hoher Grad an Sensibilität und Vorsicht, wenn es um ihre Markenkommunikation geht. Wer etwa in Australien am liebsten den anderen Burger genießen möchte und nicht den Big Mac, sucht als Neuankömmling vergebens nach einem Burger King. Die Muttergesellschaft in den Staaten ist ‚Down Under‘ zwar mit den gleichen Produkten,

Hausfarben und sogar Logos präsent wie überall auf der Welt, tritt aber nicht unter dem gleichen Namen auf. Burger King heißt auf australisch Hungry Jack, um etwaige anti-monarchistische Reflexe gar nicht erst aufkommen zu lassen.

Logodesign und Verantwortung.

Und welche Stellung nimmt in diesem Kontext der Designer ein, der die Logos, jene Artefakte des massenmedialen Zeitalters, zu gestalten hat? Er muss sich bewusst sein, dass Ästhetik eine Repräsentanz von Werten ist, dass Logogestaltung auch eine soziale Dimension hat, der nicht allein mit stilistischen Mitteln beizukommen ist. Mit anderen Worten: Verantwortung gehört zum Rüstzeug des Logodesigners. Wichtig ist die Funktion, die das zu gestaltende Zeichen zu erfüllen hat. Klar, dass ein Logo für eine freakige TV-Soap crazy und abgehoben sein kann und dasjenige für ein Finanzinstitut eine seriöse, vertrauensbildende Story zu erzählen hat. Aber zwischen diesen beiden Extremen liegt ein breites, unerschlossenes Gelände, auf dem man nie sicher ist, ob irgendwo eine Mine versteckt ist. Das permanente Hinterfragen der eigenen Arbeit gehört ebenfalls zum Job: Ist der Logo-Entwurf, der da auf dem Bildschirm entsteht, tatsächlich ‚das Gelbe vom Ei' oder rückt er womöglich nur die Identity des Designers, nicht aber diejenige der Marke ins Bild?

Manchmal ist die sinnvollste Reaktion auf einen Logoauftrag dessen Ablehnung. Als der Designer Dirk Rudolph angefragt wurde, ob er das vertraute Logo des FC Bayern München redisignen möchte, hat er abgewinkt: Er war überzeugt davon, dass die bestehende Lösung weiterhin funktioniert und ein zeitgeistiger Ersatz kontraproduktiv wirken und den ‚Spirit' der Blauweißen nicht adäquat wiedergeben würde. Logos, wie etwa die Muschel von Shell, die zu einer Ikone geworden ist – wovon selbst eine Filmstory lebt („Some like it hot") –, hat sich im Laufe der Jahrzehnte nur unwesentlich verändert: Das Unternehmen setzt auf Nachhaltigkeit! Auch die abstrahierteste Darstellung von vier Autoreifen, die das Audi-Logo prägen, folgt einer ähnlichen Philosophie. Doch es passiert auch Gegenteiliges: Manch eine vertraute nationale Marke verschwindet und mit ihr die langsam gewachsenen Vertrauensbeziehungen, wenn ein Großkonzern den Produzenten aufkauft und der Marke ein multinationales, anonymes Bild überstülpt. Da erweist sich die Integration ‚alter', bekannter Markenbilder ins neue Unternehmen als der konstruktivere Weg: Wer außer Börsenspezialisten und Wirtschaftsberatern weiß schon, dass die weltberühmte Toblerone seit geraumer Zeit schon zu einem Weltkonzern gehört, der nicht nur süße Genüsse verkauft?

Acknowledgments.

Beim ‚fact finding' für diesen Text haben mich freundlicherweise einige Fachleute unterstützt, denen ich an dieser Stelle danken möchte: Elke Schulz, Richard Feurer, Dr. Martin Fritsche, Robert Krügel und Daniel Zehntner.

# WHAT IS A LOGO?

by Norm
Manuel Krebs, Dimitri Bruni

We found out what a logo is between August 12th, 1992 and June 28th, 1994. This was a job that brought a lot of people to their knees: a logo for its own sake. It wasn't about a logotype (which we would like to distinguish clearly from the logo here: the logotype is the soft version of the logo, much easier to decipher through its written information[1]. The true and right logo is the master class (just one step below the poster): a plain sign. This good-true logo was invented in the 60s. Of course! the terms logo and sign, as equivalents to the logo, had been around long before that (†, o, x, etc.). Nevertheless the form developed at that time (the cool and functional form) is closely linked with the concept. The 60s are the antiquity of logo design.

And so we had to design a logo for ourselves. Nothing had been ruled out, and the field was a broad one. (The time available, four (4!) semesters, seemed appropriate – we were beginners.) The more designs we showed the master craftsman, the better he was pleased with us. The designs (on A4, 80 mg$^2$, white) were piled on top of each other 5 cm were obligatory. It wasn't difficult to reach this height. The master accepted even the most minimal changes, his incredible eyesight meant that he could distinguish between two identical photocopies. He knew what it was like, because his heyday, too, had been the 60s. He had seen a lot of logos. Then we were faced with a flood of designs, the fruit of an entire year's work. One design was chosen

and then developed and corrected visually over the course of another year – so that every last square now consisted entirely of curves as well. We tackled yet another flood of designs. 1000 variations of the same sign. The master pointed out the right one. The sign selected then had to be drawn on white card, in black ink and whitewash (this was not just freehand painting, as the use of a paintbrush might suggest, what was needed was a precise and pedantic final copy). Precise instructions on the paintbrushes were issued: a separate brush for each colour. It would have been a mortal sin to pollute one paint with the other colour. When pollution was really bad, we sometimes had to destroy both paintbrush and paint. That is how we created our first logo.

Not least because of this first experience we have an ambiguous relationship with logos. On the one hand we are deeply and profoundly in love with them. Yes, we love the good and true logo[2], which also has a nostalgic element, comparable to some people's devotion to 60s furniture. This is dangerous – you don't just fall in love with one part of a person's body, or at least you shouldn't: even the most beautiful hands are part of an entire being. A logo on its own does not amount to much, the crucial thing is its application, and this is the major problem: the CI manual. The logo is the flag at the CI manual masthead. These files, booklets and books that define a company's

Corporate Identity, from the company pencil to the most intimate details of company employees, create a horrendous prison (BMW's CI manual is said to consist of 10 volumes and is allegedly the most translated book after the Bible). There are few things as dreary as working with a CI manual. The concept of Corporate Identity, with applications set in stone and a logo as the identity-shaping element is not very interesting. Many things are possible and it is hard to understand why everyone still relies on the same recipe (the local butcher does not need a logo!). Maybe the logo itself is the root of all evil and the CI manual just a continuation. A logo with the weight of the CI manual behind it becomes a tyrant, dictating to and harassing its surroundings, demanding universal subordination. The logo itself is pure, faultless and always the same, it is allowed to exist in one, inviolable form only.

This must not continue. These rules (a relic of all those dull CI agencies) are nonsensical (you don't treat a lorry like an envelope) and they're boring to boot. So we need to ask ourselves whether there is such a thing as a good logo.

Never mind – all this is why, despite the fact that we adore logos, we've talked all of our clients out of them. With one exception: ourselves. So here we are again, we've just redesigned our company logo for the 17th time.

1: safe elements        a square, circle or triangle combined with the name of the firm, (in/next to the square, circle or triangle; positive-negative) set in Grotesque Bold or Helvetica Bold, hardly separated and perhaps in conjunction with ® © or ™.

2: the bad logo         Bad: screened logos
You should always be able to reproduce a logo with lines, employing any chosen technique. Semitones are firmly out of the question.
Very bad: multi-coloured logos
It should always be possible to reproduce a logo in black and white, there are no coloured logos.

Very, very bad and absolutely despicable: hand-drawn, scribbled logos or logos drawn with leisurely brushstrokes etc. (a logo is always technical).

# WAS IST EIN LOGO?

von Norm
Manuel Krebs, Dimitri Bruni

Was ein Logo ist, erfuhren wir zwischen dem 12. August 1992 und dem 28. Juni 1994. Es war die Aufgabe, an der Viele gescheitert sind: Das eigene Logo. Es ging nicht um einen Logotype (den wir an dieser Stelle klar vom Logo unterscheiden wollen: Der Logotype ist die softe Version des Logos und durch die geschrieben Information viel einfacher zu bewältigen[1]). Das wahre und richtige Logo ist die Königsklasse (knapp vor dem Plakat), ein nacktes Zeichen.

Das gute-wahre Logo wurde in den 60er Jahren erfunden. Natürlich gab es schon lange vorher den Begriff Logo sowie Zeichen (†, o, x, etc.), die der Idee des Logos entsprechen. Trotzdem ist die damals entwickelte Form (die sachliche und kühle Form) eng mit dem Begriff verknüpft. Die 60er Jahre sind die Antike des Logodesigns.

Wir mussten also ein Logo für uns selbst entwerfen. Alles war möglich, das Feld weit. (Die zur Verfügung stehende Zeit von vier (4!) Semestern schien uns angemessen – wir waren Anfänger.) Je mehr Entwürfe wir dem Meister brachten, desto günstiger war er uns gesinnt. Die Entwürfe (auf A4, 80gm$^2$, weiß) wurden auf einander gestapelt. 5 cm waren Pflicht. Es war nicht schwierig die 5 cm zu erreichen. Der Meister anerkannte kleinste Veränderungen, seine unglaublich geschärften Augen erlaubten es ihm, zwei identische Fotokopien voneinander zu unterscheiden. Er wusste wie es geht, denn auch seine Blütezeit fiel in die 60er Jahre. Viele Logos hatte er gesehen. Dann stand man vor einem Meer von Entwürfen, den Früchten von einem Jahr Arbeit. Ein Entwurf wurde ausgewählt und während eines weiteren Jahres ausgearbeitet und optisch korrigiert – so, dass auch das letzte Quadrat nur noch aus Kurven bestand. Wieder fand man sich vor einer Flut von Entwürfen. 1000 Variationen desselben Zeichens. Der Meister zeigte auf das Richtige. Mit schwarzer Tusche und Deckweiß musste das auserkorene Zeichen auf einen weißen Karton gemalt werden (hier ging es nicht um eine freie Malerei, wie es der Gebrauch der Pinsel vielleicht suggerieren könnte, verlangt war eine pedantisch-präzise Reinzeichnung). Zu den Pinseln gab es genaue Vorschriften: Für die beiden Farben gab es je einen separaten Pinsel. Die größte Sünde war, den einen Farbtopf mit dem Pinsel des andern zu verunreinigen. Verunreinigung zog in schlimmen Fällen die Vernichtung sowohl des Pinsels wie auch des Farbtopfs nach sich. So haben wir unser erstes Logo gemacht.

Vermutlich nicht zuletzt wegen dieser frühen Erfahrung ist unser Verhältnis zum Logo gespalten. Einerseits hegen wir eine innige Liebe zu Logos. Ja, wir lieben das gute, wahre Logo[2], was auch eine nostalgische Komponente hat, zu vergleichen mit der Hingabe gewisser Leute an Möbel aus den 60er Jahren. Dies ist gefährlich, man verliebt sich ja auch nicht in einen einzelnen Körperteil von jemandem, sollte es jedenfalls nicht tun, denn auch die schönsten Hände sind Teil von

einem Ganzen. Das Logo allein ist noch nicht viel, entscheidend ist, wie man es gebraucht, und da ist das große Problem des Logos: Das CI-Manual. Das Logo ist das Flaggschiff des CI-Manuals. Die Ordner, Booklets und Bücher, die das Erscheinungsbild einer Firma vom Firmenbleistift bis in die intimsten Details der Firmenangestellten festlegen, sind ein schlimmes Gefängnis (das BMW CI-Manual soll aus 10 Bänden bestehen und ist angeblich nach der Bibel das meistübersetzte Buch). Wenig ist so öde, wie mit einem CI-Manual zu arbeiten. Das Konzept des Erscheinungsbildes, mit betonierten Anwendungen und dem Logo als identitätsstiftendem Element, ist uninteressant. Vieles wäre möglich, und es ist schwer zu verstehen, warum alle dem selben Rezept vertrauen (die Metzgerei an der Ecke braucht kein Logo!). Vermutlich ist das Logo die Wurzel des Übels, das CI-Manual bloss die Fortsetzung davon. Denn das im CI-Manual verankerte Logo ist ein Tyrann, der sein Umfeld diktiert und schikaniert und dem sich alles unter ordnen muss. Pur, rein und immer gleich ist das Logo, in einer einzigen Form darf es existieren, und die ist unantastbar.

So darf es nicht sein. Diese Dogmen (für die die ganzen dumpfen CI-Agenturen gerade stehen sollen) sind unsinnig (denn ein Lastwagen erfordert nun mal eine andere Behandlung als ein Briefumschlag), und langweilig sind sie auch. Somit stellt sich die Frage, ob es das gute Logo überhaupt gibt.

Wie auch immer – aus diesen Gründen haben wir, trotz unserer heftigen Liebe zum Logo, noch jedem Kunden erfolgreich von einem Logo abgeraten. Außer einem: Uns selbst. Da wären wir wieder: Eine Aufgabe, an der viele gescheitert sind, wir haben eben zum 17. Mal unser Firmenlogo redesignt.

| 1: Sichere Werte | Quadrat, Kreis oder Dreieck kombiniert mit dem Namen der Firma, (im/neben dem Quadrat, Kreis, Dreieck; positiv-negativ) gesetzt in Akzidenz Grotesk-Bold oder Helvetica Bold, ganz leicht gesperrt, evtl. mit ® © oder ™ versehen. |
| --- | --- |
| 2: Das schlechte Logo | Schlecht: aufgerasterte Logos |

2: Das schlechte Logo

Schlecht: aufgerasterte Logos
Ein Logo ist immer im Strich reproduzierbar, es lässt sich problemlos in allen technischen Verfahren reproduzieren. Halbtöne kommen überhaupt nicht in Frage.

Sehr schlecht: mehrfarbige Logos
Ein Logo muss immer schwarz-weiß reproduzierbar sein, es gibt keine farbigen Logos.

Sehr, sehr schlecht und absolut hassenswert: handgezeichnete, gekritzelte, mit lockerem Pinselstrich o.ä. gemachte Logos (ein Logo ist technisch).

# LOGOS

# LOGOS

The logo is presented as a sign, its classic basic form, in the first chapter of this collection of sample trade marks from all over the world, compiled for LosLogos. But it is soon becomes clear that the word 'classic' is no longer appropriate. "Breaking Corporate Design dogma rules" seem to have become a leitmotif for young designers. A leitmotif that also suggests a reluctance to accept unduly streamlined signs without corners or edges (CD dogma insists that these run counter to the harmony beloved by identity strategists).

Im ersten Kapitel des in LosLogos versammelten aktuellen Markenzeichenspektrums aus aller Welt präsentiert sich das Logo als Zeichen: die klassische Grundform des Logos. Wobei jedoch sehr schnell deutlich wird, dass ‚klassisch' kein adäquater Begriff mehr ist. „Breaking the rules of the Corporate Design Dogma" scheint bei den jungen Designern zu so etwas wie einem Leitmotiv geworden zu sein. Ein Leitmotiv, das auch Abgrenzung signalisiert: gegenüber dem allzu stromlinienförmigen Zeichen, das keinerlei Ecken und Kanten mehr aufweist (weil diese dem Harmoniebedürfnis der Identity-Strategen zuwiderlaufen).

# CONTENT INHALT

Iconographic:
Pages 022 – 023

Pictorial signs, 'icons' that use photographic processes or realistic representations to communicate.

Ikonografische:
Seiten 022 – 023

Bildhafte Zeichen, 'Ikonen', die über fotografische Umsetzungen oder realistische Darstellungen mit den Rezipienten kommunizieren.

Illustrative:
Pages 024 – 027

Signs that translate their message into drawn or ornamental language.

Illustrative:
Seiten 024 – 027

Zeichen, die ihre Aussage in eine zeichnerische oder ornamentale Sprache übersetzen.

Pictographic:
Pages 028 – 036

Signs as pictograms which pinpoint an idea or message, in a graphically reduced form.

Pictografische:
Seiten 028 – 036

Zeichen als Piktogramme, die eine Idee oder Message in grafisch reduzierter Form auf den Punkt bringen.

Ideographic:
Pages 037 – 077

Highly abstract signs that convey a feeling, a form, a movement, an idea. Their content or meaning is not revealed at a glance, but requires a certain 'willingness to read'.

Ideografische:
Seiten 037 – 077

Zeichen mit einem hohen Abstraktionsgrad, die ein Gefühl, eine Form, eine Bewegung, eine Idee transportieren, deren Sinn und Inhalt sich nicht auf den ersten Blick erschließt, sondern eine gewisse 'Lesebereitschaft' erfordert.

022.01 Luca Ionescu Design

022.02 typotherapy

022.03 benjamin guedel

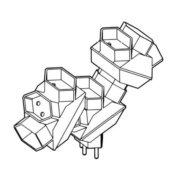

022.04 Fourskin®

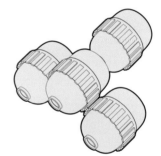

022.05 Woodtli

022.06 FORMGEBER

023.01 Disco Döner

023.02 re-p

024.01 BlackDog

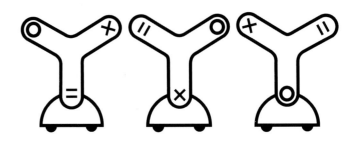

024.02 IKU

024.03 Chris Hutchinson

024.04 Electronic Curry Ltd.

025.01 Electronic Curry Ltd.

026.01 Chris Hutchinson

026.02 Luca Ionescu Design

026.03 Tsuyoshi Kusano

026.04 jum

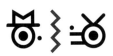

026.05 BlackDog

026.06 Rinzen

026.07 jum

026.08 nothing medialab

026.09 Guadamur

026.10 Norm

026.11 Guadamur

026.12 Guadamur

026.13 BlackDog

026.14 BlackDog

026.15 BlackDog

026.16 BlackDog

027.01 hungryfordesign

027.02 hungryfordesign

027.03 Tsuyoshi Kusano

027.04 Tsuyoshi Kusano

027.05 forcefeed:swede

027.06 benjamin guedel

027.07 moniteurs

027.08 inTEAM Graphics

027.09 CODE

027.10 jum

027.11 IKU

027.12 BlackDog

028.01 WG Berlin          028.02 MASA Colectivo Gráfico    028.03 Alphabetical Order    028.04 Blammo

029.01 Gregory Gilbert-Lodge

030.01 New Future People

031.01 MASA Colectivo Gráfico

031.02 phunk

365**DAYS**

7 DAYS A WEEK, ALL THROUGH THE YEAR,
WHAT I DREAM ABOUT IS SHOPPING.

032.01 Blammo

032.02 Power Graphixx

032.03 Niels Meulman

032.04 PCT

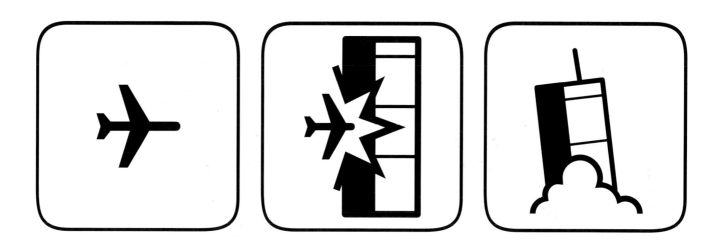

033.01 incorect

034.01 phunk

034.02 Tsuyoshi Kusano

034.03 phunk

034.04 Power Graphixx

034.05 Tsuyoshi Kusano

034.06 jum

034.07 hungryfordesign

034.08 MASA Colectivo Gráfico

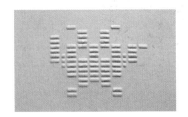

034.09 tronics

034.10 Tsuyoshi Kusano

034.11 MASA Colectivo Gráfico

034.12 Sweden

035.01 Tsuyoshi Kusano

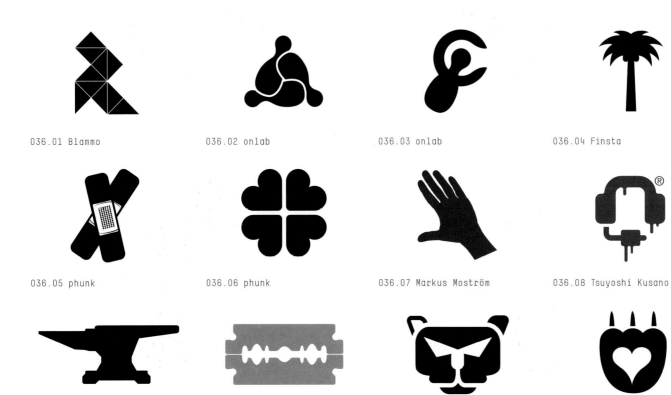

036.01 Blammo

036.02 onlab

036.03 onlab

036.04 Finsta

036.05 phunk

036.06 phunk

036.07 Markus Moström

036.08 Tsuyoshi Kusano

036.09 phunk

036.10 Tim Jester

036.11 Deanne Cheuk

036.12 IKU

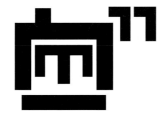

037.01 HandGun

037.02 re-p

037.03 Lobo

037.04 Norm

038.01 Luca Ionescu Design

038.02 Norm

038.03 Tsuyoshi Kusano

038.04 MASA Colectivo Gráfico

038.05 MASA Colectivo Gráfico

038.06 kong.gmbh

038.07 Raoul SINIER

038.08 nothing medialab

038.09 minigram

038.10 minigram

038.11 minigram

038.12 ghs web graphica

039.01 New Future People

040.01 MASA Colectivo Gráfico

040.02 MASA Colectivo Gráfico

040.03 kong.gmbh

040.04 BlackDog

041.01 MASA Colectivo Gráfico

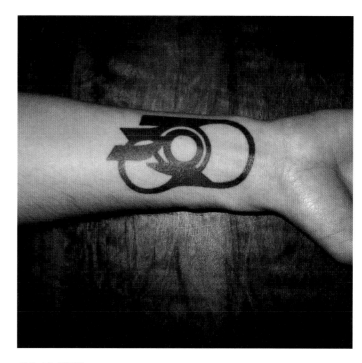

041.02 CISMA

041.03 Tsuyoshi Kusano

041.04 Nendo Grafic Squad

042.01 automatic art and design

042.02 BlackDog

042.03 BlackDog

042.04 BlackDog

042.05 Dopepope

042.06 Power Graphixx

042.07 minigram

042.08 FORMGEBER

042.09 Ross Imms

042.10 STRADA

042.11 Tsuyoshi Kusano

042.12 Ben Mulkey

043.01 Little Eskimo

043.02 Form®

043.03 designershock/DSOS1

043.04 Lobo

043.05 Lobo

043.06 Lobo

043.07 Tsuyoshi Kusano

043.08 OCKTAK

043.09 minigram

043.10 OCKTAK

043.11 OCKTAK

043.12 New Future People

044.01 hungryfordesign

044.02 hungryfordesign

044.03 hungryfordesign

044.04 hungryfordesign

044.05 hungryfordesign

044.06 hungryfordesign

044.07 hungryfordesign

044.08 hungryfordesign

044.09 hungryfordesign

044.10 hungryfordesign

044.11 FORMGEBER

044.12 jum

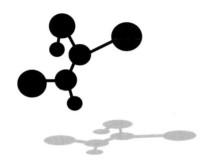

045.01 MK12

045.02 onlab

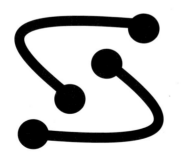

045.03 FORMGEBER

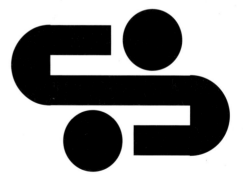

045.04 FORMGEBER

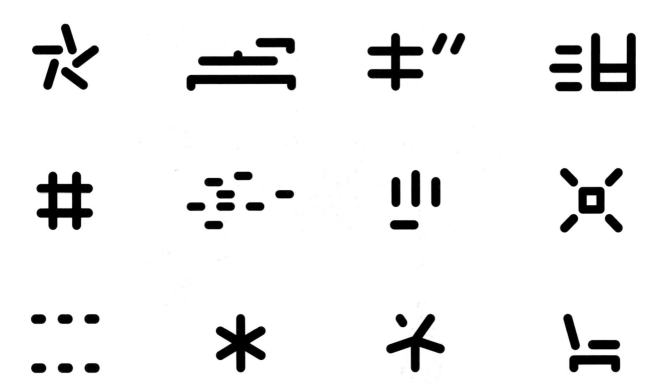

046.01 yippieyeah

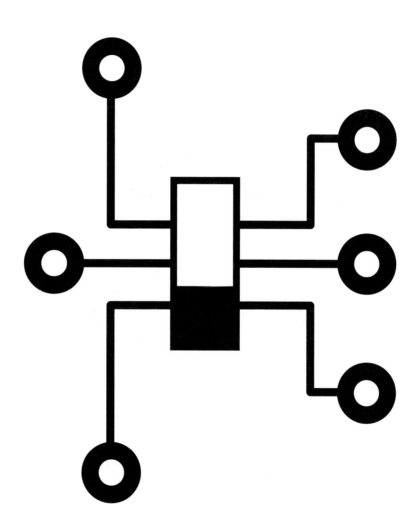

047.01 forcefeed:swede

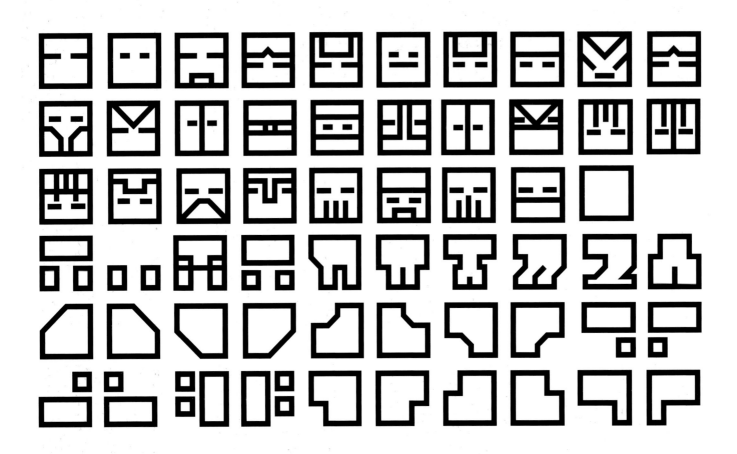

048.01 New Future People

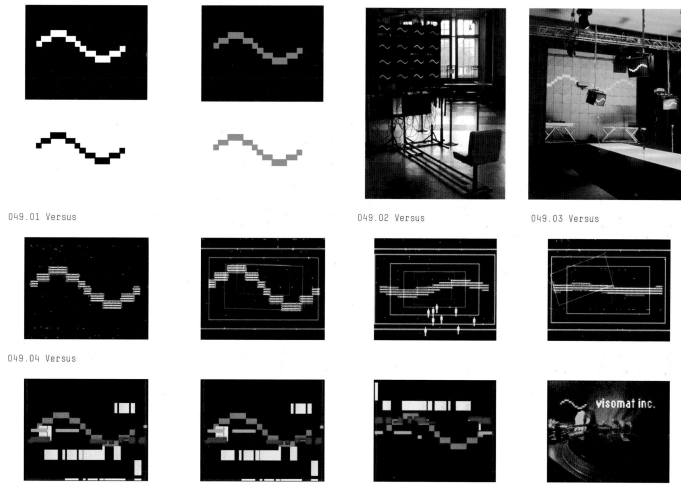

049.01 Versus

049.02 Versus

049.03 Versus

049.04 Versus

049.05 Versus

050.01 New Future People

050.02 New Future People      050.03 New Future People      050.04 New Future People      050.05 New Future People

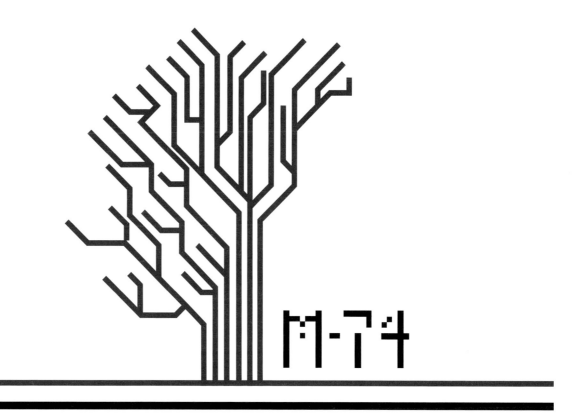

051.01 New Future People

052.01 augenbluten

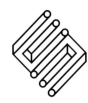

052.02 MASA Colectivo Gráfico

052.03 Luca Ionescu Design

052.04 Syrup Helsinki

052.05 Tsuyoshi Kusano

052.06 Machine

052.07 Luca Ionescu Design

052.08 Tsuyoshi Kusano

052.09 OCKTAK

052.10 OCKTAK

052.11 OCKTAK

052.12 Dirk Rudolph

053.01 OCKTAK

053.02 Alphabetical Order

053.03 Dirk Rudolph

053.04 FORMGEBER

053.05 Alphabetical Order

053.06 re-p

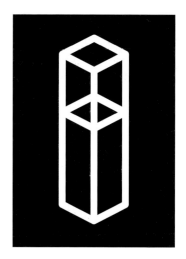

053.07 Tsuyoshi Kusano

053.08 minigram

053.09 Dirk Rudolph

053.10 Syrup Helsinki

054.01 IKU

054.02 Tsuyoshi Kusano

054.03 Tsuyoshi Kusano

054.04 CISMA

054.05 HandGun

054.06 Luca Ionescu Design

054.07 Dirk Rudolph

054.08 minigram

054.09 FORMGEBER

054.10 FORMGEBER

054.11 archetype:interactive

054.12 H617

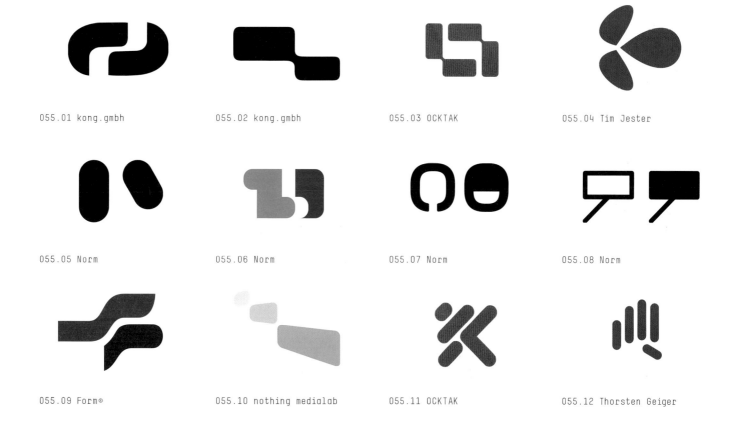

055.01 kong.gmbh          055.02 kong.gmbh          055.03 OCKTAK          055.04 Tim Jester

055.05 Norm               055.06 Norm               055.07 Norm            055.08 Norm

055.09 Form©              055.10 nothing medialab   055.11 OCKTAK          055.12 Thorsten Geiger

056.01 nothing nmedialab

056.02 FORMGEBER

056.03 nothing nmedialab

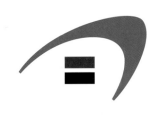

056.04 nothing nmedialab

056.05 hungryfordesign

056.06 FORMGEBER

056.07 Tim Jester

056.08 hausgrafik

057.01 Alphabetical Order

057.02 Marc Kappeler

057.03 FORMGEBER

057.04 Dirk Rudolph

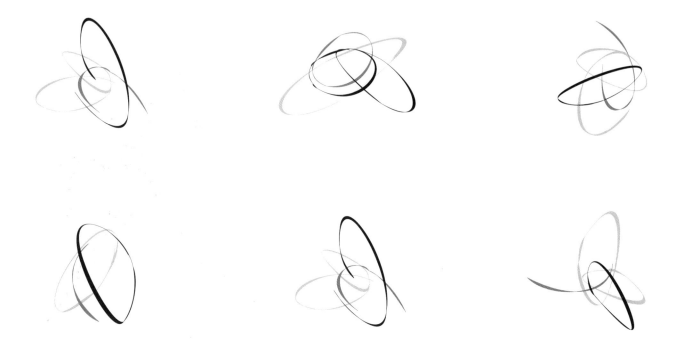

058.01 Move Design

059.01 SuperHappyBunny Company                                    059.02 Dirk Rudolph

060.01 Tim Jester

060.02 augenbluten

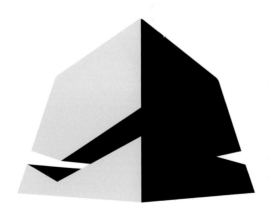

060.03 FORMGEBER

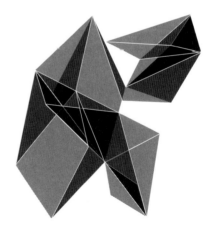

060.04 augenbluten

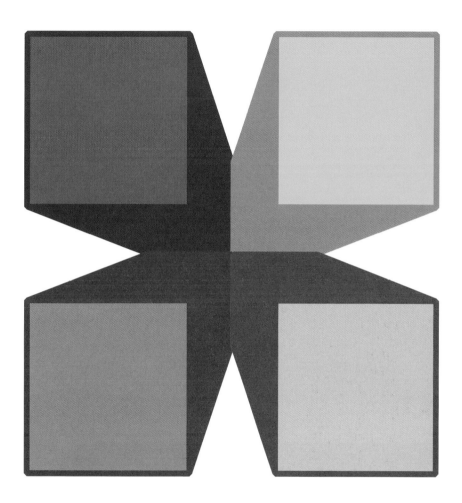

061.01 Superpopstudio

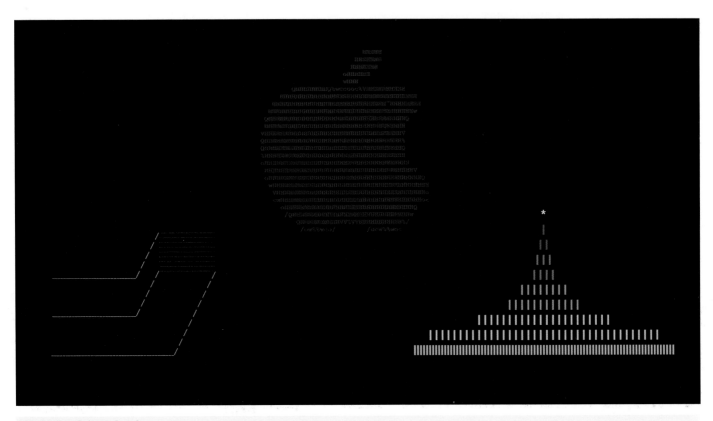

062.01 New Future People

063.01 New Future People

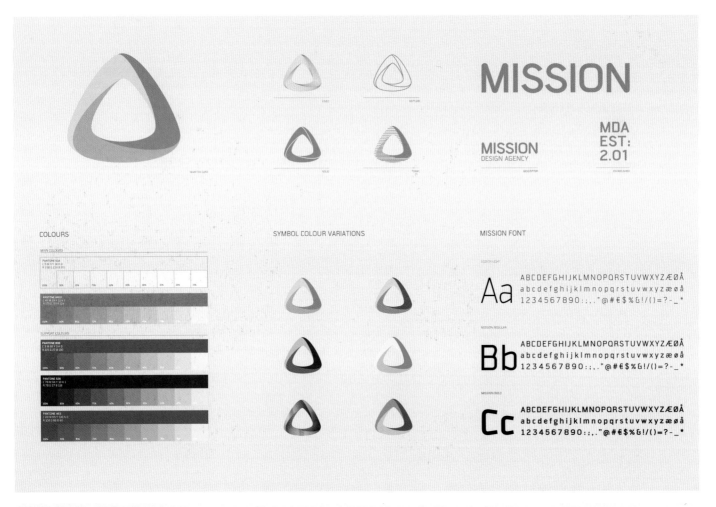

COLOURS

SYMBOL COLOUR VARIATIONS

MISSION FONT

065.01 Tim Jester

065.02 Tim Jester

065.03 Tim Jester

065.04 MASA Colectivo Gráfico

065.05 Tim Jester

065.06 Tim Jester

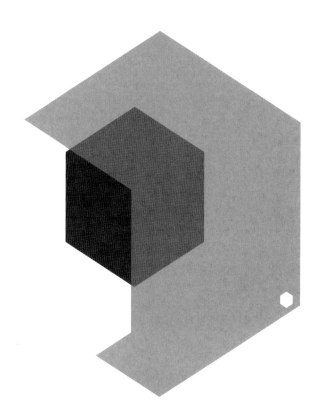

065.07 MASA Colectivo Gráfico

066.02 Dirk Rudolph

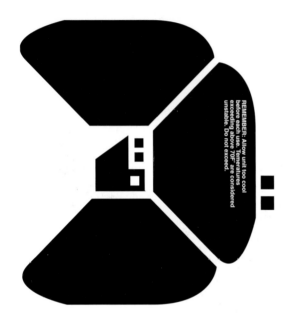

REMEMBER: Allow unit too cool before each use. Temeratures exceeding above 70F are considered unstable. Do not exceed.

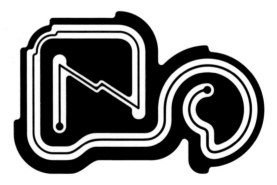

066.01 Luca Ionescu Design

066.03 hungryfordesign

067.01 Tsuyoshi Kusano

068.01 OCKTAK

068.02 OCKTAK

068.03 OCKTAK

068.04 OCKTAK

068.05 OCKTAK

068.06 OCKTAK

068.07 OCKTAK

068.08 OCKTAK

068.09 OCKTAK

068.10 OCKTAK

068.11 OCKTAK

068.12 OCKTAK

069.01 OCKTAK

069.02 OCKTAK

069.03 OCKTAK

069.04 OCKTAK

069.05 OCKTAK

069.06 OCKTAK

069.07 OCKTAK

069.08 OCKTAK

069.09 OCKTAK

069.10 OCKTAK

069.11 OCKTAK

069.12 OCKTAK

070.01 Norm

070.02 phunk

070.03 Bitsteam

070.04 raum mannheim

070.05 Eboy

070.06 Norm

070.07 kong.gmbh

070.08 PXPress

070.09 Chris Hutchinson

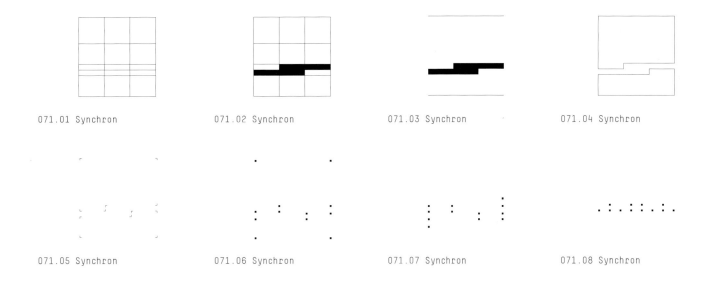

071.01 Synchron    071.02 Synchron    071.03 Synchron    071.04 Synchron

071.05 Synchron    071.06 Synchron    071.07 Synchron    071.08 Synchron

071.09 Synchron

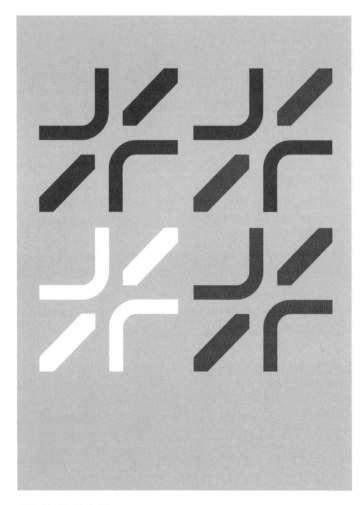

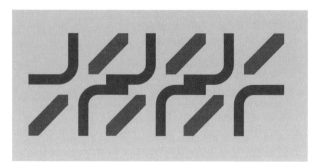

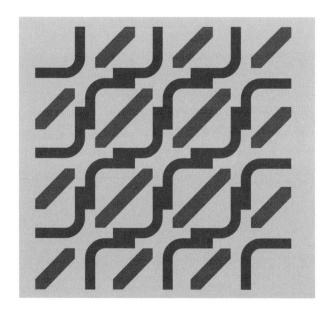

072.01 Digitalultras

073.01 minigram

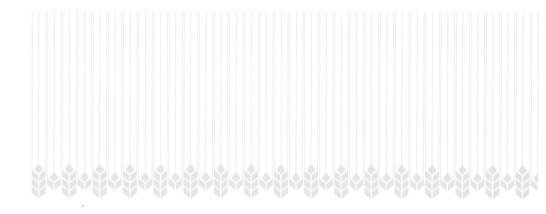

073.02 minigram

073.03 minigram

073.04 minigram

073.05 minigram

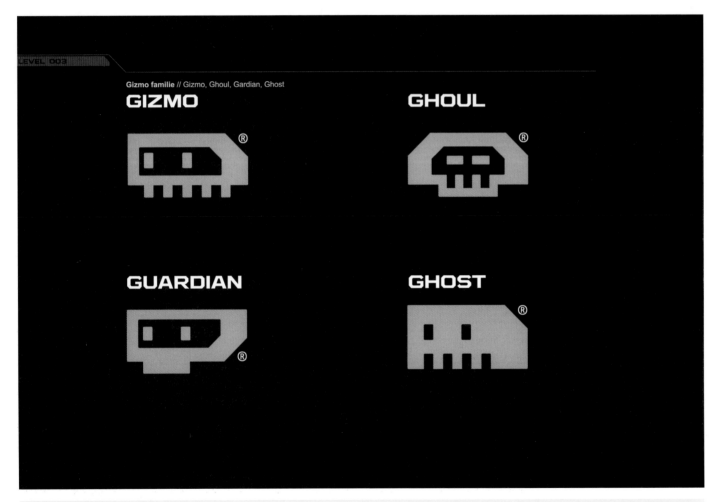

075.01 e-Types

075.02 e-Types

075.03 e-Types

075.04 e-Types

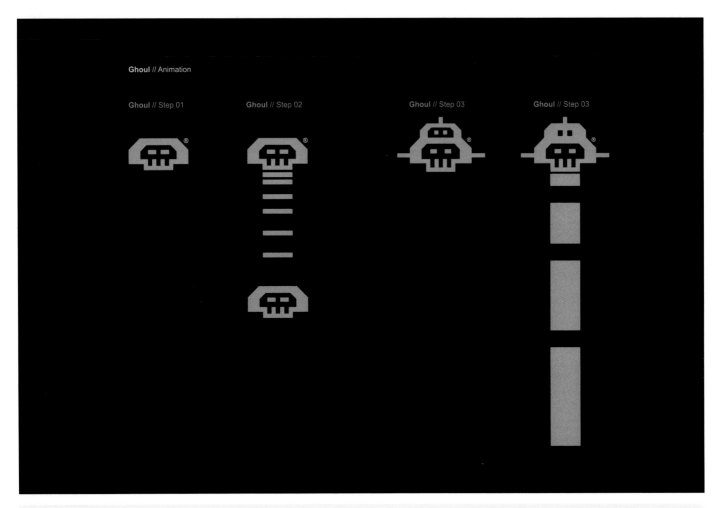

Ghoul // Animation

Ghoul // Step 01    Ghoul // Step 02    Ghoul // Step 03    Ghoul // Step 03

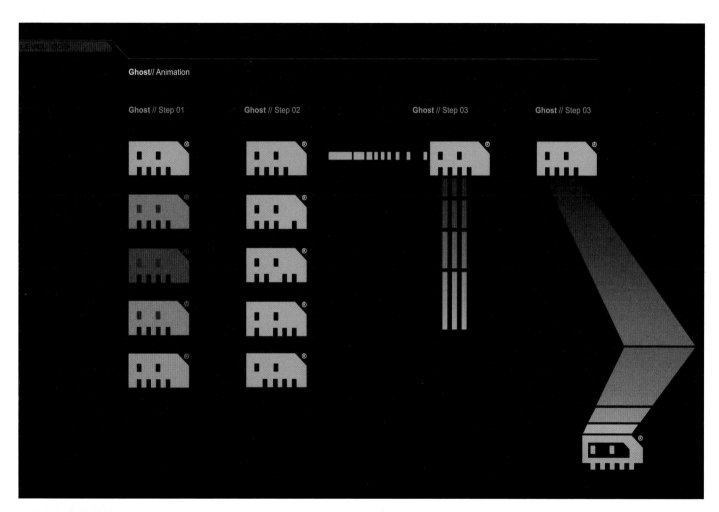

Ghost// Animation

Ghost // Step 01          Ghost // Step 02          Ghost // Step 03          Ghost // Step 03

# LETTERING

# SCHRIFTZÜGE

The letters as 'building material' for the construction of logos: when designers create logos as lettering, with existing typefaces or newly developed fonts, they return to the early days when type was still pictographic. As early as the fourth century before Christ the Sumerians were reducing elements from the world around them – animals, plants, people – to their pictorial essence, as signs. A visual language, in other words, to convey meaning rapidly and unmistakably. And this communicative mechanism works for modern sign-like lettering as well: the choice of a particular kind of font – perhaps for the company name – reveals the character, content and approach behind the firm or brand. Abstract, neutral lettering becomes pictographic again.

Das Medium Schrift als ‚Baumaterial' für die Konstruktion von Logos: Indem Designer aus bestehenden Schriften oder neu entwickelten Fonts Logos in Form von Schriftzügen kreieren, gehen sie zurück zu den Ursprüngen, als die Schrift noch Bilderschrift war. Bereits im 4. Jahrtausend v. Chr. reduzierten die Sumerer Dinge aus ihrer Umwelt – Tiere, Pflanzen, Menschen – auf ihre bildliche Zeichenhaftigkeit. Auf eine Bilderschrift also, die ihre Bedeutungsinhalte rasch und unmissverständlich kommuniziert. Ein kommuniktiver Mechanismus, der auch bei modernen zeichenhaften Schriftzügen funktioniert: Durch die Wahl einer bestimmten Schriftart – etwa für einen Firmennamen – und ihrer typografischen Gestaltung werden Charakter, Inhalte und Haltung sichtbar, die sich hinter der Firma oder Marke verbergen. Abstrakte, neutrale Schrift wird zurück verwandelt in Bilderschrift.

# CONTENT     INHALT

Type as type:
Pages 080 – 103

Lettering developed from existing type-faces, consistently avoiding additional graphic elements and other interventions.

Schrift als Schrift:
Seiten 080 – 103

Schriftzüge, die aus vorhandenen Schriften entwickelt wurden; mit konsequentem Verzicht auf zusätzliche grafische Elemente und andere Eingriffe.

Type as a brand:
Pages 104 – 133

Fonts whose independent qualities have been enhanced by typographic manipulation.

Schrift als
Wortmarke:
Seiten 104 – 133

Schriftzüge, bei denen vermittels typografischer Eingriffe eine gesteigerte Eigenständigkeit erreicht wurde.

Pictorial type:
Pages 134 – 155

Lettering in which additional graphic elements communicate content.

Bildliche Schrift:
Seiten 134 – 155

Schriftzüge, bei denen zum Kommunizieren der Inhalte zusätzliche grafische Elemente verwendet worden sind.

Type as pictures:
Pages 156 – 189

Lettering that gains its significance from the free approach to characters, the typography broken down to the point of illegibility.

Schrift als Bild:
Seiten 156 – 189

Schriftzüge, die ihre Signifikanz aus einem sehr freien Umgang mit Lettern erreichen, wobei sich die Typografie bis zur Unleserlichkeit auflöst.

Asian type:
pages 190 – 203

Typography (Type as type, Type as a brand, pictorial type and Type as pictures) making use of asian characters.

Asiatische Schrift:
Seiten 190 – 203

Schriftzüge (Schrift als Schrift, Schrift als Wortmarke, bildliche Schrift und Schrift als Bild) unter Verwendung asiatischer Schriftzeichen.

EUROWOMAN

080.01 e-Types

aperto

080.02 DSOS1

Landscape™

080.03 Form®

essence

080.04 FORMGEBER

SinnerSchrader

080.05 Mutabor

CONDOR

080.06 CODE

korridor

080.07 augenbluten

HIRMER

080.08 STRADA

neksis

080.09 typotherapy

flava

080.10 phunk

dori dock

080.11 Défil Inc.

Chocolate©

080.12 Blammo

econa

080.13 DSOS1

primitive™

080.14 Power Graphixx

solid.™

080.15 Method

UnBuiltMart
EVERYWHERE BUT NOWHERE / TWENTY FOUR HOURS OF FAKE

080.16 Power Graphixx

**CiaopanicAirlines**®

081.01 ghs web graphica

resonancecommunication

081.02 B.ü.L.b grafix

**working class hero***
**02** どぜりにが

081.03 Luca Ionescu Design

**one/fifteen**<sup>1/15</sup>

081.04 typotherapy

**inbetweendub.**

081.05 typotherapy

081.06 OCKTAK

*composite*

081.07 ASYL DESIGN Inc.

# CASETTE VISION

082.01 Tsuyoshi Kusano

# MNOPQR

082.02 Norm

# CONTINUE

082.03 ASYL DESIGN Inc.

# WASHOE.

082.04 BlackDog

# NORM

082.05 Norm

**NEUT. 002**
alt. designers media

082.06 ASYL DESIGN Inc.

# FRANTIČEK KLOSSNER

082.07 hausgrafik

082.08 Eboy

082.09 augenbluten

belief

083.01 Power Graphixx

083.02 Luca Ionescu Design

083.03 Luca Ionescu Design

083.04 Luca Ionescu Design

083.05 Tsuyoshi Kusano

083.06 Luca Ionescu Design

**FONT FRONTLINE 01**

084.01 Maniackers Design

**the next LeveL**

084.02 augenbluten

084.03 raum mannheim

**timecrusher**

084.04 augenbluten

**drum and bass**

084.05 OCKTAK

**bullit.proof**

084.06 OCKTAK

**LAST SEASON**

085.01 augenbluten

**Sanana**

085.02 Niels Jansson

**magma girl**

085.03 Maniackers Design

**balibioskop**

085.04 Electronic Curry Ltd.

**ROOMNOVI**

085.05 ghs web graphica, english version.

**ル-ムナウ゛**

085.06 ghs web graphica, japanese version.

# FUSION-INC.NL

086.01 OCKTAK

# FUSION

086.02 OCKTAK

# FULL·ON

086.03 OCKTAK

# uptone

086.04 OCKTAK

# thing

086.05 OCKTAK

087.01 OCKTAK

088.01 OCKTAK

088.02 Luca Ionescu Design

088.03 CODE

088.04 CODE

088.05 SAKAMOTO

088.06 CODE

T O CC O

089.01 tankdesign

FR. E I GH T8

089.02 Luca Ionescu Design

DIGITAL DIAGIREF

090.01 Tsuyoshi Kusano

AUTOBAHN

090.02 Tsuyoshi Kusano

FIRMABONN

090.03 Disko Döner

KEN ISHII MISPROGRAMMED DAY

091.01 ASYL DESIGN Inc.

antikarma.com

091.02 Niels Jansson

BIT GENERATION

091.03 Tsuyoshi Kusano

# ~scape

092.01 STRADA

# (STRADA

092.02 STRADA

# :pepper

092.03 CODE

092.04 OCKTAK

092.05 büro destruct

092.06 Niels Jansson

## ›»/ UNDER CONSTRUCTION

093.01 Kathrin Jachmann

## //typologophonics

093.02 typotherapy

## [ planquadrat ]

093.03 raum mannheim

SNEAKER® NATION

094.01 Alphabetical Order

PANZER FRONT

094.02 Tsuyoshi Kusano

BREAK THROUGH

094.03 Tsuyoshi Kusano

ブ.ランド
BRAND STRATEGY OPERATING
3RAND

094.04 Tsuyoshi Kusano

LOCUS IS drawn

094.05 Tsuyoshi Kusano

ONLINE OFFICE

094.06 DSOS1

element of time

094.07 Designunion

babylon motorhome™

094.08 MAGNETOFONICA

THE MAD CAPSULE MARKETS

094.09 POSITRON CO., LTD.

HOTLINE
All Japan records compilation series

094.10 Tsuyoshi Kusano

HONGKONG EXPRESS

094.11 ASYL DESIGN Inc.

SPINNIPS
gallery

094.12 typotherapy

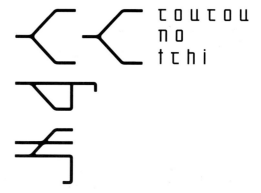

095.01 ASYL DESIGN Inc.                              095.02 ASYL DESIGN Inc.

# DESIGNERDOCK®

096.01 DSOS1

# wahlıɾueflı

096.02 kong.gmbh

# bluewin

096.03 anja klausch

# turicer

096.04 CODE

096.05 blindresearch

## think

096.06 p*star

# bullit.PROOF

096.07 OCKTAK

# PLAYER1

096.08 OCKTAK

# INPUT

096.09 OCKTAK

096.10 OCKTAK

096.11 Form®

096.12 Dopepope

*Schmuckpreis*

096.13 Marc Kappeler

# no|type

096.14 nothing medialab

097.01 CODE

097.02 raum mannheim

097.03 Disko Döner

097.04 Tim Jester

097.05 ghs web graphica

097.06 ghs web graphica

097.07 tankdesign

097.08 dubius?

098.01 Tina Backmann                          098.02 Digitalultras

HEKTIK URBAN
APPAREL 02™

HEKTIK CASUAL APPAREL
FOR THE URBAN ESCAPIST
WEAR WITH CAUTION. READ RIGHT WAY UP!

099.01 Luca Ionescu Design

PICTURE TRACK

100.03 Jorge Alderete

SUPERFURNITURE™

100.04 dubius?

100.01 typotherapy          100.02 benjamin guedel          100.05 CRAIG ROBINSON

101.01 Blammo

101.02 kong.gmbh

101.03 Jorge Alderete

101.04 CRAIG ROBINSON

atomikXT

A B C D E
F G H I J K
L M N O P
Q R S T U
V W X Y Z

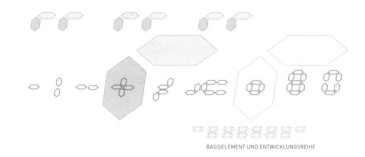

BASISELEMENT UND ENTWICKLUNGSREIHE

102.02 Artificial Environments

1 2 3 4 5 6 7 8 9 0   P
3   5   7 8 9          schoenes
5   7   99             sonderelement

E E E F N G  J L C P Q U R  S T V X Z
E E E F F N 9  J L C P Q U R S   V   Z

102.01 Artificial Environments

OFFIS   OLDENBURGER FORSCHUNGS- UND
ENTWICKLUNGSINSTITUT FÜR
INFORMATIK-WERKZEUGE UND -SYSTEME

102.03 Artificial Environments

103.01 Finsta

104.01 Rinzen

104.02 Bionic System

104.03 MAGNETOFONICA

104.04 Tycoon Graphics

104.05 CODE

104.06 Rinzen

104.07 typotherapy

104.08 Norm

104.09 Power Graphixx

104.10 Niels Meulman

104.11 Power Graphixx

104.12 24HR

104.13 Power Graphixx

104.14 Rio Grafik

104.15 Rio Grafik

balduin

105.01 büro destruct

phaeno

105.02 büro destruct

105.03 SAKAMOTO

essense

105.04 SAKAMOTO

105.05 Move Design

105.06 Rinzen

105.07 Rinzen

106.01 LEVEL1

106.02 Luca Ionescu Design

106.03 Um|bruch Gestaltung

106.04 Tsuyoshi Kusano

106.05 Luca Ionescu Design

106.06 balsi

106.07 Sweden

106.08 Norm

106.09 Um|bruch Gestaltung

106.10 OCKTAK

106.11 tankdesign

106.12 24HR

106.13 Markus Moström

106.14 Finsta

106.15 Deanne Cheuk

107.01 Niels Meulman

107.02 Bionic System

107.03 ColdWater Graphiix

107.04 Luca Ionescu Design

107.05 Power Graphixx     107.06 Machine     107.07 Power Graphixx     107.08 Machine

FIRECRACKER

108.01 Tsuyoshi Kusano

108.02 FORMGEBER

PROFILAGER

108.03 Disco Döner

108.04 FORMGEBER

108.05 Dopepope

SKYWALK
PARAGLIDERS

108.06 FORMGEBER

.com

108.07 Hendrik Hellige

THE HOSPI+AL
MUSIC, ART AND FILM CENTRE

108.08 Form®

# typotherapy+design ⟩

109.01 typotherapy

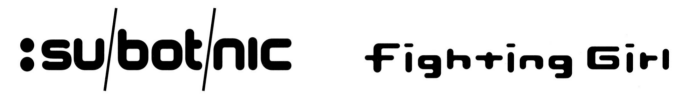

:su/bot/nic

109.02 moniteurs

Fighting Girl

109.03 ASYL DESIGN Inc.

RESIST!

109.04 Mutabor

sakamoto™

109.05 SAKAMOTO

DIRECTLY          RAUSCH▮              GO:Rilla          CÏBONE

109.06 Power Graphixx    109.07 minimise        109.08 Mutabor        109.09 POSITRON CO., LTD.

110.01 büro destruct

110.02 balsi

110.03 büro destruct

110.04 Syrup Helsinki

110.05 Niels Meulman

110.06 phunk

110.07 Electronic Curry Ltd.

110.08 Um|bruch Gestaltung

110.09 Tsuyoshi Kusano

110.10 Marc Kappeler

110.11 ghs web graphica

110.12 Luca Ionescu Design

111.01 Machine

111.02 Tsuyoshi Kusano

111.03 Hendrik Hellige

111.04 büro destruct

111.05 büro destruct

111.06 phunk

111.07 Rinzen

111.08 Machine

111.09 Hendrik Hellige

111.10 Maniackers Design

112.01 büro destruct

112.02 Fourskin®

112.03 Machine

112.04 Deanne Cheuk

112.05 DED Associates

112.06 MASA Colectivo Gráfico

112.07 Machine

112.08 büro destruct

112.09 Maniackers Design

112.10 Jorge Alderete

113.01 344 Design

113.02 ColdWater Graphiix

113.03 balsi

113.04 Machine

113.05 Eboy

114.01 Luca Ionescu Design

114.02 Machine

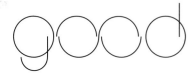

114.03 Machine

114.04 MAGNETOFONICA

114.05 Rinzen

114.06 raum mannheim

114.07 Matthias Hübner

114.08 raum mannheim

Sick Bag™

115.01 Machine

WAR™

115.02 Machine

116.01 344 Design

116.02 Bionic System

116.03 Niels Meulman

117.01 Gregory Gilbert-Lodge

118.01 OCKTAK

118.02 OCKTAK

118.03 kong.gmbh

118.04 Hendrik Hellige

118.05 CODE

118.06 CODE

118.07 Kathrin Jachmann

118.08 344 Design

119.01 CODE

119.02 CODE

119.03 Bionic System

119.04 raum mannheim

119.05 MIGUEL ANGEL LEYVA

119.06 Bionic System

119.07 Bionic System

119.08 Bionic System

119.09 CODE

119.10 Bionic System

120.01 Luca Ionescu Design

120.02 Cyclone Graphix

120.03 QuickHoney

120.04 CODE

120.05 tikkigirl

120.06 Bas Visual Concepts

120.07 Lindedesign

120.08 HandGun

120.09 büro destruct

120.10 inTEAM Graphics

120.11 OCKTAK

120.12 nothing medialab

121.01 CODE

121.02 raum mannheim

121.03 Finsta

121.04 Tycoon Graphics

121.05 Bas Visual Concepts

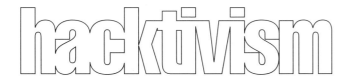

121.06 Fourskin®

121.07 OCKTAK

122.01 Sweden

122.02 Niels Jansson

122.03 Luca Ionescu Design

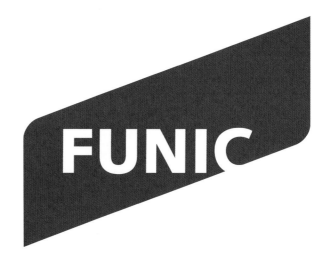

122.04 kong.gmbh

123.01 Bionic System

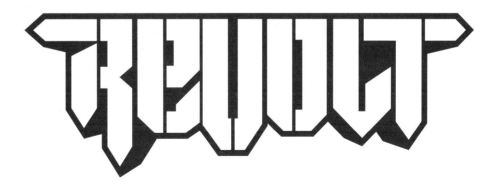

123.02 Machine

124.01 Eboy

124.02 benjamin guedel

124.03 benjamin guedel

124.04 Machine

124.05 Luca Ionescu Design

124.06 benjamin guedel

124.07 benjamin guedel

124.08 benjamin guedel

124.09 Machine

124.10 Machine

124.11 Machine

124.12 Machine

125.01 benjamin guedel

125.02 Superpopstudio

125.03 hausgrafik

125.04 benjamin guedel

125.05 archetype:interactive

125.06 Syrup Helsinki

125.07 Machine

125.08 Norm

125.09 Hendrik Hellige

125.10 Eboy

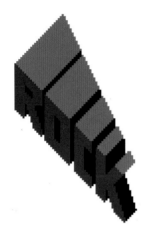

126.01 Eboy

126.02 Eboy

126.03 Eboy

126.04 Eboy

126.05 Eboy

126.06 Eboy

127.01 Menatry

127.02 344 Design

127.03 Eboy

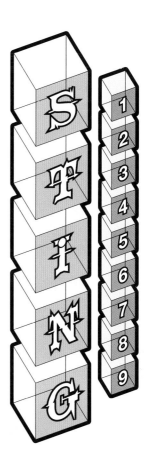

127.04 344 Design

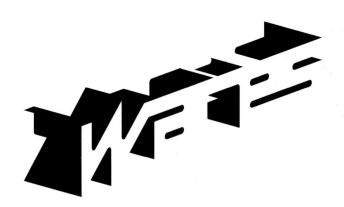

128.01 Tsuyoshi Kusano

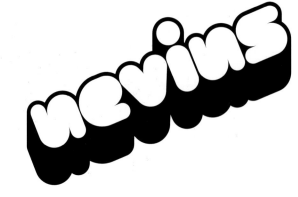

128.02 augenbluten

128.03 augenbluten

128.04 Hendrik Hellige

©2001 cleaning
SUPPORTED BY
POWER GRAPHIXX

129.01 Power Graphixx

129.02 OhioGirl

129.03 Machine

130.01 Tsuyoshi Kusano

130.02 Syrup Helsinki

131.01 Rinzen

131.02 Rinzen

131.03 Rinzen

131.04 Rinzen

131.05 Rinzen

132.01 tronics

132.02 Um|bruch Gestaltung

132.03 Um|bruch Gestaltung

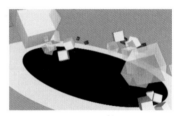

132.04 Um|bruch Gestaltung

132.05 tronics

132.06 Um|bruch Gestaltung

132.07 Um|bruch Gestaltung

132.08 Um|bruch Gestaltung

132.09 tronics

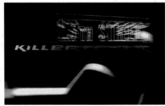

132.10 Um|bruch Gestaltung

132.11 Um|bruch Gestaltung

132.12 Um|bruch Gestaltung

133.01 Rinzen                                      133.02 TOI Inc.

134.01 123KLAN

134.02 123KLAN

134.03 123KLAN

134.04 123KLAN

135.01 123KLAN

136.01 CODE

136.02 CODE

136.03 CISMA

136.04 FORMGEBER

136.05 OCKTAK

137.01 büro destruct

137.02 Jorge Alderete

137.03 Rinzen

137.04 Luca Ionescu Design

138.01 344 Design

138.02 phunk

138.03 hausgrafik

138.04 Luca Ionescu Design

139.01 Luca Ionescu Design

140.01 Power Graphixx

140.02 Niels Meulman

140.03 Machine

140.04 Machine

141.01 büro destruct

141.02 michele del nobolo

142.01 DSOS1

142.02 MASA Colectivo Gráfico

142.03 DSOS1

142.04 DED Associates

142.05 Machine

142.06 Sweden

142.07 John J. Candy Design

142.08 büro destruct

142.09 Machine

142.10 büro destruct

142.11 Niels Meulman

142.12 Rinzen

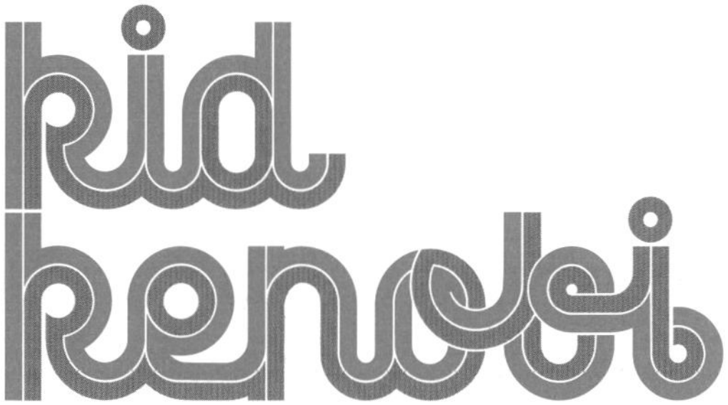

143.01 Rinzen

143.02 Rinzen

143.03 Rinzen

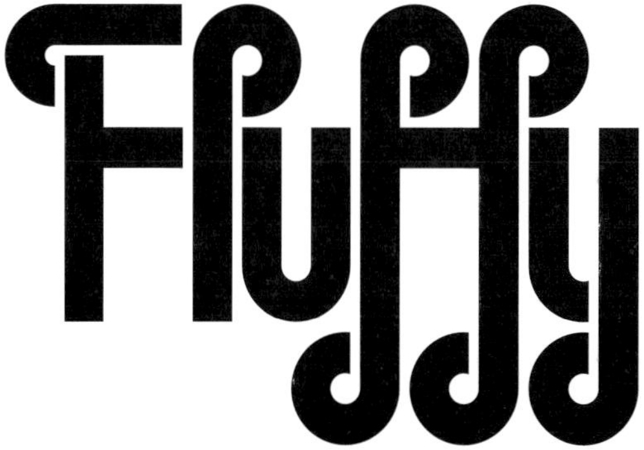

143.04 Rinzen

144.01 Norm

144.02 Norm

144.03 Norm

144.04 Norm

144.05 Sanjai Bhana

144.06 Blammo

144.07 phunk

144.08 benjamin guedel

144.09 dubius?

144.10 Alphabetical Order

144.11 Pictomat

144.12 Electronic Curry Ltd.

144.13 STRADA

144.14 B.ü.L.b grafix

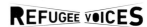

144.15 balsi

144.16 B.ü.L.b grafix

145.01 Luca Ionescu Design

145.02 Luca Ionescu Design

145.03 büro destruct

145.04 büro destruct

146.01 DSOS1

146.02 DSOS1

146.03 DSOS1

146.04 DSOS1

UALLEY FIESTA

JULY 13-15 2001
BRUNSWICK STREET AND CHINATOWN MALLS

147 01 Rinzen

MUSIC FASHION ARTS

147.02 Rinzen

148.01 Hendrik Hellige

148.02 Tsuyoshi Kusano

148.03 Pfadfinderei

148.04 tankdesign

148.05 Rinzen

148.06 Rinzen

swissrain

149.01 316tn

149.02 344 Design

149.03 WG Berlin

149.04 Hendrik Hellige

149.05 Form®

149.06 augenbluten

150.01 Machine

150.02 p*star

150.03 archetype:interactive

150.04 Hintze.gruppen

151.01 CODE

151.02 Form®

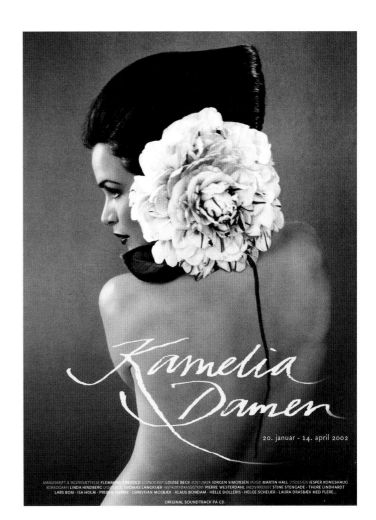

151.03 e-Types

152.01 tankdesign

152.02 tankdesign

152.03 Versus

152.04 unikum graphic design

152.05 Eboy

152.06 Menatry

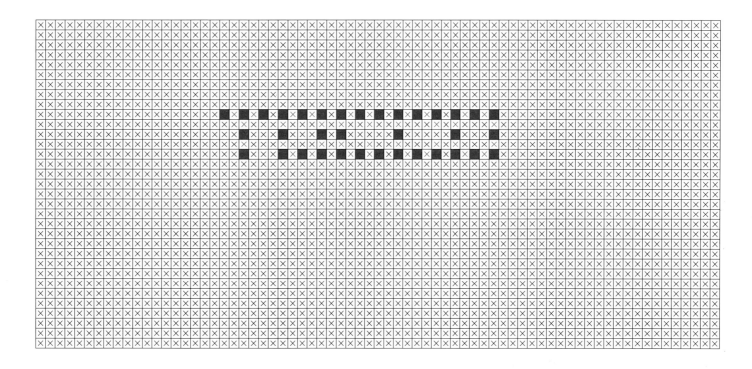

153.01 tankdesign

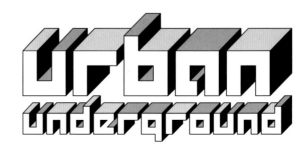

154.02 Zip Design

154.01 Electronic Curry Ltd.                                    154.03 HandGun

155.01 LEVEL1

156.01 MASA Colectivo Gráfico

156.02 MASA Colectivo Gráfico

156.03 123KLAN

156.04 123KLAN

157.01 123KLAN

158.01 phunk

158.02 phunk

158.03 phunk

158.04 Tim Jester

158.05 forcefeed:swede

158.06 123KLAN

158.07 123KLAN

158.08 dubius?

158.09 Tim Jester

158.10 Tim Jester

159.01 POSITRON CO., LTD.

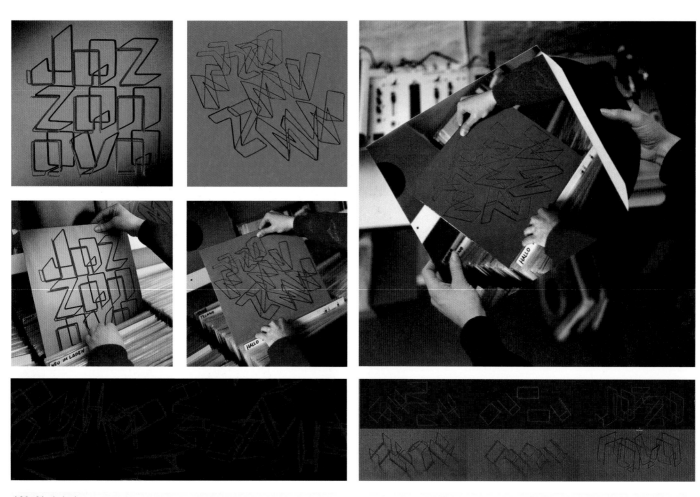

160.01 jutojo

161.01 jutojo

162.01 Marc Kappeler

162.02 Machine

162.03 Rinzen

162.04 blindresearch

162.05 Rinzen

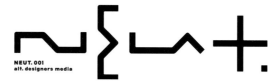

162.06 ASYL DESIGN Inc.

bausparer

163.01 augenbluten

datagirl

163.02 augenbluten

excellence

163.03 augenbluten

163.04 augenbluten

163.05 grasp at the air Co.,LTD

164.01 Luca Ionescu Design

164.02 Luca Ionescu Design

164.03 Luca Ionescu Design

164.04 Power Graphixx

164.05 Machine

164.06 grasp at the air Co.

164.07 Tsuyoshi Kusano

164.08 Luca Ionescu Design

164.09 Machine

165.01 Rinzen

165.02 Luca Ionescu Design

165.03 ghs web graphica

165.04 Power Graphixx

165.05 Matthias Hübner

165.06 Luca Ionescu Design

165.07 Bionic System

165.08 Power Graphixx

165.09 Luca Ionescu Design

165.10 Luca Ionescu Design

165.11 LEVEL1

165.12 onlab

166.01 Luca Ionescu Design

166.02 Rinzen

FAMILY™

167.01 Rinzen

167.02 Rinzen

**EXTENDED FAMILY . LEVEL FOUR . OPENING SOON**

FAMILY CLIMBS A STEP CLOSER TO HEAVEN WITH THE OPENING OF LEVEL FOUR,
OUR TOP-FLOOR GARDEN OF DELIGHTS, INCLUDING:

**THE COCKTAIL LOUNGE**
ELEVATED SEATING AND STAGE SPACES FOR QUIET, MORE INTIMATE SESSIONS.
LAID BACK MUSIC, A MIXTURE OF RECORDINGS, DJS, AND LIVE ACTS. LOUNGE BOOTHS
WILL BE AVAILABLE FOR RESERVATION FOR MEMBERS.

**THE POD**
A SELF CONTAINED SENSORY OVERLOAD ENVIRONMENT REINFORCED WITH AUSTRALIA'S
LARGEST STATE OF THE ART SOUND SYSTEM.

**SAT 25.08.01**
**CHRIS WILSON . MARK BRIAIS . JULES CAMPAIN**
WITH SPECIAL GUEST
**DECLAN LEE** (SYDNEY/CHINESE LAUNDRY, CHINA WHITE)

**FAMILY**™

**8 McLACHLAN STREET FORTITUDE VALLEY**
WWW.THEFAMILY.COM.AU
DOORS OPEN AT 9PM.
MANAGEMENT RESERVES RIGHT TO REFUSE ENTRY.
PHOTO ID MAY BE REQUIRED.

169.01 Rinzen                                            169.02 Rinzen

170.01 Blammo

170.02 Machine

170.03 Machine

170.04 hausgrafik

170.05 hausgrafik

170.06 Blammo

170.07 Niels Meulman

171.01 Blammo

171.02 Blammo

EXHALE
EXHALE EXHALE
EXHALE EXHALE EXHALE
EXHALE EXHALE EXHALE EXHALE
EXHALE EXHALE EXHALE EXHALE
EXHALE EXHALE EXHALE EXHALE EXHALE
EXHALE EXHALE EXHALE EXHALE
EXHALE EXHALE EXHALE EXHALE
EXHALE EXHALE EXHALE EXHALE
EXHALE EXHALE EXHALE EXHALE
EXHALE EXHALE EXHALE EXHALE
EXHALE EXHALE EXHALE
EXHALE EXHALE EXHALE
EXHALE EXHALE EXHALE
EXHALE
EXHALE
EXHALE
EXHALE
EXHALE
EXHALE
EXHALE

172.01 Blammo

172.02 Marc Kappeler

172.03 LEVEL1

172.04 Tsuyoshi Kusano

172.05 Blammo

172.06 Tsuyoshi Kusano

173.01 Pfadfinderei

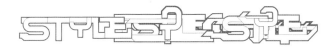

173.02 Pfadfinderei

173.03 OCKTAK

173.04 OCKTAK

173.05 forcefeed:swede

173.06 Machine

174.01 LEVEL1

174.02 augenbluten

174.03 Tsuyoshi Kusano

174.04 Norm

174.05 Tsuyoshi Kusano

174.06 Tsuyoshi Kusano

174.07 Tsuyoshi Kusano

174.08 Tsuyoshi Kusano

174.09 Tsuyoshi Kusano

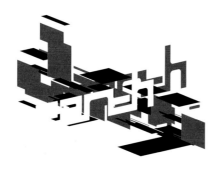

175.01 Tsuyoshi Kusano

175.02 phunk

175.03 GRIFF

175.04 phunk

176.01 A'

177.01 A'

178.01 vektor3          178.02 vektor3              178.03 vektor3              178.04 vektor3

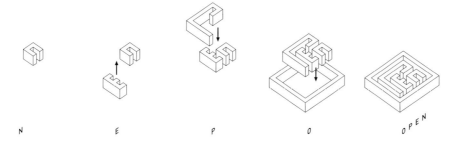

N                 E                 P                 O                 OPEN

OPEN®

179.01 yippieyeah

180.01 Woodtli

180.02 Woodtli

180.03 Woodtli

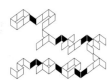

180.04 Woodtli

180.05 Woodtli

180.06 Woodtli

180.07 Woodtli

180.08 Woodtli

| ↑ | a | !, | c | d | e | f | g | h | i | j | k | l | m | n | o | p | q | ? | ! | _ | # |
|---|---|----|---|---|---|---|---|---|---|---|---|---|---|---|---|---|---|---|---|---|---|
|   |   |    |   |   |   |   |   |   |   |   |   |   |   |   |   |   |   |   |   |   |   |

| ↑ | r | s | t | u | v | w | x | y | z | $ | 0 | 1 | 2 | 3 | 4 | 5 | 6 | 7 | 8 | 9 | , |
|---|---|---|---|---|---|---|---|---|---|---|---|---|---|---|---|---|---|---|---|---|---|
|   |   |   |   |   |   |   |   |   |   |   |   |   |   |   |   |   |   |   |   |   |   |

181.01 Woodtli

| ↑ | a | !, | c | d | e | f | g | h | i | j | k | l | m | n | o | p | q | ? | ! | _ | # |
|---|---|----|---|---|---|---|---|---|---|---|---|---|---|---|---|---|---|---|---|---|---|
|   |   |    |   |   |   |   |   |   |   |   |   |   |   |   |   |   |   |   |   |   |   |

| ↑ | r | s | t | u | v | w | x | y | z | $ | 0 | 1 | 2 | 3 | 4 | 5 | 6 | 7 | 8 | 9 | , |
|---|---|---|---|---|---|---|---|---|---|---|---|---|---|---|---|---|---|---|---|---|---|
|   |   |   |   |   |   |   |   |   |   |   |   |   |   |   |   |   |   |   |   |   |   |

181.02 Woodtli

| ↑ | a | !, | c | d | e | f | g | h | i | j | k | l | m | n | o | p | q | ? | ! | _ | # |
|---|---|----|---|---|---|---|---|---|---|---|---|---|---|---|---|---|---|---|---|---|---|
|   |   |    |   |   |   |   |   |   |   |   |   |   |   |   |   |   |   |   |   |   |   |

| ↑ | r | s | t | u | v | w | x | y | z | $ | 0 | 1 | 2 | 3 | 4 | 5 | 6 | 7 | 8 | 9 | , |
|---|---|---|---|---|---|---|---|---|---|---|---|---|---|---|---|---|---|---|---|---|---|
|   |   |   |   |   |   |   |   |   |   |   |   |   |   |   |   |   |   |   |   |   |   |

181.03 Woodtli

182.01 augenbluten

182.02 jutojo

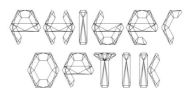

182.03 augenbluten

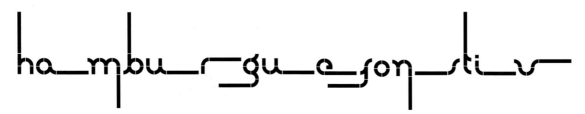

182.04 MAGNETOFONICA

# THE FEELGOOD MUSIC COLLECTION

183.01 gottfolk / fiskar

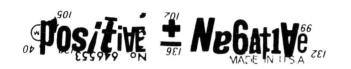

183.02 HandGun

183.03 Matthias Hübner

183.04 raum mannheim

183.05 raum mannheim

183.06 Tina Backmann

183.07 Tsuyoshi Kusano

183.08 Hendrik Hellige

183.09 Alphabetical Order

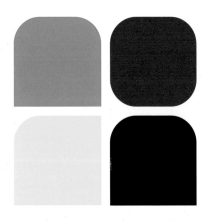

184.01 Norm

184.02 hausgrafik

184.03 Machine

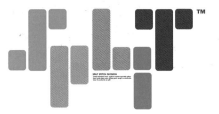

184.04 Luca Ionescu Design

184.05 Machine

184.06 augenbluten

184.07 Machine

185.01 Rinzen

185.02 Rinzen

185.03 Rinzen

186.01 Machine

186.02 Rinzen

187.01 Rinzen

187.02 Rinzen

187.03 Form®

187.04 Luca Ionescu Design

**DANISH FILM INSTITUTE**

188.01 e-Types

188.02 e-Types

188.03 e-Types

188.04 e-Types

189.01 Trixi Barmettler

189.02 Trixi Barmettler

189.03 Trixi Barmettler

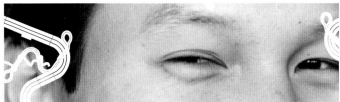

189.04 Trixi Barmettler

189.05 Trixi Barmettler

189.06 Trixi Barmettler

190.01 LEVEL1

190.02 LEVEL1

190.03 Nendo Grafic Squad

190.04 Nendo Grafic Squad

190.05 Nendo Grafic Squad

190.06 Nendo Grafic Squad

191.01 LEVEL1

191.02 LEVEL1

弐千大阪

192.01 Nendo Grafic Squad

光速船

192.02 Nendo Grafic Squad

モリソバ

192.03 Nendo Grafic Squad

192.04 Nendo Grafic Squad

ウィッギト

192.05 OCKTAK

192.06 LEVEL1

东京麦代

193.01 Nendo Grafic Squad

弐千东奈

193.02 Nendo Grafic Squad

文化計画

193.03 Maniackers Design

194.01 Nendo Grafic Squad

194.02 Nendo Grafic Squad

194.03 LEVEL1

194.04 Power Graphixx

194.05 Nendo Grafic Squad

194.06 hungryfordesign

MAGOKORO BROTHERS. P.D.C.NOTE

195.01 Tsuyoshi Kusano

中野ブロードウェイ大全

The unauthorized exploration guide for "Nakano Broadway"

195.02 Nendo Grafic Squad

196.01 Nendo Grafic Squad

吉本新喜劇弐千

196.02 Nendo Grafic Squad

ドリバシャフトレコーデング"プレゼンツ
リターンオブ ザ キラードリハ

196.03 Nendo Grafic Squad

197.01 LEVEL1

音楽と人

G戦場ヘヴンズドア

週刊日南橋ヨヨコ
™

若者のすべて

198.01 Maniackers Design     198.02 Maniackers Design 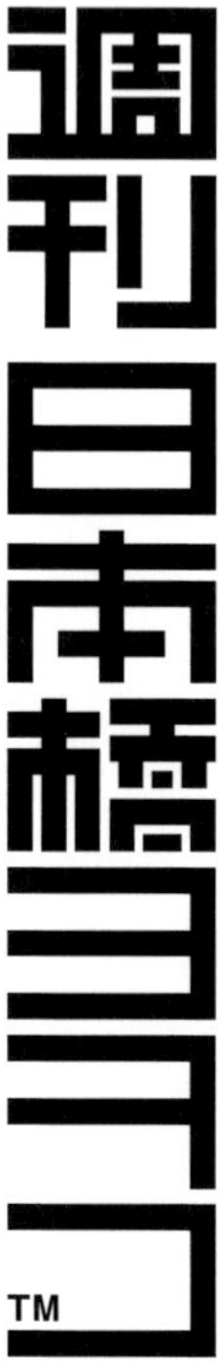    198.03 Maniackers Design     198.04 Tsuyoshi Kusano

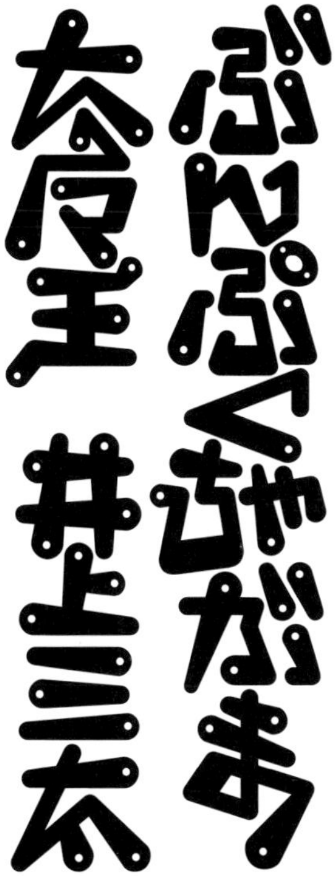

ぷんぷくちゃがま
大倉王 井上三太

南無阿弥陀佛

ホリデイ計画

199.01 Nendo Grafic Squad                                     199.02 Nendo Grafic Squad     199.03 Maniackers Design

アリアケ

**NENDO TYPEFACE SERIES**
POSTSCRIPT TYPE-I Formats Enclosed

アイウエオカキク
ケコサシスセソタ
チツテトナニヌネ
ノハヒフヘホマミ

200.02 Power Graphixx

200.03 phunk

200.01 Tsuyoshi Kusano

200.04 Nendo Grafic Squad

201.01 LEVEL1

202.01 Maniackers Design

202.02 Nendo Grafic Squad

202.03 Tsuyoshi Kusano

202.04 LEVEL1

202.05 grasp at the air Co.,LTD

202.06 Maniackers Design

203.01 ghs web graphica

203.02 OCKTAK

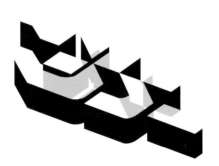

203.03 Tsuyoshi Kusano

203.04 Tsuyoshi Kusano

# TYPOGRAMS

# TYPOGRAMME

How do designers handle the building blocks of language: the characters? There are countless of answers to this question, from the classical approach via alienation, transformation, ornamental gimmicks and proportional changes to actual disruption, sometimes even breaking down the barriers erected around legibility. It is essential to display originality amongst the constant deluge of attention-seeking trade marks. Original in terms of contemporary aesthetic sensibilities (breaking rules and provoking people can be 'beautiful' as well), but original – and ultimately this is what it is all about – in a way that reflects the client's interests as unambiguously as possible. An exciting task. How do you work with somewhat 'heavy' company initials, seemingly set in stone, when they stand for a light, airy, finely-spun product? It doesn't matter how, the main thing is to use appropriate design to escape anonymity and head straight for for the recipients sensual receptors!

Wie gehen Gestalter mit den Bausteinen der Sprache um: mit den Schriftzeichen? Darauf gibt es unzählige Antworten, die von der klassischen Herangehensweise über Verfremdungen, Transformationen, ornamentale Gimmicks und proportionale Veränderungen bis hin zu eigentlichen Irritationen reichen und auch schon einmal die Grenzpfähle zum Territorium der Unleserlichkeit nieder reißen. In der ständig steigenden Flut der um Aufmerksamkeit buhlenden Markenzeichen ist Originalität gefragt. Originalität, die das zeitgeistige ästhetische Empfinden trifft (auch Regelbrüche und Provokationen können ‚schön' sein), die jedoch auch – und darauf kommt es schlussendlich an – das Anliegen des Absenders möglichst unmissverständlich reflektiert. Eine spannende Aufgabe. Wie setzt man etwa die wie in Stein gemeißelten, massig ‚schweren' Initialen eines Unternehmens um, wenn sich dahinter ein luftig-leichtes, filigran ‚gestricktes' Produkt verbirgt? Egal wie, Hauptsache mit adäquatem Design heraus aus der Anonymität, hinein in die sinnlichen Wahrnehmungszonen der Rezipienten!

CONTENT

INHALT

# PRJ/17.

206.01 Power Graphixx

# 123KLVN

206.02 123KLAN

# B.Q.E.

206.03 Power Graphixx

# TYO.

206.04 Power Graphixx

# TGNG

206.05 Tsuyoshi Kusano

# NYDP.

206.06 Dopepope

# S I

206.07 re-p

# US40

206.08 STRADA

# Red

206.09 Ben Mulkey

# dp

206.10 Dopepope

206.11 FORMGEBER

206.12 Blammo

207.01 Tsuyoshi Kusano

207.02 CODE

ATNY

207.03 Tsuyoshi Kusano

207.04 kong.gmbh

207.05 123KLAN

FCDAV

207.06 B.ü.L.b grafix

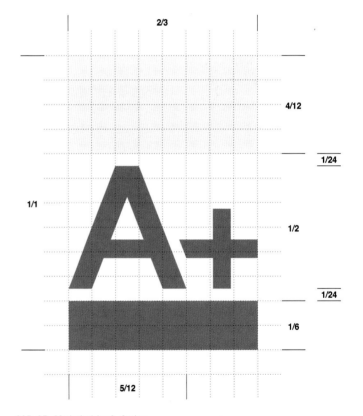

207.07 Alphabetical Order

208.01 Maniackers Design

208.02 Tycoon Graphics

208.03 Power Graphixx

208.04 Sanjai Bhana

208.05 Power Graphixx

208.06 Tsuyoshi Kusano

208.07 Dopepope

208.08 Norm

208.09 Pfadfinderei

208.10 Pfadfinderei

208.11 raum mannheim

208.12 Bionic System

209.01 FORMGEBER

209.02 typotherapy

209.03 RosendahlGrafik

209.04 Dopepope

209.05 p*star

209.06 Form®

209.07 Form®

**Australian Boarders Inc.**

209.08 Luca Ionescu Design

209.09 jum

209.10 jum

209.11 New Future People

209.12 New Future People

210.01 Tsuyoshi Kusano

210.02 Maniackers Design

210.03 Luca Ionescu Design

210.05 Markus Moström

210.06 augenbluten

210.04 Power Graphixx

210.07 DED Associates

210.08 Ross Imms

211.01 24HR

212.01 B.ü.L.b grafix

212.02 Fourskin®

212.03 Power Graphixx

212.04 Gregory Gilbert-Lodge

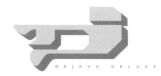

212.05 123KLAN

212.06 Machine

212.07 Tsuyoshi Kusano

212.08 Matthias Hübner

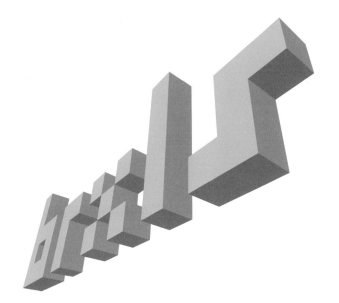

213.01 dubius?                                    213.02 dubius?

214.01 Maniackers Design

214.02 123KLAN

214.03 Power Graphixx

214.04 Luca Ionescu Design

214.05 Power Graphixx

214.06 DED Associates

214.07 büro destruct

214.08 Power Graphixx

214.09 designershock/DSOS1

214.10 Tsuyoshi Kusano

214.11 Power Graphixx

214.12 Power Graphixx

215.01 balsi

215.02 Luca Ionescu Design

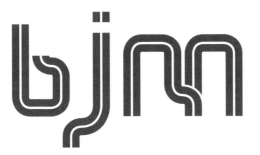

215.03 Ben Mulkey

215.04 Tsuyoshi Kusano

216.01 Dopepope

216.02 jum

216.03 Form®

216.04 Tsuyoshi Kusano

216.05 Chris Hutchinson

216.06 Form®

216.07 344 Design

216.08 re-p

216.09 BlackDog

216.10 archetype:interactive

216.11 kong.gmbh

216.12 BlackDog

217.01 LEVEL1

217.02 Lobo

217.03 nothing medialab

217.04 Form®

217.05 archetype:interactive

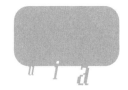

217.06 archetype:interactive

217.07 BlackDog

217.08 MIGUEL ANGEL LEYVA

217.09 anja klausch

217.10 Norm

217.11 jum

217.12 Form®

218.01 yippieyeah

218.02 OhioGirl

218.03 Ana Starling

218.04 Dopepope

219.01 Woodtli

219.02 Woodtli

219.03 Woodtli

219.08 Syrup Helsinki

219.04 Woodtli

219.05 Woodtli

219.06 Woodtli

219.07 Woodtli

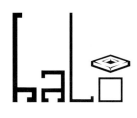

219.09 hungryfordesign

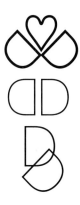

219.10 New Future People

220.01 123KLAN

220.02 Tsuyoshi Kusano

220.03 Blammo

220.04 123KLAN

220.05 123KLAN

220.06 123KLAN

221.01 Blammo

222.01 jum                222.02 Blammo                222.03 Blammo                222.04 jum

222.05 phunk              222.06 Niels Meulman          222.07 Blammo                222.08 Move Design

223.01 Tsuyoshi Kusano

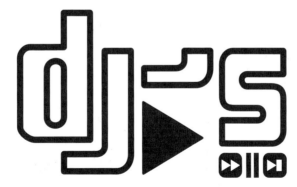

223.02 büro destruct

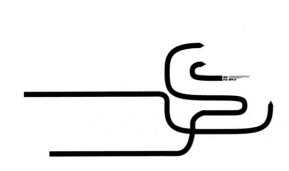

224.01 Luca Ionescu Design

224.02 Luca Ionescu Design

224.03 Luca Ionescu Design

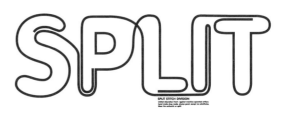

224.04 Luca Ionescu Design

225.01 Finsta

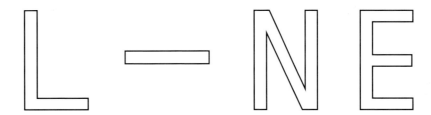

225.02 Taylor Deupree

226.01 büro destruct

226.02 Machine

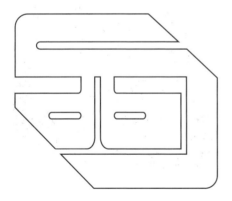

226.03 CODE

226.04 Machine

227.01 CODE

227.02 Sanjai Bhana

227.03 Machine

227.04 büro destruct

228.01 Dopepope

228.02 Dopepope

228.03 POSITRON CO., LTD.

228.04 Sanjai Bhana

228.05 Dopepope

228.06 Dopepope

228.07 MASA Colectivo Gráfico    228.08 Tycoon Graphics

228.09 Dopepope

228.10 p*star

229.01 phunk

230.01 Tsuyoshi Kusano

230.02 Tsuyoshi Kusano

230.03 Tsuyoshi Kusano

230.04 Tsuyoshi Kusano

230.05 augenbluten

230.06 phunk

230.07 Tsuyoshi Kusano

230.08 Power Graphixx

230.09 augenbluten

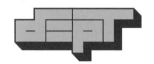

230.10 Machine

230.11 Tsuyoshi Kusano

230.12 Niels Jansson

231.01 vektor3

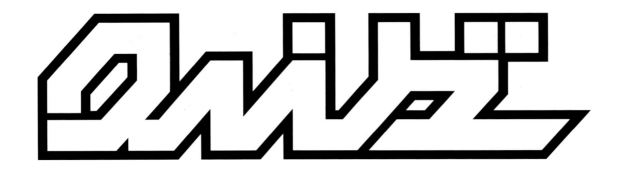

232.01 Power Graphixx

232.02 Luca Ionescu Design

232.03 Tsuyoshi Kusano

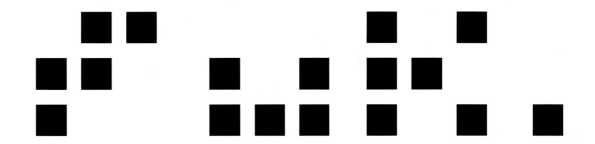

233.01 DED Associates

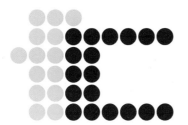

233.02 p*star                                                              233.03 SAKAMOTO

234.01 Hendrik Hellige

234.02 Hendrik Hellige

234.03 FORMGEBER

234.04 Tsuyoshi Kusano

234.06 SAKAMOTO

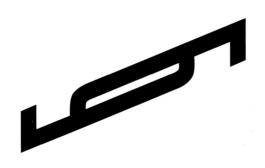

234.05 kong.gmbh

234.07 Form®

235.01 Zip Design

235.02 TOI Inc.

236.01 Alphabetical Order

236.02 phunk        236.03 Luca Ionescu Design

236.05 Rinzen

236.06 Rinzen

236.04 Lobo       236.07 Digitalultras      236.08 Rinzen

**SPLIT STITCH DIVISION**
United Liberation Front : against machine operated artillery
hand made shop made. always good. except no substitutes.
Wear the authentic or split!

237.01 Luca Ionescu Design

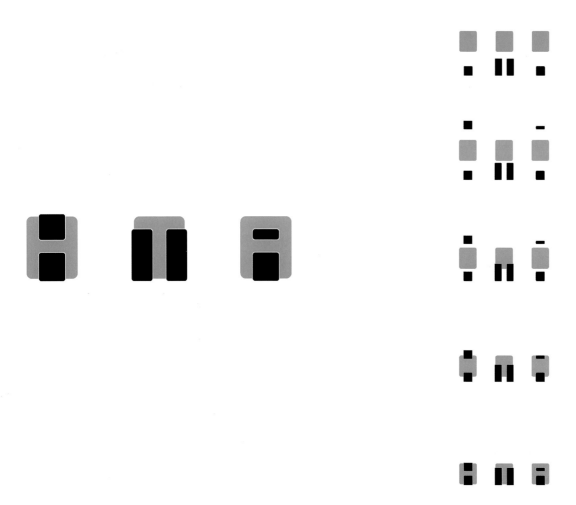

238.01 buffet für gestaltung

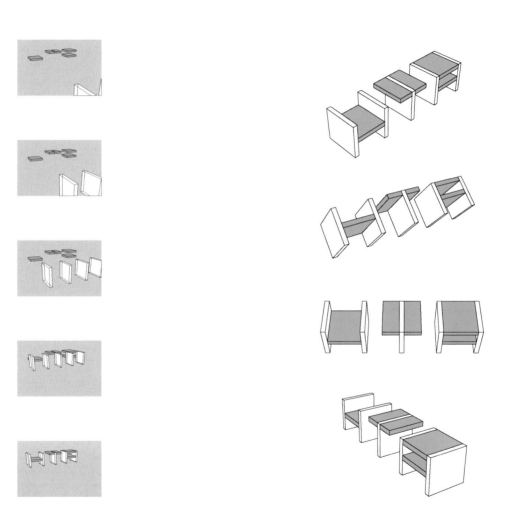

239.01 buffet für gestaltung

240.01 ghs web graphica

240.02 ghs web graphica

240.03 Sanjai Bhana

240.04 archetype:interactive

240.05 ghs web graphica

240.06 LEVEL1

240.07 Sanjai Bhana

240.08 Power Graphixx

その先の言葉　五つの赤い風船

241.01 Tsuyoshi Kusano          241.02 ghs web graphica          241.03 LEVEL1          241.04 Nendo Grafic Squad

242.01 Cyclone Graphix

242.02 Cyclone Graphix

242.03 123KLAN

242.04 Disco Döner

243.01 LEVEL1

243.02 Tycoon Graphics

243.03 ASYL DESIGN Inc.

244.01 blindresearch

244.02 Mutabor

244.03 Mutabor

244.04 nothing medialab

244.05 dubius?

244.06 RosendahlGrafik

245.01 Planet Pixel

245.02 Planet Pixel

245.03 Bionic System

245.04 Power Graphixx

245.05 typotherapy

245.06 büro destruct

**EXTRA-BREATHABLE
ALL-ROUND PROTECTION**

246.01 Um|bruch Gestaltung

**EXTRA-LIGHT
INVISIBLE PROTECTION**

246.02 Um|bruch Gestaltung

246.03 Um|bruch Gestaltung

**EXTRA-DRY
ALL-TERRAIN PROTECTION**

246.04 Um|bruch Gestaltung

246.05 Um|bruch Gestaltung

**EXTRA-DRY
ALL-TERRAIN PROTECTION**

246.06 Um|bruch Gestaltung

 | SENSOR

247.01 Um|bruch Gestaltung

 | REAKTOR

247.02 Um|bruch Gestaltung

247.03 CODE

247.04 blindresearch

247.05 moniteurs

247.06 B.ü.L.b grafix

248.01 Syrup Helsinki

248.02 ColdWater Graphiix

248.03 STRADA

248.04 p*star

248.05 Todd Hansson

248.06 BlackDog

248.07 ColdWater Graphiix

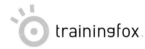

248.08 B.ü.L.b grafix

248.09 Power Graphixx

248.10 BlackDog

248.11 forcefeed:swede

248.12 Thorsten Geiger

INTEL STUDENT DESIGN COMPETITION

249.01 Move Design

    CAMELOT  FILMPRODUKTIONEN

249.02 raum mannheim

249.03 Mutabor            249.04 Taylor Deupree        249.05 Machine            249.06 nothing medialab

250.01 Bionic System

250.02 augenbluten

250.03 CODE

250.04 jutojo

250.05 New Future People

250.06 Form®

250.07 büro destruct

250.08 DED Associates

250.09 xonetik

250.10 xonetik

250.11 Fourskin®

250.12 tankdesign

 **Gut Boltenhof**

251.01 anja klausch

 BIKE STATION

251.02 kong.gmbh

 Red Establishment

251.03 Ben Mulkey

 **GRÜNDER**
PARTNER FÜR BERLIN

251.04 Thorsten Geiger

 POWERPLAY

251.05 FORMGEBER

251.06 AREADESIGN

252.01 CODE

252.02 Bionic System

252.03 SAKAMOTO

252.04 Maniackers Design

252.05 Maniackers Design

252.06 Bionic System

ZEONIC™

252.07 Power Graphixx

Zwinemn™

252.08 Power Graphixx

 fruchtig

252.09 raum mannheim

 fieldwork

252.10 Sweden

 streetwork

252.11 nothing medialab

* bluetec

252.12 nothing medialab

253.01 tronics

253.02 Mutabor

253.03 FORMGEBER

253.04 STRADA

253.05 Sanjai Bhana

253.06 344 Design

253.07 typotherapy

253.08 Designunion

253.09 büro destruct

253.10 Mutabor

253.11 DED Associates

253.12 jutojo

254.01 Sweden

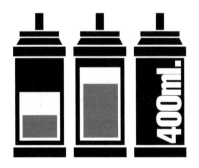

254.02 123KLAN

254.03 123KLAN

255.01 Zookeeper

255.02 Power Graphixx

workplace

256.01 typotherapy

256.02 Mutabor

256.03 Mutabor

 **DISTEFORA**

256.04 Mutabor

 linde design

256.05 Lindedesign

Fanfare
by CLASSEN

257.01 Mutabor

257.02 Mutabor          257.03 Mutabor          257.04 Mutabor          257.05 Mutabor

./ logicaland

258.01 re-p

258.02 Luca Ionescu Design

merz+partner_events

258.03 CODE

258.04 gottfolk / fiskar

braus.ch

dynAmisch digitales

258.05 tankdesign

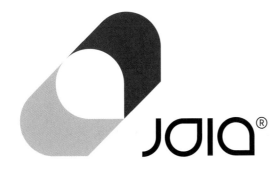

259.01 24HR

259.02 anja klausch

259.03 John J. Candy Design

259.04 anja klausch

260.01 e-Types

260.02 e-Types

260.03 e-Types

260.04 e-Types

261.01 e-Types

262.01 OCKTAK

262.02 OCKTAK

262.03 OCKTAK

262.04 OCKTAK

263.01 24HR

263.02 OCKTAK

263.03 OCKTAK

263.04 Rinzen

263.05 OCKTAK

264.01 Electronic Curry Ltd.

264.02 Electronic Curry Ltd.

265.01 Alphabetical Order

265.02 Lobo

265.03 CODE

265.04 CODE

265.05 raum mannheim

265.06 Move Design

266.01 ghs web graphica

266.02 Mutabor

266.03 Tycoon Graphics

266.04 forcefeed:swede

266.05 Pictomat

266.06 Mutabor

267.01 Luca Ionescu Design

267.02 Luca Ionescu Design

267.03 Dopepope

267.04 Sanjai Bhana

267.05 balsi

267.06 Luca Ionescu Design

268.01 Lobo

268.02 xonetik

**Audi Speed Challenge**

268.03 anja klausch

269.01 tankdesign

269.02 Mutabor

269.03 Mutabor

270.01 dubius?

270.02 augenbluten

270.03 Mutabor

270.04 Power Graphixx

271.01 xonetik

recordings
of substance<sup>HD</sup>

PO Box 23137 London SE1 3ZW

271.02 DED Associates

271.03 nothing medialab

271.04 CRAIG ROBINSON

271.05 grasp at the air Co.,LTD

271.06 123KLAN

272.01 dubius?

272.02 BlackDog

272.03 Tsuyoshi Kusano

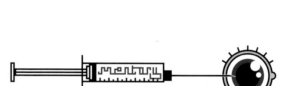

272.04 Mentary

272.05 Chris Hutchinson

272.06 Blammo

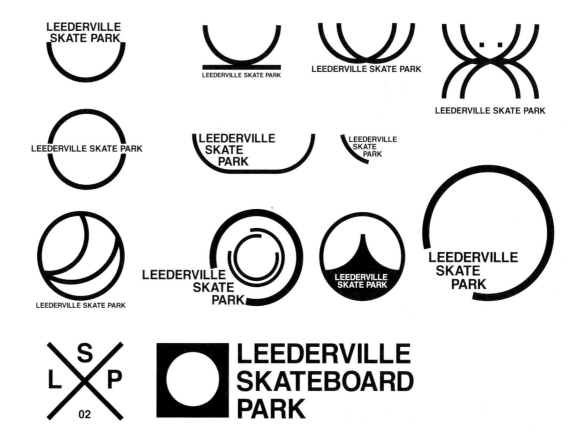

Leederville Skateboard Park - Perth, Australia

WETWARE

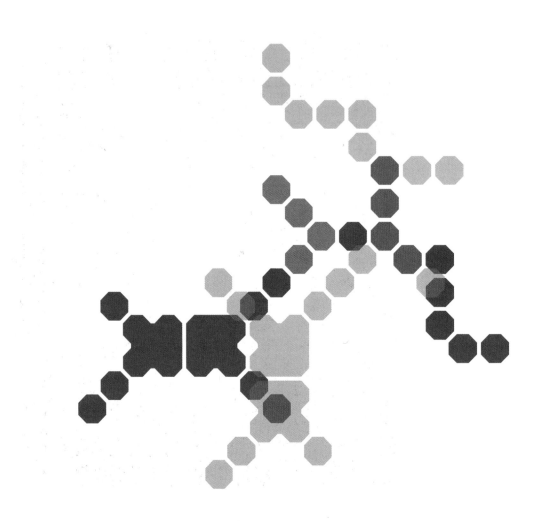

東京地下製造

madentyourgd™

275.01 Cyclone Graphix

276.01 Nendo Grafic Squad

276.02 Tycoon Graphics

kemab
elnät

kemab
elnät

kemab
elnät

kemab
kraft

kemab
kraft

kemab
kraft

kemab
kraft

kemab
kraft

k          e          s          m

kemab
miljö

kemab
miljö

kemab
miljö

kemab
kraft

kemab
kraft

kemab
kraft

kemab
kraft

Realizers™

278.01 büro destruct

AS/REC

278.02 Bionic System

NIGHTCRAWLER

278.03 blindresearch

ANTI*TAINMENT*

278.04 blindresearch

composite station

278.05 Nendo Grafic Squad

Primal Music®

278.06 24HR

278.07 ghs web graphica

DexeeDinner

278.08 POSITRON CO., LTD.

HIMIT

278.09 ghs web graphica

Offspring

278.10 Zip Design

Khnm

278.11 Power Graphixx

子供銀行

278.12 Nendo Grafic Squad

PARADISE

278.13 Tsuyoshi Kusano

LEVEL1

278.14 LEVEL1

有限会社 池越玉堂社

278.15 ghs web graphica

BOOMBEAT
MUSIC

278.16 archetype:interactive

**HOTRODS**

279.01 Chris Hutchinson

**BEER**

279.02 Chris Hutchinson

**HOOCHIES**

279.03 Chris Hutchinson

279.04 Chris Hutchinson

8180.com

279.05 archetype:interactive

chocolate

279.06 CODE

TRADING|POST
AT THE END OF THE UNIVERSE

279.07 Artificial Environments

279.08 Matthias Hübner

InterEgo

279.09 gottfolk / fiskar

itokenstein

279.10 Tsuyoshi Kusano

IGNTE

279.11 Zookeeper

**Destination Paradise**

279.12 artetic

DAVID BRESKIN
varied interests

279.13 BlackDog

spidergalaxy

279.14 CODE

**BQE CUSTOM**

279.15 Power Graphixx

279.16 büro destruct

280.01 MASA Colectivo Gráfico

280.02 büro destruct

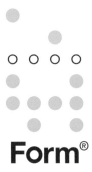

280.03 Form®

280.04 archetype:interactive

280.05 MAGNETOFONICA

280.06 MASA Colectivo Gráfico

281.01 POSITRON CO., LTD.

281.02 ColdWater Graphiix

281.03 Sweden

281.04 John J. Candy Design

281.05 Power Graphixx

lucious™

281.06 Luca Ionescu Design

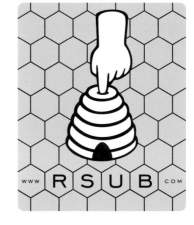

281.07 o-matic corp.

Atom

282.01 Method

blitztrade

282.02 FORMGEBER

UPLOAD

282.03 Lobo

SCIENCE FICTION
BOKHANDELN

282.04 John J. Candy Design

Club iT

282.05 Tsuyoshi Kusano

sydney|side

282.06 Luca Ionescu Design

industria

282.07 DED Associates

phoenix & dragon trust

282.08 archetype:interactive

282.09 Hirschindustries

organic

282.10 dubius?

COMPANY

282.11 Niels Meulman

the9thFLOOR

282.12 Deanne Cheuk

283.01 jutojo

283.02 Bionic System

283.03 WG Berlin

283.04 Electronic Curry Ltd.

283.05 Machine

283.06 Tsuyoshi Kusano

283.07 LEVEL1

283.08 Sweden

283.09 Tycoon Graphics

283.10 AREADESIGN

284.01 HandGun

284.02 hungryfordesign

284.03 Zookeeper

284.04 Zookeeper

284.05 MASA Colectivo Gráfico

284.06 phunk

BAD IDEA JEANS

285.01 Sweden

285.02 ala webstatt

285.03 Sweden

285.04 Power Graphixx

286.01 Power Graphixx

286.02 augenbluten

286.03 augenbluten

286.04 Ross Imms

286.05 büro destruct

286.06 Luca Ionescu Design

286.07 Luca Ionescu Design

286.08 büro destruct

286.09 Tsuyoshi Kusano

286.10 augenbluten

286.11 büro destruct

286.12 büro destruct

286.13 Ross Imms

286.14 Tsuyoshi Kusano

286.15 Power Graphixx

286.16 Tycoon Graphics

287.01 Pfadfinderei

287.02 p*star

287.03 WG Berlin

287.04 archetype:interactive

287.05 archetype:interactive    287.06 archetype:interactive    287.07 DED Associates

288.01 Tsuyoshi Kusano

288.06 Deanne Cheuk

288.02 LEVEL1

288.03 OhioGirl

288.04 Power Graphixx

288.05 Power Graphixx

288.07 Luca Ionescu Design

288.08 OhioGirl

288.09 büro destruct

288.10 augenbluten

289.01 Dirk Rudolph        289.02 Move Design        289.03 DED Associates        289.04 Zip Design

289.05 DED Associates      289.06 balsi        289.07 grasp at the air Co.,LTD  289.08 Hirschindustries

DED industria

290.01 DED Associates

hellvetica™

290.02 New Future People

mute

290.03 grasp at the air Co.,LTD

minimise

290.04 minimise

Lid Design

290.05 Luca Ionescu Design

stewarts

290.06 Luca Ionescu Design

EU|UPPLYSNINGEN
SVERIGES RIKSDAG

290.07 John J. Candy Design

ELEIJEGA

290.08 MASA Colectivo Gráfico

BEEP™

290.09 Luca Ionescu Design

norm

290.10 Norm

artificialenvironments

290.11 Artificial Environments

TELEMETRIC

290.12 Hirschindustries

291.01 Tsuyoshi Kusano

291.02 Zip Design

291.03 Luca Ionescu Design

291.04 MASA Colectivo Gráfico

291.05 HandGun

291.06 büro destruct

291.07 büro destruct

291.08 MIGUEL ANGEL LEYVA

291.09 LEVEL1

291.10 büro destruct

291.11 DED Associates

291.12 balsi

PRIMER
SALON NACIONAL
DE
**ACUARELAS**

292.01 MAGNETOFONICA                              292.02 Dopepope              292.03 benjamin guedel

293.01 Luca Ionescu Design

293.02 Planet Pixel

293.03 ghs web graphica

293.04 ghs web graphica

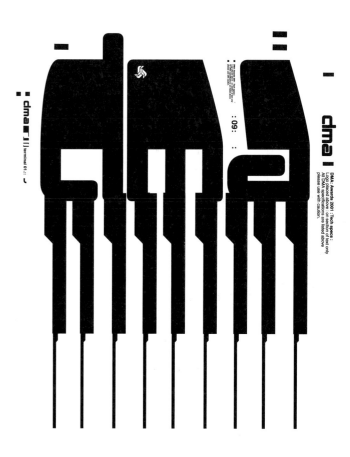

293.05 Luca Ionescu Design

294.01 büro destruct

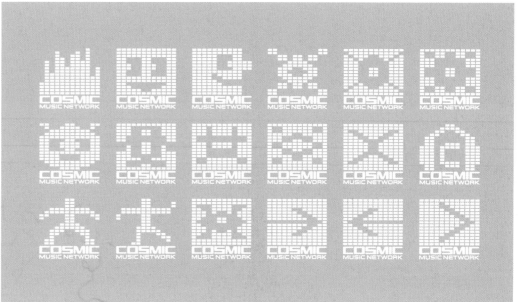

295.01 Move Design

295.02 Move Design

296.01 nothing medialab

296.02 nothing medialab

296.03 nothing medialab

296.04 nothing medialab

296.05 nothing medialab

296.06 nothing medialab

296.07 nothing medialab

296.08 nothing medialab

296.09 nothing medialab

296.10 nothing medialab

296.11 nothing medialab

296.12 Eboy

297.01 nothing medialab

297.02 MELON DEZIGN

297.03 nothing medialab

297.04 MASA Colectivo Gráfico

297.05 nothing medialab

297.06 Electronic Curry Ltd.

298.01 Syrup Helsinki

298.02 Move Design

298.03 Matthias Hübner

298.04 nothing medialab

298.05 Planet Pixel

298.06 CODE

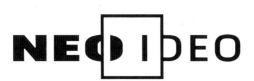

298.07 e-Types

298.08 Hendrik Hellige

299.01 Woodtli

299.02 büro destruct

299.03 POSITRON CO., LTD.

299.04 Luca Ionescu Design

299.05 Sanjai Bhana

299.06 Form©

299.07 Form©

299.08 HandGun

299.09 Form©

299.10 Form©

299.11 Form©

299.12 balsi

299.13 tankdesign

299.14 Todd Hansson

299.15 Alphabetical Order

299.16 Form©

300.01 Gobler Toys

300.02 Planet Pixel

300.03 grasp at the air Co.,LTD

300.04 CODE

300.05 jum

300.06 GRIFF

300.07 Nendo Grafic Squad

300.08 büro destruct

300.09 büro destruct

300.10 24HR

300.11 hausgrafik

300.12 Niels Meulman

300.13 Cyclone Graphix

300.14 SuperHappyBunny Company

300.15 24HR

300.16 Disco Döner

301.01 John J. Candy Design

301.02 Form®

301.03 Alphabetical Order

301.04 DSOS1

302.01 Form®

302.02 büro destruct

302.03 Sanjai Bhana

302.04 Bas Visual Concepts

302.05 ghs web graphica

302.06 Dirk Rudolph

302.07 123 KLAN

302.08 Tim Jester

302.09 tankdesign

302.10 büro destruct

302.11 Sanjai Bhana

302.12 Tim Jester

303.01 Dirk Rudolph          303.02 phunk              303.03 Mutabor              303.04 vektor3

303.05 Dopepope              303.06 Niels Meulman       303.07 benjamin guedel      303.08 Tim Jester

304.01 Zip Design

304.02 Zip Design

304.03 Raoul SINIER

304.04 moniteurs

305.01 raum mannheim

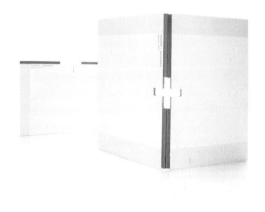

306.01 e-Types

306.02 e-Types                        306.03 e-Types

# NASCENT™
## Organic Vitality

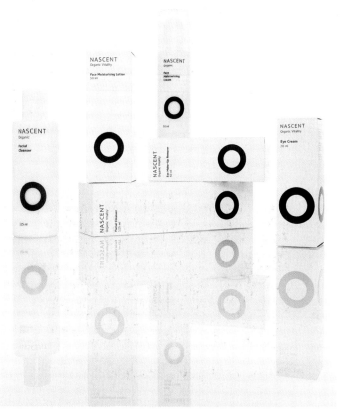

307.01 e-Types

307.02 e-Types

308.02 kong.gmbh

fusionOne

308.03 Method

308.01 Rinzen

308.04 Method

BERLIN CLUB_VIDEO

309.01 Versus

309.03 tankdesign

309.02 U.R.L. Agentur für Informationsdesign GmbH

F F F

fotografie franziska frutiger.

309.04 kong.gmbh

309.05 U.R.L. Agentur für Informationsdesign GmbH

310.01 MASA Colectivo Gráfico

FREHNER CONSULTING

310.02 p*star

310.03 24HR

Centre PasquArt

310.04 re-p

BLINDRESEARCH

310.05 blindresearch

310.06 balsi

310.07 balsi

310.08 büro destruct

310.09 Electronic Curry Ltd.

311.01 DED Associates

311.02 DED Associates

311.03 Form®

311.04 typotherapy

311.05 Luca Ionescu Design

311.06 FORMGEBER

311.07 CISMA

311.08 Bionic System

311.09 FORMGEBER

# Bionic Systems.

312.01 Bionic System

312.02 STRADA

312.03 123KLAN

**Wettbewerbskommission**
**Commission de la concurrence**
**Commissione della concorrenza**

312.04 316tn

313.01 Electronic Curry Ltd.

313.02 DED Associates

313.03 typotherapy

313.04 New Future People

313.05 MASA Colectivo Gráfico

313.06 dubius?

313.07 jutojo

313.08 24HR

313.09 RosendahlGrafik

313.10 Bionic System

313.11 OCKTAK

313.12 Disco Döner

314.01 Luca Ionescu Design

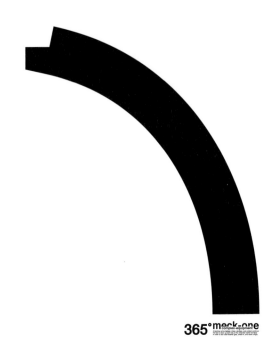

314.02 Luca Ionescu Design

314.03 Luca Ionescu Design

314.04 inTEAM Graphics

315.01 Luca Ionescu Design

315.02 Luca Ionescu Design

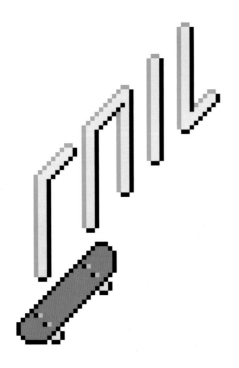

316.01 Eboy

316.02 Zip Design

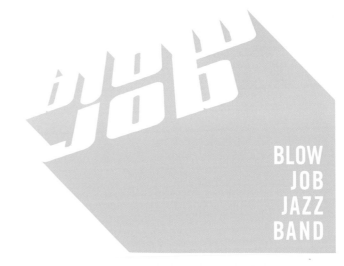

316.03 p*star

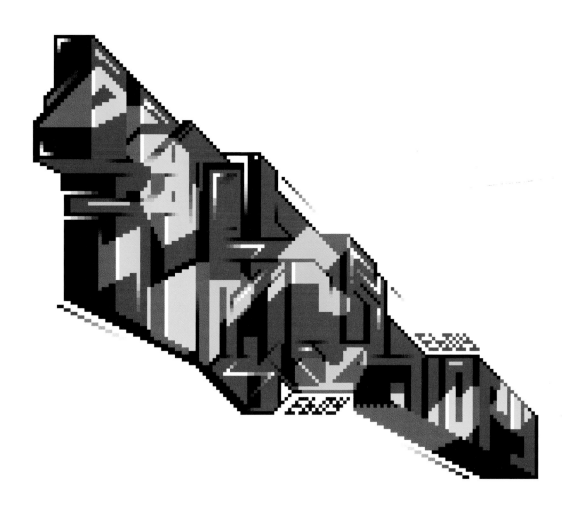

317.01 Eboy

318.01 Planet Pixel

318.02 jum

318.03 kong.gmbh

318.04 Disco Döner

318.05 BlackDog

318.06 Eboy

318.07 Form®

318.08 GRIFF

318.09 büro destruct

318.10 Eboy

318.11 Tim Jester

318.12 büro destruct

319.01 anja klausch

319.02 Disco Döner

319.03 Tsuyoshi Kusano

319.04 Chris Hutchinson

STUDIO BERLIN

319.05 RosendahlGrafik

319.06 tankdesign

319.07 buka grafik

319.08 BlackDog

319.09 GRIFF

319.10 nothing medialab

319.11 Rio Grafik

319.12 Mutabor

320.01 Eboy

320.02 Eboy

320.03 123KLAN

320.04 ghs web graphica

321.01 Rinzen

321.02 Mutabor

321.03 Rinzen

321.04 Sweden

322.01 BlackDog

322.02 24HR

322.03 Lobo

322.04 Gregory Gilbert-Lodge

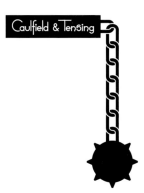

327.01 Niels Meulman

327.02 Blammo

327.03 phunk

327.04 OhioGirl

328.01 GRIFF

328.02 Disco Döner

328.03 jum

328.04 jum

328.05 GRIFF

328.06 jum

328.07 jum

328.08 Form®

328.09 Teamchman

328.10 Maniackers Design

328.11 GRIFF

328.12 michele del nobolo

329.01 Rinzen

329.02 Sanjai Bhana

329.03 MAGNETOFONICA

329.04 Luca Ionescu Design

# COLLECTED THEMES

# THEMEN-SAMMLUNG

What's to be done if a number of examples illustrating the LosLogos theme from countries all over the world refuse to fit in with the book's original categories? It would be destructive, and therefore wrong, to leave them out. So we went for the constructive approach and created a new category: productions.

Firstly, the productions take place on a world stage, where familiar and unfamiliar actors unwittingly take part in various brand and identity comedies.

Secondly, productions are the alienation and distortion of sometimes threatening signs and signals, playing exactly the same part as a 'normal' logo in their new context. But in a different way – and thus perhaps far more poignantly.

And last but not least this chapter presents logos staged in a thematic context. Real interiors for example, with the logo appearing and developing its effect as an integral part of the furniture. Or – as in the case of TOI – it is about a staging the logo of Ooze, a mysterious virtual city, dissolving the boundaries between fiction and reality.

Was tun, wenn zahlreiche, das Thema LosLogos illustrierende Beispiele aus vielen Ländern der Erde partout nicht in die anfänglich festgelegten Kategorien dieses Buches hineinpassen wollen? Eliminieren wäre die destruktive und somit falsche Methode. Also haben wir den konstruktiven Weg gewählt und eine neue Kategorie geschaffen: Inszenierungen.

Die Inszenierungen finden zum Einen auf einer Art Weltbühne statt, auf der bekannte und unbekannte Protagonistinnen und Protagonisten unbefragt Rollen in verschiedenen Marken- und Identity-Komödien zu spielen haben.

Inszenierungen meint zum Zweiten ironische Zweckentfremdungen bekannter, zum Teil auch bedrohlicher Zeichen und Signale, die in ihrem neuen Kontext die gleichen Funktionen erfüllen wie ein ganz 'normales' Logo. Eben nur anders – und damit vielleicht pointierter.

Last but not least präsentiert dieses Kapital auch Logos, deren Inszenierung in einem thematischen Umfeld stattfindet. Dabei geht es beispielsweise um ganz reale Innenräume, in denen die Logo-Inszenierung als integraler Bestandteil des Mobiliars seine Wirkung entfaltet. Oder es geht – wie im Fall TOI – um die Logo-Inszenierung der rätselhaften virtuellen Stadt Ooze, in der sich die Grenze zwischen Fiktion und Realität aufgelöst hat.

CONTENT

INHALT

Pages 332 – 391

Political activists, icons of the pop era, Jesus Christ Superstar, Hollywood B–movie stars, pixel creatures with manga and other traits, the late Ronald Reagan, unknown 'faces in the crowd', kids & pets, robots, cover girls and others.

Fire and flames, Guns without Roses, skulls and Gothic lettering, but also star-collecting, dairy cows or tools like record players or floppy disks are part of this inventory.

Seiten 332 – 391

Polit–Aktivisten, Ikonen der Pop Ära, Jesus Christ Superstar, B–Movie Stars aus Holly-wood, Pixelwesen mit mangahaften und an-deren Zügen, the late Ronald Reagan in Per-son, unbekannte 'faces in the crowd', Kids & Pets, Robots & Cover Girls und andere.

Feuer und Flammen, Guns without Roses, Totenköpfe und Schriftzüge aus Gothic Novels; aber auch Sterne vom Himmel holen, Milchkühe oder Tools wie Platten-spieler oder Floppy Discs gehören zu diesem Inventar.

**SOUMI DESIGN**

332.01 Syrup Helsinki                                    332.02 MASA Colectivo Gráfico

333.01 Luca Ionescu Design

333.02 Luca Ionescu Design

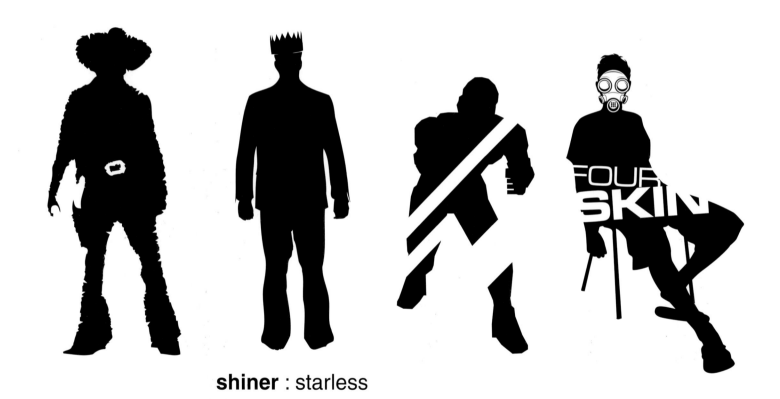

**shiner** : starless

334.01 benjamin guedel          334.02 OhioGirl          334.03 Tsuyoshi Kusano          334.04 Fourskin®

335.01 Norm

335.02 Die Gestalten

335.03 Norm

335.04 Tod Hansson

335.05 phunk

336.01 Dopepope

336.02 Planet Pixel

336.03 ColdWater Graphiix

336.04 Rio Grafik

337.01 Rinzen

337.02 Luca Ionescu Design

337.03 CODE

337.04 Rinzen

338.01 Rinzen        338.02 Rinzen        338.03 Rinzen        338.04 jum

338.05 incorect      338.06 incorect      338.07 incorect      338.08 Dopepope

339.01 jum

339.02 jum

339.03 jum

339.04 jum

339.05 jum

339.06 jum

340.03 Fourskin®

340.04 Blammo

340.05 Blammo

340.06 jum

340.01 Gregory Gilbert-Lodge    340.02 Luca Ionescu Design    340.07 Blammo    340.08 123KLAN

341.01 jum

341.02 Syryp Helsinki

341.03 jum

341.04 Judith Zaugg

341.05 hungryfordesign

342.01 jum

342.02 jum

342.03 jum

342.04 tikkigirl

342.05 nothing medialab

342.06 LEVEL1

342.07 designershock/DSOS1

342.08 unikum graphic design

342.09 Zinc

342.10 Zinc

342.11 Form®

342.12 Form®

343.01 xonetik

343.02 BlackDog

343.03 John J. Candy Design

343.04 MASA Colectivo Gráfico

343.05 LEVEL1

343.06 Gregory Gilbert-Lodge

343.07 jum

343.08 Gregory Gilbert-Lodge

343.09 MK12

343.10 MK12

343.11 nothing medialab

343.12 Move Design

344.01 LEVEL1                                    344.02 LEVEL1

344.03 incorect                                  344.04 Chris Hutchinson

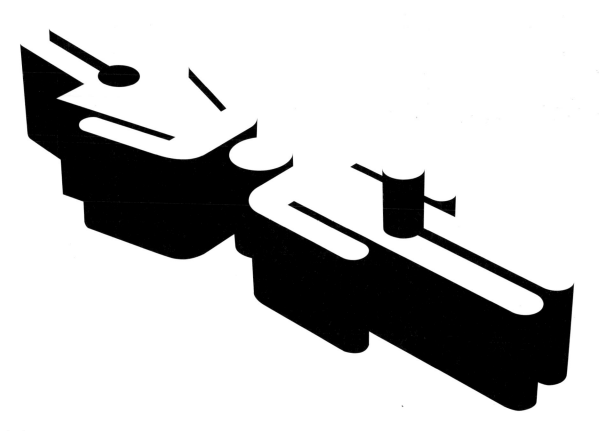

345.01 phunk

**fortyeightk**

346.01 jum                                      346.02 Ross Imms          346.03 phunk

347.01 Derrick Hodgson

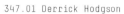

347.02 Derrick Hodgson

347.03 Derrick Hodgson

348.01 Dopepope

**IMPORTED NINJA UNIFORM**
Premium Grade • Made in Japan
**BLACK Ninja Uniform**
Shown at right.
No. 301
$39.95

—

**CAMOUFLAGE**
**Ninja Uniform**
**Woodland Green Color**
**Not Shown.**
**No.320**
**$44.95**

**NIN Patch**
Symbol of Ninjitsu.
Black & White. 3" in
diameter.
No. 4172........$1.50

348.02 Dopepope

dopepope:
hands free technology

349.01 Dopepope

350.01 OhioGirl

350.02 bigsexyland

350.03 Zookeeper

350.04 michele de nobolo

350.05 inTEAM Graphics

350.06 Zookeeper

351.01 incorect                                                    351.02 Superpopstudio

352.01 MAGNETOFONICA

352.02 Tsuyoshi Kusano

352.03 phunk

352.04 BlackDog

352.05 Disco Döner

353.01 phunk

353.02 Hellgolfers

353.03 dubius?

353.04 Power Graphixx

353.05 Planet Pixel

353.06 Planet Pixel

353.07 Rinzen

354.01 ghs web graphica        354.02 Blammo              354.03 Fourskin®           354.04 Superpopstudio

354.05 Dopepope                354.06 Fourskin®           354.07 Blammo              354.08 Nendo Grafic Squad

355.01 Fourskin®

355.02 Luca Ionescu Design

355.03 Luca Ionescu Design

355.04 Cyclone Graphix

355.05 Gregory Gilbert-Lodge

355.06 incorect

355.07 Luca Ionescu Design

355.08 Nendo Grafic Squad

356.01 Blammo

356.02 Blammo

356.03 phunk

356.04 Blammo

356.05 Blammo

356.06 Blammo

356.07 Blammo

356.08 Fourskin®

357.01 tankdesign

357.02 tankdesign

357.03 Blammo

357.04 Zip Design

357.05 hungryfordesign

357.06 Alphabetical Order

357.07 incorect

357.08 incorect

358.01 Mutabor

358.02 jum

358.03 Cyclone Graphix

358.04 Mutabor

358.05 MK12

358.06 Dopepope

358.07 Electronic Curry Ltd.

358.08 24HR

358.09 Luca Ionescu Design

358.10 Hirschindustries

359.01 AREADESIGN

359.02 Jorge Alderete

359.03 Yipyop

359.04 MASA Colectivo Gráfico

359.05 Niels Jansson

359.06 Luca Ionescu Design

359.07 Blammo

359.08 123KLAN

359.09 Mutabor

359.10 Syrup Helsinki

359.11 xonetik

359.12 Zookeeper

360.01 automatic art and design

360.02 phunk

360.03 Artificial Environments

360.04 MASA Colectivo Gráfico

360.05 New Future People

360.06 PXPress

360.07 büro destruct

360.08 MIGUEL ANGEL LEYVA

360.09 Fourskin®

360.10 Chris Hutchinson

360.11 OCKTAK

360.12 New Future People

360.13 Judith Zaugg

360.14 tomotomo.net

360.15 Luca Ionescu Design

360.16 Alphabetical Order

361.01 tokidoki

361.02 New Future People

361.03 balsi

361.04 Hendrik Hellige

361.05 jum

361.06 Power Graphixx

361.07 Thomas Mischler

361.08 SAKAMOTO

361.09 jum

361.10 Thomas Mischler

361.11 Rinzen

361.12 Eboy

361.13 Gobler Toys

361.14 augenbluten

361.15 phunk

362.01 Rinzen                  362.02 Mirko Borsche              362.03 Mirko Borsche

363.01 Gregory Gilbert-Lodge

364.01 Teamchman

364.02 Teamchman

364.03 Teamchman

364.04 moniteurs

364.05 Artificial Environments

364.06 Artificial Environments

364.07 Artificial Environments

364.08 Artificial Environments

364.09 AREADESIGN

364.10 büro destruct

364.11 jum

364.12 AREADESIGN

365.01 BlackDog

365.02 BlackDog

365.03 Norm

365.04 Blammo

365.05 automatic art and design    365.06 Form®

365.07 DED Associates

365.08 incorect

365.09 DED Associates

365.10 DSOS1

366.01 tankdesign

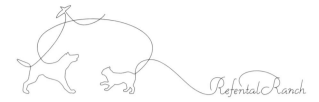

366.02 tankdesign

366.03 Zip Design

366.04 Mutabor

366.05 phunk

366.06 123KLAN

366.07 GRIFF

366.08 Bionic System

366.09 Alphabetical Order

366.10 Luca Ionescu Design

366.11 Luca Ionescu Design

366.12 SuperHappyBunny Company

366.13 phunk

367.01 Luca Ionescu Design

367.02 Disco Döner

367.03 e-Types

367.04 blindresearch

367.05 Blammo

367.06 Blammo

367.07 Luca Ionescu Design

367.08 Luca Ionescu Design

367.09 phunk

367.10 New Future People

367.11 Maniackers Design

367.12 Tim Jester

367.13 blindresearch

368.01 Gregory Gilbert-Lodge

368.02 minigram

368.03 Hirschindustries

369.01 Blammo

370.01 Menatry

370.02 CODE

370.03 phunk

370.04 incorect

370.05 Blammo

370.06 Blammo

370.07 phunk

370.08 jum

370.09 Luca Ionescu Design

370.10 Blammo

370.11 Blammo

370.12 Blammo

370.13 minigram

370.14 automatic art and design   370.15 Blammo

370.16 Blammo

371.01 HandGun

371.02 Mika Mischler

371.03 Deanne Cheuk

371.04 designiskinky

372.01 minigram

373.01 minigram

374.01 lasercade

374.02 lasercade

374.03 Mentary

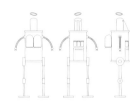

374.04 POSITRON CO., LTD.

374.05 Tsuyoshi Kusano

374.06 Teamchman

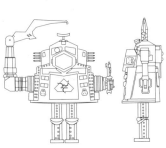

374.07 Mentary

374.08 Dopepope

374.09 hungryfordesign

374.10 Apakstudio

375.01 Luca Ionescu Design

375.02 123KLAN

375.05 Bionic System

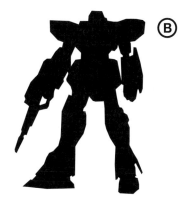

375.03 Bionic System

375.04 Sanjai Bhana

376.01 CODE

376.02 grasp at the air Co.,LTD

376.03 Hirschindustries

376.04 Mutabor

376.05 HandGun

376.06 moniteurs

376.07 incorect

376.08 123KLAN

376.09 büro destruct

376.10 Alphabetical Order

376.11 BlackDog

376.12 BlackDog

376.13 Luca Ionescu Design

376.14 Bionic System

377.01 raum mannheim

377.02 Rot

377.03 344 Design

377.04 Fernando Leal

377.05 HandGun

377.06 Form®

378.01 HandGun

378.02 benjamin guedel

378.03 HandGun

378.04 Blammo

378.05 HandGun

378.06 123KLAN

378.07 jum

378.08 Chris Hutchinson

378.09 Blammo

378.10 hungryfordesign

379.01 nothing medialab

379.02 John J. Candy Design

379.03 Trixi Barmettler

379.04 phunk

379.05 DED Associates

379.06 Tsuyoshi Kusano

379.07 Zinc

379.08 p*star

379.09 New Future People

380.01 123KLAN

380.02 FORMGEBER

380.03 Tim Jester

380.04 Sweden

380.05 Nendo Grafic Squad

380.06 nothing medialab

380.07 Thomas Mischler

380.08 Blammo

380.09 tankdesign

380.10 CODE

380.11 phunk

380.12 Tsuyoshi Kusano

381.01 Machine

381.02 Cyclone Graphix

381.03 Luca Ionescu Design

381.04 Zip Design

381.05 p*star

381.06 MASA Colectivo Gráfico

381.07 Zip Design

381.08 123KLAN

381.09 yippieyeah

381.10 nothing medialab

381.11 FORMGEBER

382.01 tankdesign

382.02 büro destruct

382.03 Bionic System

382.04 augenbluten

382.05 Form®

382.06 ColdWater Graphiix

382.07 phunk

382.08 p*star

382.09 tankdesign

382.10 büro destruct

383.01 Blammo

383.02 Form®

383.03 Blammo

383.04 minigram

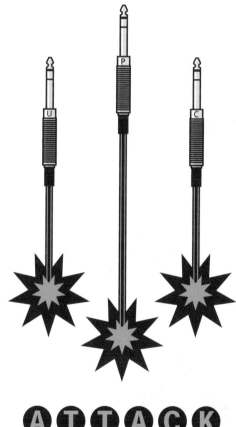

383.05 Mentary

384.01 Hirschindustries

384.02 Blammo

384.03 Zip Design

384.04 Finsta

384.05 Finsta

384.06 Finsta

384.07 FORMGEBER

384.08 Deanne Cheuk

384.09 Luca Ionescu Design

384.10 Sanjai Bhana

384.11 Disco Döner

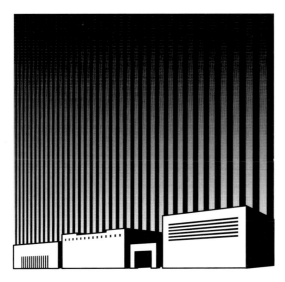

**STUDIO BERLIN**

M O T I O N   P I C T U R E S

385.01 RosendahlGrafik

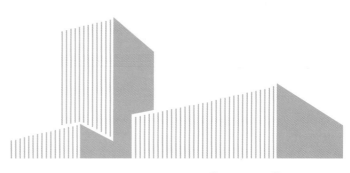

*stufenbau*

385.02 p*star

385.03 Planet Pixel    385.04 Deanne Cheuk    385.05 John J. Candy Design    385.06 WG Berlin

386.01 TOI Inc.

386.02 TOI Inc.

387.01 TOI Inc.                    387.02 TOI Inc.

388.01 Mirko Borsche                                    388.02 Mirko Borsche

NO DISK_

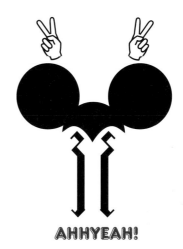

AHHYEAH!

389.01 Mirko Borsche          389.02 Mirko Borsche          389.03 Mirko Borsche          389.04 Mirko Borsche

**FF TradeMarker    SansLight**

FAMILY                WEIGHT

TYPESET

ABCDEFGHIJKLMNOPQRSTUVWXYZ
abcdefghijklmnopqrstuvwxyzß
0123456789[]::;<=>+,-.~?!"#$%&'*
@®©™¢£¥€{}[\]{/}§•¶

SAMPLE

Jackdåws love my big sphinx of quartz.
Blowzy red vixeñs fight for a quick jump?
The five "boxing wîzards" jump quickly.


**FF TradeMarker    SansBold**

FAMILY                WEIGHT

TYPESET

ABCDEFGHIJKLMNOPQRSTUVWXYZ
abcdefghijklmnopqrstuvwxyzß
0123456789[]::;<=>+,-.~?!"#$%&'*
@®©™¢£¥€{}[\]{/}§•¶

SAMPLE

Jackdåws love my big sphinx of quartz.
Blowzy red vixeñs fight for a quick jump?
The five "boxing wîzards" jump quickly.


**FF TradeMarker    SansBold**

FAMILY                WEIGHT

TYPESET

ABCDEFGHIJKLMNOPQRSTUVWXYZ
abcdefghijklmnopqrstuvwxyzß
0123456789[]::;<=>+,-.~?!"#$%&'*
@®©™¢£¥€{}[\]{/}§•¶

SAMPLE

Jackdåws love my big sphinx of quartz.
Blowzy red vixeñs fight for a quick jump?
The five "boxing wîzards" jump quickly.


**FF TradeMarker    SansLightItalic**

FAMILY                WEIGHT

TYPESET

ABCDEFGHIJKLMNOPQRSTUVWXYZ
abcdefghijklmnopqrstuvwxyzß
0123456789[]::;<=>+,-.~?!"#$%&'*
@®©™¢£¥€{}[\]{/}§•¶

SAMPLE

Jackdåws love my big sphinx of quartz.
Blowzy red vixeñs fight for a quick jump?
The five "boxing wîzards" jump quickly.


**FF TradeMarker    SansBoldItalic**

FAMILY                WEIGHT

TYPESET

ABCDEFGHIJKLMNOPQRSTUVWXYZ
abcdefghijklmnopqrstuvwxyzß
0123456789[]::;<=>+,-.~?!"#$%&'*
@®©™¢£¥€{}[\]{/}§•¶

SAMPLE

Jackdåws love my big sphinx of quartz.
Blowzy red vixeñs fight for a quick jump?
The five "boxing wîzards" jump quickly.


**FF TradeMarker    SansBoldItalic**

FAMILY                WEIGHT

TYPESET

ABCDEFGHIJKLMNOPQRSTUVWXYZ
abcdefghijklmnopqrstuvwxyzß
0123456789[]::;<=>+,-.~?!"#$%&'*
@®©™¢£¥€{}[\]{/}§•¶

SAMPLE

Jackdåws love my big sphinx of quartz.
Blowzy red vixeñs fight for a quick jump?
The five "boxing wîzards" jump quickly.

ASTEROIDS

**NENDO TYPEFACE SERIES**
POSTSCRIPT TYPE-I Formats Enclosed

ISHIMARU

**NENDO TYPEFACE SERIES**
POSTSCRIPT TYPE-I Formats Enclosed

391.01 Tsuyohsi Kusano

391.02 Tsuyohsi Kusano

# STATISTICS

# STATISTIKEN

Find out more about the background of the designers featured in LosLogos: four sets of statistics clearly show the distribution of designers and studios across various geographical regions and their preference for the possible approaches.

The statistics focus on chapters 1-3 (Logos, Lettering, Typograms). From the Japanese submissions examples were chosen which clearly describe a particular approach. We have not provided any statistics for chapter 4 and 5 (combinations and collected themes) because the work spans too broad range to fit into a precise typology.

Hier geht es um die Herkunft der am Werk LosLogos beteiligten Gestalter: In vier Statistiken wird anschaulich dargestellt, wie sich die Designer und Studios auf verschiedene geografische Regionen verteilen und welches ihre Präferenzen bezüglich der verschiedenen Umsetzungsarten sind.

Die Statistiken sind auf die Kapitel 1-3 (Logos, Schriftzüge, Typogramme) fokussiert. Von den Einsendungen japanischen Ursprungs wurden Beispiele ausgewählt, die klar einer bestimmten Usetzungsart zugeordnet werden können. Bei Kapitel 4 und 5 (Kombinationen und Themensammlungen) haben wir auf eine Statitsik verzichtet, weil sich die grosse Bandbreite der Umsetzungen einer geordneten Typologie entzieht.

CONTENT INHALT

Logos, lettering, typograms:
Pages 394 – 401

Illustrates the number of submissions, the proportional percentage across the various approaches and shows the distribution of the logos, lettering and typograms in the book across the different approaches.

Logos, Schriftzüge, Typogramme:
Seiten 394 – 401

Veranschaulicht die Anzahl der Zusendungen, die prozentualen Anteile an den verschiedenen Umsetzungsarten und zeigt auf, wie sich die im Buch gezeigten Logos, Schriftzüge und Typogramme auf die verschiedenen Umsetzungsarten verteilen.

Origins of the logos:
Pages 402 – 403

Shows the number of submissions, the geographical origins of the logos published in LosLogos and their designers.

Herkunft der Logos:
Seiten 402 – 403

Veranschaulicht die Anzahl der Zusendungen und zeigt die geografische Herkunft der in Los Logos publizierten Logos und ihrer Gestalter.

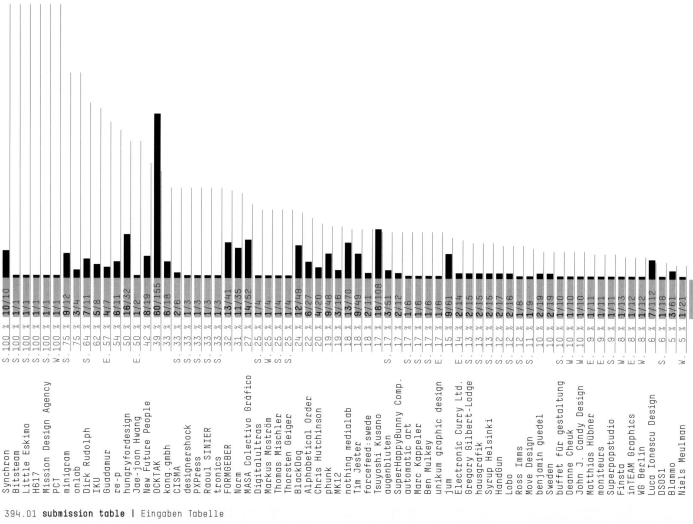

Logos/total number of the entries.
Logos/Gesamteinsendung.

Percentage of logos submitte
Prozentsatz der Gesamteinse
dung.

N. S. W. E. :
Specific poles of production.
Spezifische Produktionspole.

designers

| designer | N.S.W.E. | logos/total | % |
|---|---|---|---|
| Synchron | S. | 10/10 | 100 % |
| Bitsteam | S. | 1/1 | 100 % |
| Little Eskimo | S. | 1/1 | 100 % |
| H617 | S. | 1/1 | 100 % |
| Mission Design Agency | W. | 1/1 | 100 % |
| PCT | S. | 1/1 | 100 % |
| minigram | S. | 9/12 | 75 % |
| onlab | | 3/4 | 75 % |
| Dirk Rudolph | S. | 7/11 | 64 % |
| IKU | | 5/8 | 62 % |
| Guadamur | E. | 4/7 | 57 % |
| re-p | | 6/11 | 54 % |
| hungryfordesign | | 16/32 | 50 % |
| Jae-joon Hwang | E. | 1/2 | 50 % |
| New Future People | | 8/19 | 42 % |
| OCKTAK | | 60/155 | 39 % |
| kong.gmbh | S. | 6/18 | 33 % |
| CISMA | S. | 2/6 | 33 % |
| designershock | S. | 1/3 | 33 % |
| PXPress | S. | 1/3 | 33 % |
| Raoul SINIER | S. | 1/3 | 33 % |
| tronics | S. | 1/3 | 33 % |
| FORMGEBER | | 13/41 | 32 % |
| Norm | | 11/35 | 31 % |
| MASA Colectivo Gráfico | | 14/52 | 27 % |
| Digitalultras | S. | 1/4 | 25 % |
| Markus Moström | W. | 1/4 | 25 % |
| Thomas Mischler | | 1/4 | 25 % |
| Thorsten Geiger | S. | 1/4 | 25 % |
| BlackDog | | 12/49 | 24 % |
| Alphabetical Order | | 6/27 | 22 % |
| Chris Hutchinson | | 4/20 | 20 % |
| phunk | | 9/48 | 19 % |
| MK12 | | 3/16 | 19 % |
| nothing medialab | | 13/70 | 18 % |
| Tim Jester | | 9/49 | 18 % |
| forcefeed:swede | | 2/11 | 18 % |
| Tsuyoshi Kusano | S. | 18/108 | 17 % |
| augenbluten | | 3/51 | 17 % |
| SuperHappyBunny Comp. | S. | 2/12 | 17 % |
| automatic art | S. | 1/6 | 17 % |
| Marc Kappeler | S. | 1/6 | 17 % |
| Ben Mulkey | S. | 1/6 | 17 % |
| unikum graphic design | E. | 1/6 | 17 % |
| jüm | | 9/61 | 15 % |
| Electronic Curry Ltd. | E. | 2/14 | 14 % |
| Gregory Gilbert-Lodge | S. | 2/15 | 13 % |
| hausgrafik | S. | 2/15 | 13 % |
| Syrup Helsinki | S. | 2/15 | 13 % |
| HandGun | S. | 2/17 | 12 % |
| Lobo | S. | 2/16 | 12 % |
| Ross Imms | S. | 1/8 | 12 % |
| Move Design | | 1/9 | 11 % |
| benjamin guedel | S. | 2/19 | 10 % |
| Sweden | | 2/19 | 10 % |
| buffet für gestaltung | W. | 1/10 | 10 % |
| Deane Cheuk | W. | 1/10 | 10 % |
| John J. Candy Design | E. | 1/11 | 9 % |
| Matthias Hübner | E. | 1/11 | 9 % |
| moniteurs | | 1/11 | 9 % |
| Superpopstudio | W. | 1/13 | 8 % |
| Finsta | E. | 1/12 | 8 % |
| inTEAM Graphics | W. | 1/12 | 8 % |
| WG Berlin | | 7/112 | 6 % |
| Luca Ionescu Design | S. | 1/18 | 6 % |
| DSOS1 | | 3/61 | 5 % |
| Blammo | | 1/21 | 5 % |
| Niels Meulman | W. | | |

394.01 **submission table** | Eingaben Tabelle

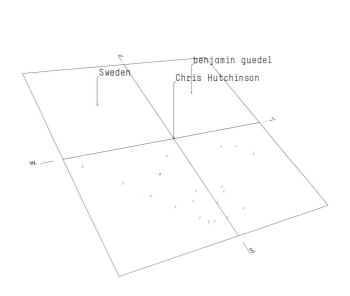

positioning   Positionierung

N. iconographic   Ikonografisch
S. ideographic   Ideografisch
W. pictographic   Pictografisch
E. illustrative   Illustrativ

395.01 **iconographical region** | ikonografische Region

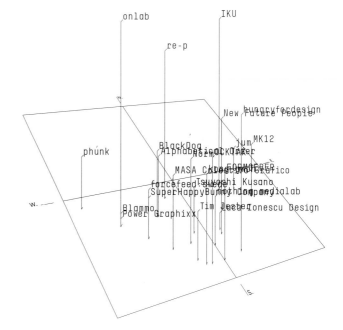

positioning   Positionierung

N. iconographic   Ikonografisch
S. ideographic   Ideografisch
W. pictographic   Pictografisch
E. illustrative   Illustrativ

395.02 **ideographical region** | ideografische Region

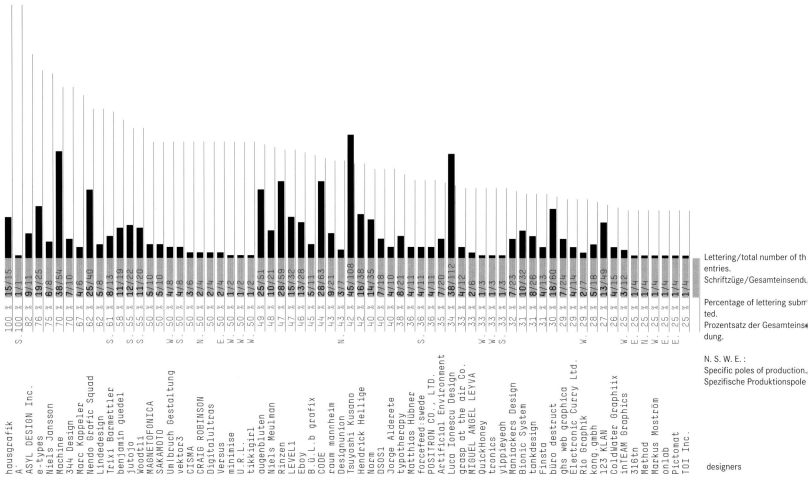

Lettering/total number of the entries.
Schriftzüge/Gesamteinsendu...

Percentage of lettering subm...
ted.
Prozentsatz der Gesamteins...
dung.

N. S. W. E. :
Specific poles of production.
Spezifische Produktionspole

designers

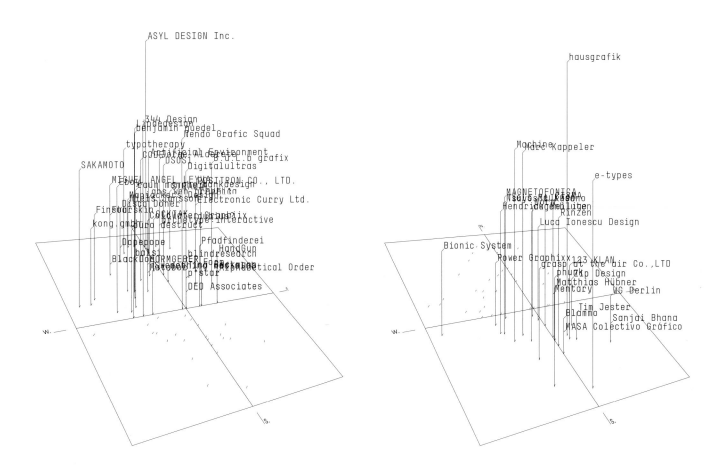

positioning   Positionierung

N. type as type    Schrift als Schrift
S. type as pictures    Schrift als Bild
W. type as a brand    Schrift als Wortmarke
E. pictorial type    Bildliche Schrift

**397.01 typographical region** | typografische Region

positioning   Positionierung

N. type as type    Schrift als Schrift
S. type as pictures    Schrift als Bild
W. type as a brand    Schrift als Wortmarke
E. pictorial type    Bildliche Schrift

**397.02 pictorial region** | bildlische Region

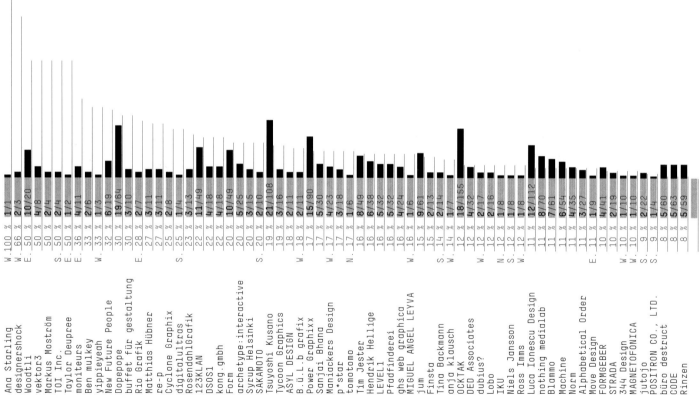

Typograms/total number of the entries.
Typogramme/Gesamteinser
dung.

Percentage of typograms submitted.
Prozentsatz der Gesamteins
dung.

N. S. W. E.:
Specific poles of production
Spezifische Produktionspole

| | | | |
|---|---|---|---|
| Ana Starling | W. 100 % | 1/1 | |
| designershock | W. 66 % | 2/3 | |
| Woodtli | E. 50 % | 10/20 | |
| vektor3 | 50 % | 4/8 | |
| Markus Moström | S. 50 % | 2/4 | |
| TOI Inc. | E. 50 % | 2/4 | |
| Taylor Deupree | 50 % | 1/2 | |
| moniteurs | E. 36 % | 4/11 | |
| Ben mulkey | 33 % | 2/6 | |
| yippieyeah | W. 33 % | 1/3 | |
| New Future People | 32 % | 6/19 | |
| Doppope | 30 % | 19/64 | |
| buffet für gestaltung | 30 % | 3/10 | |
| Rio Grafik | E. 28 % | 2/7 | |
| Matthias Hübner | 27 % | 3/11 | |
| re-p | 27 % | 3/11 | |
| Cyclone Graphix | 25 % | 2/8 | |
| digitalultras | S. 25 % | 1/4 | |
| Rosendahl Grafik | 23 % | 3/13 | |
| 123KLAN | 22 % | 11/49 | |
| DSOS1 | 22 % | 4/18 | |
| kong.gmbh | 22 % | 4/18 | |
| Form | 20 % | 10/49 | |
| archetype:interactive | 20 % | 5/25 | |
| Syrup Helsinki | 20 % | 3/15 | |
| SAKAMOTO | S. 20 % | 2/10 | |
| Tsuyoshi Kusano | 19 % | 21/108 | |
| Tycoon Graphics | 19 % | 3/16 | |
| ASYL DESIGN | 18 % | 2/11 | |
| B.ü.L.b grafix | W. 18 % | 2/11 | |
| Power Graphixx | 17 % | 15/90 | |
| Sanjai Bhana | W. 17 % | 4/23 | |
| Maniackers Design | 17 % | 3/18 | |
| p*star | N. 17 % | 1/6 | |
| tomotomo | 17 % | 1/6 | |
| Tim Jester | 16 % | 8/49 | |
| Hendrik Hellige | 16 % | 6/38 | |
| LEVEL1 | 16 % | 5/32 | |
| Pfadfinderei | 16 % | 5/32 | |
| ghs web graphica | 16 % | 4/24 | |
| MIGUEL ANGEL LEYVA | W. 16 % | 1/6 | |
| jum | 15 % | 9/61 | |
| Finsta | S. 15 % | 2/13 | |
| Tina Backmann | 14 % | 2/14 | |
| anja klausch | W. 14 % | 1/7 | |
| OCKTAK | 12 % | 18/155 | |
| DED Associates | 12 % | 4/32 | |
| dubius? | W. 12 % | 2/17 | |
| Lobo | 12 % | 2/16 | |
| IKU | N. 12 % | 1/8 | |
| Niels Jansson | S. 12 % | 1/8 | |
| Ross Imms | W. 12 % | 1/8 | |
| Luca Ionescu Design | 11 % | 12/112 | |
| nothing medialab | 11 % | 8/70 | |
| Blammo | 11 % | 7/61 | |
| Machine | 11 % | 6/54 | |
| Norm | 11 % | 4/35 | |
| Alphabetical Order | 11 % | 3/27 | |
| Move Design | E. 11 % | 1/9 | |
| FORMGEBER | 10 % | 4/41 | |
| STRADA | 10 % | 2/19 | |
| 344 Design | W. 10 % | 1/10 | |
| MAGNETOFONICA | W. 10 % | 1/10 | |
| jutojo | S. 9 % | 2/22 | |
| POSITRON CO., LTD. | 9 % | 1/4 | |
| büro destruct | 8 % | 5/60 | |
| CODE | 8 % | 5/63 | |
| Rinzen | 8 % | 5/59 | |

designers

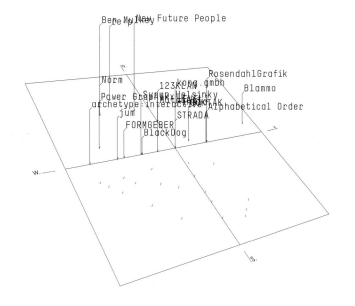

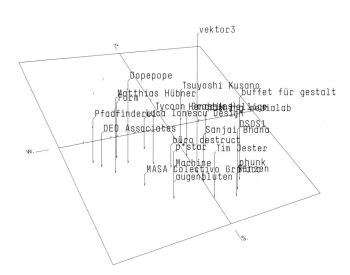

positioning   Positionierung

N.  type as type    Schrift als Schrift
S.  type as pictures    Schrift als Bild
W.  type as a brand    Schrift als Wortmarke
E.  pictorial type    Bildliche Schrift

positioning   Positionierung

N.  type as type    Schrift als Schrift
S.  type as pictures    Schrift als Bild
W.  type as a brand    Schrift als Wortmarke
E.  pictorial type    Bildliche Schrift

399.01 **typographical region** | typografische Region

399.02 **pictographical region** | pictografische Region

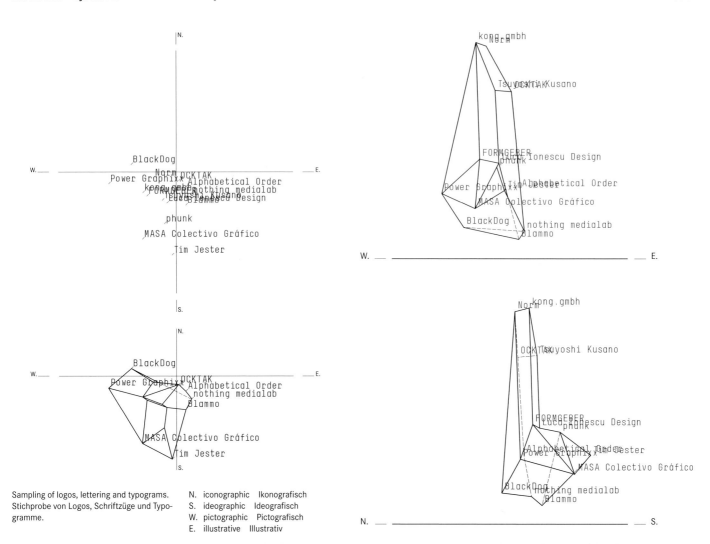

Sampling of logos, lettering and typograms.
Stichprobe von Logos, Schriftzüge und Typogramme.

N. iconographic   Ikonografisch
S. ideographic    Ideografisch
W. pictographic   Pictografisch
E. illustrative   Illustrativ

400.01 **extract** | Auszug

400.02 **sections (W-E)+(N-S)** | Schnitte (W-E)+(N-S)

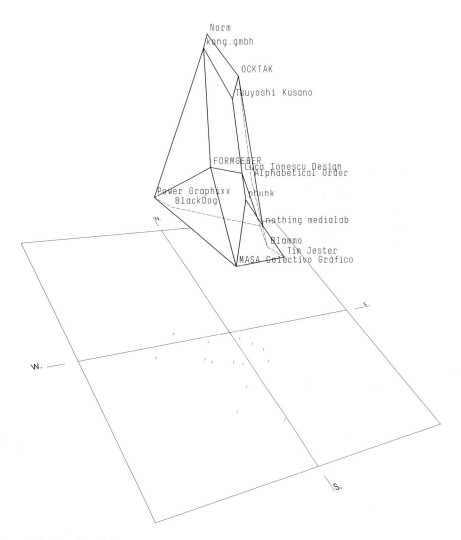

Norm
kong.gmbh

OCKTAK

Tsuyoshi Kusano

FORMGEBER
Luca Ionescu Design
Alphabetical Order

Power Graphixx    nhunk
BlackDog

nothing medialab

Blammo
Tim Jester
MASA Colectivo Gráfico

N.

E.

W.

S.

401.01 **tip of the iceberg** | Spitze des Eisberges

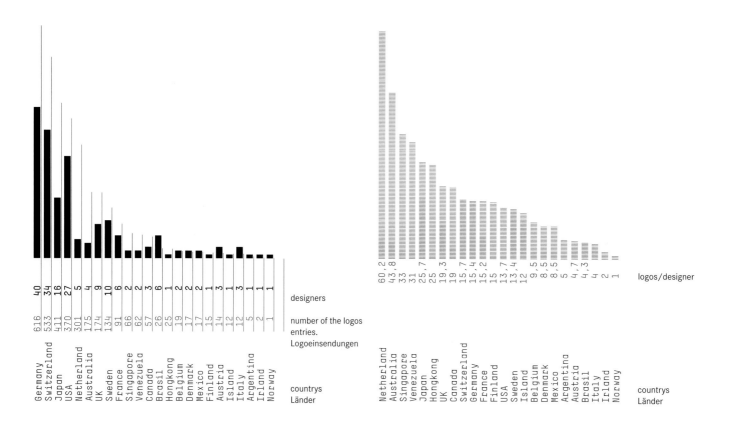

**402.01 submission table** | Eingaben Tabelle                    **402.02 production of logos/designer** | Logoproduktion/Designer

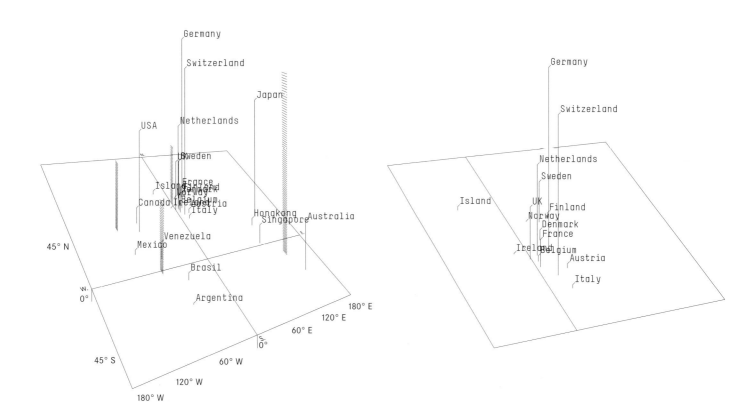

Germany
Switzerland
Japan
USA
Netherlands
Sweden
France
Island
Canada Ireland
Italy
Hongkong
Singapore   Australia
Venezuela
45° N
Mexico
Brasil
W.
0°
Argentina
180° E
120° E
60° E
S.
0°
45° S
60° W
120° W
180° W

Germany
Switzerland
Netherlands
Sweden
Island
UK   Finland
Norway
Denmark
France
Ireland   Belgium
Austria
Italy

Continental production of logos/designer.        32 l./d.: Asia+Australia   Asien+Australien
Kontinental Logoproduktion/Designer.             16 l./d.: North America   Nordamerika
                                                 14 l./d.: Europe   Europa
                                                 12 l./d.: South America   Südamerika

403.01 **origins and prod. proportions** | Herkunft und Prod.Anteil    403.02 **Europe detail** | Europa Detail

# INDEX

**#**

**123KLAN**, France
134, 135, 156, 157, 158, 206,
207, 212, 214, 220, 302, 242,
254, 271, 312, 320, 340, 359,
366, 375, 376, 378, 380, 381
Scien & Klor
scien-klor@123klan.com
ww.123klan.com

**24HR**, Sweden
104, 106, 211, 259, 263, 278,
300, 310, 313, 322, 323
Ricky Tillblad
ricky@24hr.se
ww.24hr.se

**316tn**, Switzerland
149, 312
316tn - interaktive und
klassische Medien GmbH
irene@316tn.com
ww.316tn.ch

**344 Design**, USA
113, 116, 118, 127, 138, 149,
216, 253, 377
344 Design, LLC
info@344design.com
ww.344design.com

**A**

**A'**, Brasil
176, 177
A', Clarissa Tossin
clarissa@a-linha.org
ww.a-linha.org

**ala webstatt**, Switzerland
285
info@ala.ch, rek@chmork.net
ww.ala.ch, ww.chmork.net

**Jorge Alderete**, Mexico
100, 101, 112, 137, 359
contacto@jorgealderete.com
ww.jorgealderete.com

**Alphabetical Order**, Sweden
028, 053, 057, 094, 144, 183,
207, 236, 265, 299, 301, 357,
360, 366, 376
everyone@alphabeticalorder.com
ww.alphabeticalorder.com

**Apakstudio**, USA
374
Aaron Piland
aaron@apakstudio.com
ww.apakstudio.com

**archetype:interactive**, Hongkong
054, 125, 150, 216, 217, 240,
278, 279, 280, 282, 287
info@a-i.com.hk
ww.a-i.com.hk

**AREADESIGN**, Switzerland
251, 283, 359, 364
Alberto Russo
info@areadesign.ch
ww.areadesign.ch

**artetic**, Germany
279
Irene Marx
irene@artetic.com
ww.artetic.com

**Artificial Environments**, UK
102, 279, 290, 360, 364
monitor@ae-pro.com
ww.ae-pro.com

**ASYL DESIGN Inc.**, Japan
081, 082, 091, 094, 095, 109,
162, 243
contact@asyl.co.jp
ww.asyl.co.jp

**augenbluten**, Germany
052, 060, 080, 082, 084, 085,
128, 149, 163, 174, 182, 184,
210, 230, 250, 270, 286, 288,
361, 382
interfaces - symposium über
schrift und sprache
info@augenbluten.com
ww.augenbluten.com

**automatic art and design**, USA
042, 360, 365, 370
charles wilkin,
info@automatic-iam.com
ww.automatic-iam.com

**B**

**Tina Backmann**, Sweden
098, 183, 277
Tina Backmann
anitba@hotmail.com

**balsi**, Switzerland
106, 110, 113, 144, 215, 267,
289, 291, 299, 310, 361
balsi lefthanded grafics,
christoph baalsiger
mail@balsigrafik.ch
ww.balsigrafik.ch

**Trixi Barmettler**, Switzerland
189, 379
sun@tag-inn.ch

**Bas Visual Concepts**, Netherlands
120, 121, 302
bas@basvisualconcepts.com
ww.basvisualconcepts.com

**Sanjai Bhana**, Canada
144, 208, 227, 228, 240, 253,
267, 299, 302, 329, 375, 384
Sanjai Bhana
Illustration & Design
esanjai@hotmail.com
ww.portfolios.com/sanjai

**bigsexyland**, Germany
350
Björn Hansen
bjoern@bigsexyland.de
ww.bigsexyland.de

**Bionic System**, Germany
104, 107, 116, 119, 123, 165,
208, 245, 250, 252, 278, 283,
311, 312, 313, 323, 366, 375,
376, 382
contact@Bionic-Systems.com
ww.Bionic-Systems.com

**Bitsteam**, Germany
070
Stephan Mathieu
mathieu@bitsteam.de
ww.bitsteam.de

**BlackDog**, USA
024, 026, 027, 040, 042, 082,
216, 217, 248, 272, 279, 318,
319, 322, 343, 352, 365, 376
Mark Fox
mfox@blackdogma.com
ww.blackdogma.com

**Blammo**, Netherlands
028, 032, 036, 080, 101, 144,
170, 171, 172, 206, 220, 221,
222, 272, 327, 340, 354, 356,
357, 359, 365, 367, 369, 370,
378, 380, 383, 384
Pieter Janssen aka Parra
parra@blammo.nl
ww.blammo.nl/parra

**blindresearch**, Germany
096, 162, 244, 247, 278, 310,
367
Sven Züge
sven@blindresearch.com
ww.blindresearch.com

**Mirko Borsche**, Germany
362, 388, 389
mirko.borsche@jetzt.de

**büro destruct**, Switzerland
092, 105, 110, 111, 112, 120,
137, 141, 142, 145, 214, 223,
226, 227, 245, 250, 253, 278,
279, 280, 286, 288, 291, 294,
299, 300, 302, 310, 318, 360,
364, 376, 382
Lopetz
bd@bermuda.ch,
lopetz@bermuda.ch
ww.burodestruct.net
ww.typedifferent.com

**buffet für gestaltung**, Switzerland
238, 239
markus wicki, silvio waser
buffet.f.gestaltung@bluewin.ch

**buka grafik**, Switzerland
319
franziska burkhardt
buka@datacomm.ch
www.bukagrafik.ch

**B.ü.L.b grafix**, Switzerland
081, 144, 207, 212, 247, 248
Nicolas Robel
grafix@bulbfactory.ch
www.bulbfactory.ch

**C**

**Deanne Cheuk**, USA
036, 106, 112, 282, 288, 371,
384, 385
neomuworld@aol.com
www.neomu.com

**CISMA**, Brasil
041, 054, 136, 311
cisma@cisma.com.br
www.cisma.com.br

**CODE**, Switzerland
027, 080, 088, 092, 096, 097,
104, 118, 119, 120, 121, 136,
151, 207, 226, 227, 247, 250,
252, 258, 265, 279, 298, 300,
337, 370, 376, 380
CODE. Werkstatt für Grafik
Reto Gehrig, Daniel Donati
code@code.ch
www.code.ch

**ColdWater Graphiix**, Japan
107, 113, 248, 281, 336, 382
Tabito Mizuo
tabito@xenn.com

**Cyclone Graphix**, Japan
120, 242, 275, 300, 355, 358,
381
Cyclone Graphix
info@cyclonegraphix.com
www.cyclonegraphix.com

**D**

**DED Associates**, UK
112, 142, 210, 214, 233, 250,
253, 271, 282, 287, 289, 290,
291, 311, 313, 365, 379
DED Associates
info@dedass.com
www.dedass.com

**Défil Inc.**, Japan
080
dori dock
info@mold.org
www.mold.org/dd/

**designershock**, Germany
043, 214, 342
Birte Ludwig
birte@designershock.com
www.designershock.com

**designiskinky**, Australia
371
Andrew Johnstone
andrew@designiskinky.net
www.designiskinky.net

**Designunion**, Germany
094, 253
info@designunion-berlin.de
www.designunion-berlin.de

**Taylor Deupree**, USA
225, 249
taylor@12k.com
www.12k.com

**Digitalultras**, Italy
072, 098, 236
Manuel Perfetto
info@mors.it
www.digitalultras.com

**Disco Döner**, Germany
023, 090, 097, 108, 242, 300,
313, 318, 319, 328, 352, 367,
384
nicole hackbarth
nicole@discodoener.de

**Dopepope**, USA
042, 096, 108, 206, 208, 209,
216, 218, 228, 267, 292, 303,
336, 338, 348, 349, 354, 358,
374
Joe Lucchese
joel@dopepope.com
www.dopepope.com

**DSOS1**, Germany
080, 094, 096, 142, 146, 301,
365
Stefan Gandl
stefan@dsos1.com
www.dsos1.com
www.designershock.com

**dubius?**, Sweden
097, 100, 144 ,158, 213, 244,
270, 272, 282, 313, 353
dubius?
info@thedubius.com
www.thedubius.com

**E**

**Eboy**, Germany
070, 082, 113, 124, 125, 126,
127, 152, 296, 316, 317, 318,
320, 324, 361
eboy@eboy.com
www.eboy.com

**Electronic Curry Ltd.**, Switzerland
024, 025, 085, 110, 144, 154,
264, 283, 297, 310, 313, 358
Christian Bili
contact@electroniccurry.ch
www.electroniccurry.ch

**e-Types**, Denmark
074, 075, 076, 077, 080, 151,
188, 260, 261, 274, 298, 306,
307, 367
e-Types A/S
info@e-types.com
www.e-types.com

**F**

**Finsta**, Sweden
036, 103, 106, 121, 225, 326,
384
Finn Hallin
finn.hallin@konstfack.se

**forcefeed:swede**, Sweden
027, 047, 158, 173, 248, 266
globalvegetableavoidance@for-
cefeedswede.com
www.forcefeedswede.com

**Form**, UK
043, 055, 080, 096, 108, 149,
151, 187, 209, 216, 217, 234,
250, 280, 299, 301, 302, 311,
318, 328, 342, 365, 377, 382,
383
studio@form.uk.com
www.form.uk.com

**FORMGEBER**, Germany
022, 042, 044, 045, 053, 054,
056, 057, 060, 080, 108, 136,
206, 209, 234, 251, 253, 282,
311, 380, 381, 384
atelier@formgeber.de
www.formgeber.de
www.formgeber.net

**Fourskin**, Singapore
022, 112, 121, 212, 250, 334,
340, 354, 355, 356, 360
info@fourskinstore.com
www.fourskinstore.com
www.fourskinstore.com/fourski-
nation

**G**

**Thorsten Geiger**, Germany
055, 248, 251
info@thorsten-geiger.de
www.thorsten-geiger.de

**Die Gestalten**, Germany
335
Birga Meyer
birga@die-gestalten.
www.die-gestalten.de

ghs web graphica, Japan
038, 081, 085, 097, 110, 165,
203, 240, 241, 266, 278, 293,
302, 320, 354
AKIHIRO IKEGOSHI - GWG
ikegoshi@ghs.net
ww.ghs.net

Gobler Toys, USA
300, 361
Steve Casino
iragobler@goblertoys.com
ww.goblertoys.com

gottfolk / fiskar, Island
183, 258, 279
Dagur Hilmarsson
dagur@gottfolk.is
ww.gottfolk.is
ww.fiskar.is

grasp at the air Co.,LTD, Japan
163, 164, 202, 271, 289, 290,
300, 326, 376
info@grasp.co.jp
ww.grasp.co.jp

Gregory Gilbert-Lodge, Switzerland
029, 117, 212, 322, 340, 343,
355, 363, 368
gilbert-lodge@mydiax.ch

GRIFF, UK
175, 300, 318, 319, 328, 366
griff@worldofputty.com
ww.worldofputty.com

Guadamur, Mexico
026
Miki Guadamur
guadahm@yahoo.com
ww.geocities.com/guadahm
ww.fuga.com.mx/guadamur

benjamin guedel, Switzerland
022, 027, 100, 124, 125, 144,
292, 303, 334, 378
benjamin@guedel.biz
ww.guedel.biz

H

H617, Japan
054
Takeshi Hamada
617@gmx.net
ww.64.124.215.177/617/

HandGun, USA
037, 054, 120, 154, 183, 284,
291, 299, 371, 376, 377, 378
david zack custer
zack@hand-gun.org
ww.hand-gun.org

Tod Hansson, Australia
335, 248, 299
plazma@gil.com.au
ww.gasket.ws

hausgrafik, Switzerland
056, 082, 125, 138, 170, 184,
300
Urs Althaus
urs@hausgrafik.ch
ww.hausgrafik.ch

Hellgolfers, Switzerland
353
Thomas Berger, Jonas Ganz
peanutz@gmx.ch,
erdnuss1@gmx.ch
ww.funkenflug.ch

Hendrik Hellige, Germany
108, 111, 118, 125, 128, 148,
149, 183, 234, 298, 361
henni@die-gestalten.de
ww.die-gestalten.de

Hintze.gruppen, Denmark
150
Jesper Hintze Vildbrad
hintze.gruppen@get2net.dk

Hirschindustries, Germany
282, 289, 290, 358, 368, 376,
384
ollie@hirschindustries.de
ww.hirschindustries.de

Derrick Hodgson, Canada
347
derrick@madreal.com
ww.madreal.com

Matthias Hübner, Germany
114, 165, 183, 212, 279, 298
matthias@bordfunk.de
ww.bordfunk.de

hungryfordesign, USA
027, 034, 044, 056, 066, 219,
284, 341, 357, 374, 378
Nando Costa
nando@hungryfordesign.com
ww.hungryfordesign.com

Chris Hutchinson, USA
024, 026, 070, 216, 272, 279,
319, 344, 360, 378
chris@heightlab.com
ww.heightlab.com

I

IKU, USA
024, 027, 036, 054
Ilan Katin
ikulius@ikuchiku.com
ww.ikuchiku.com

Ross Imms, USA
042, 210, 286, 346
rossperran@aol.com
ww.fortyeightk.com

incorect, France
033, 338, 344, 351, 355, 357,
365, 370, 376
Izo9000, Nogam, yogo.o
contact@incorect.com
ww.incorect.com

inTEAM Graphics, Switzerland
027, 120, 314, 350
inteam@bluewin.ch

Luca Ionescu Design, Australia
022, 026, 038, 052, 054, 066,
081, 083, 088, 089, 099, 106,
107, 110, 114, 120, 122, 124,
137, 138, 139, 145, 164, 165,
166, 184, 187, 209, 210, 214,
215, 224, 232, 236, 237, 258,
267, 281, 282, 286, 288, 290,
291, 293, 299, 311, 314, 315,
323, 329, 333, 337, 340, 355,
358, 359, 360, 366, 367, 370,
375, 376, 381, 384
acul@optushome.com.au
ww.luca.com.au

J

Kathrin Jachmann, Germany
093, 118
kj@diamond-gestaltung.de
ww.diamond-gestaltung.de

Niels Jansson, Belgium
085, 091, 092, 122, 230, 359
Njansson@sanana.com
ww.kay-kay.com

Tim Jester, USA
036, 055, 056, 060, 065, 097,
158, 302, 303, 318, 367, 380
jester@j6studios.com

John J. Candy Design, Sweden
142, 259, 281, 282, 290, 301,
343, 379, 385
bigboss@johnjcandy.com
ww.johnjcandy.com

jum, Germany
026, 027, 034, 044, 209, 216,
217, 222, 300, 318, 328, 338,
339, 340, 341, 342, 343, 346,
358, 361, 364, 370, 378
Jens Meyer
jum@jumabc.de
ww.jumabc.de

jutojo, Germany
160, 161, 182, 250, 253, 283,
313
julie gayard
ju@jutojo.de
ww.jutojo.de

**K**
Marc Kappeler, Switzerland
057, 096, 110, 162, 172
marc kappeler.moiré
marc@soda.ch

anja klausch, Germany
096, 217, 251, 259, 268, 319
anja@klausch.de
www.klausch.de

kong.gmbh, Switzerland
038, 040, 055, 070, 096, 101,
118, 122, 207, 216, 234, 251,
308, 309, 318
wir@kong.ch
www.kong.ch

Tsuyoshi Kusano, Japan
026, 027, 034, 035, 036, 038,
041, 042, 043, 052, 053, 054,
067, 082, 083, 090, 091, 094,
106, 108, 110, 111, 128, 130,
148, 164, 172, 174, 175, 183,
195, 198, 200, 202, 203, 206,
207, 208, 210, 212, 214, 215,
216, 220, 223, 230, 232, 234,
241, 272, 278, 279, 282, 283,
286, 288, 291, 319, 334, 352,
374, 379, 380, 391
tsuyos-k@momo.so-net.ne.jp

**L**

lasercade, USA
325, 374
Michael Murphy
murphy@lasercade.com
www.lasercade.com

Fernando Leal, Brasil
377
fernando@cisorium.com
www.cisorium.com

LEVEL1, Japan
106, 155, 165, 172, 174, 190,
191, 192, 194, 197, 201, 202,
217, 240, 241, 243, 278, 283,
288, 291, 342, 343, 344
Tsuyoshi Hirooka
hiro-ka@wa2.so-net.ne.jp
www.hello.to/level1

MIGUEL ANGEL LEYVA, UK
119, 217, 291, 360
CONTACT@FUNKYMONKEY.COM
www.FUNKYMONKEY.COM

Lindedesign, Germany
120, 256
Christian Lindemann
linderockt@web.de
www.lindedesign.de

Little Eskimo, Sweden
043
Jonas Loefgren
j@little-eskimo.com
www.little-eskimo.com

Lobo, Brasil
037, 043, 217, 236, 265, 268,
282, 322
info@lobo.cx
www.lobo.cx
Carlos Bêla
carlosbela@goldenshower.gs
www.goldenshower.gs

**M**

Machine, Netherlands
052, 107, 111, 112, 113, 114,
115, 123, 124, 125, 129, 140,
142, 150, 162, 164, 170, 173,
184, 186, 212, 226, 227, 230,
249, 283, 381
we@ourmachine.com
www.ourmachine.com

MAGNETOFONICA, Venezuela
094, 104, 114, 182, 280, 292,
329, 352
Dario Alejandro Utreras Obando
d@magnetofonica.net
www.magnetofonica.net

Maniackers Design, Japan
084, 085, 111, 112, 193, 198,
199, 202, 208, 210, 214, 252,
328, 367
sato@mks.jp.org
www.mks.jp.org

MASA Colectivo Gráfico, Venezuela
028, 031, 034, 038, 040, 041,
052, 065, 112, 142, 156, 228,
280, 284, 290, 291, 297, 310,
313, 332, 343, 359, 360, 381
info@masa.com.ve
www.masa.com.ve

MELON DEZIGN, France
297
infos@melondezign.com
www.melondezign.com

Mentary, Switzerland
127, 152, 272, 370, 374, 383
gregory chapuisat
gregory@mentary.com
www.mentary.com

Method, USA
080, 282, 308
info@method.com
www.method.com

Niels Meulman, Netherlands
032, 104, 107, 110, 116, 140,
142, 170, 222, 282, 300, 303,
327
n.meulman1@chello.nl

minigram, Germany
038, 042, 043, 053, 054, 073,
368, 370, 372, 373, 383
in@minigram.de
www.minigram.de

minimise, Ireland
109, 290
info@minimise.com
www.minimise.com

Mika Mischler, Switzerland
371
mika@matik.de

Thomas Mischler, Switzerland
361, 380
r3dstar@cr-entertainment.ch

Mission Design Agency, Norway
064
Nicolai Schaanning Larsen,
Kjetil Devig, Gary Swindell,
Marc Ligeti
hello@mission.no
www.mission.no

MK12, USA
045, 343, 358
John Dretzka
info@mk12.com
www.mk12.com,
www.dontyoufeelbetter.com

moniteurs, Germany
027, 109, 247, 304, 364, 376
Sibylle Schlaich
sibylle@moniteurs.de
www.moniteurs.de

Markus Moström, Sweden
036, 106, 210
markus@mostromdesign.se
www.mostromdesign.se

Move Design, USA
058, 105, 222, 249, 265, 289,
295, 298, 343
Peter Spreenberg
peter@movedesign.com
www.movedesign.com

Roland Müller, Switzerland
003 - 015 foreword
rjmueller@access.ch

Ben Mulkey
042, 206, 215, 251
ben@benmulkey.com
www.benmulkey.com

Mutabor, Germany
080, 109, 244, 249, 253, 256,
257, 266, 269, 270, 303, 319,
321, 358, 359, 366, 376
Mutabor Design GmbH
info@mutabor.de
www.mutabor.com

**N**

**Nendo Grafic Squad,** Japan
041, 190, 192, 193, 194, 195,
196, 199, 200, 202, 241, 276,
278, 300, 325, 354, 355, 380
Quentaro "Nendo ANI" Fujimoto
quen@nendo.com
ww.nendo.com

**New Future People,** UK
030, 039, 043, 048, 050, 051,
062, 063, 209, 219, 250, 273,
290, 313, 360, 361, 367, 379
contact@newfuturepeople.com
ww.newfuturepeople.com

**michele del nobolo,** Italy
141, 328, 350
dokrobei@supereva.it
ww.web.tiscali.it/dokrobei

**Norm,** Switzerland
026, 037, 038, 055, 070, 082,
104, 106, 125, 144, 174, 184,
208, 217, 290, 335, 365
abc@norm.to
ww.norm.to

**nothing medialab,** Switzerland
026, 038, 055, 056, 096, 120,
217, 244, 249, 252, 271, 296,
297, 298, 319, 324, 342, 343,
379, 380, 381
bastiaan van rooden
spot@nothing.ch
ww.nothing.ch

**O**

**OCKTAK,** Netherlands
043, 052, 053, 055, 068, 069,
081, 084, 086, 087, 088, 092,
096, 106, 118, 120, 121, 136,
173, 192, 203, 262, 263, 313,
360
Paul Rickus
OK@OCKTAK.NL
ww.OCKTAK.NL

**OhioGirl,** USA
129, 218, 288, 327, 334, 350
Andy Mueller, OhioGirl Design
andy@ohiogirl.com
ww.ohiohgirl.com

**onlab,** Switzerland
036, 045, 165
in@onlab.ch
ww.onlab.ch

**o-matic corp.,** USA
281
Marina Zurkow
marina@o-matic.com
ww.o-matic.com

**P**

**p*star,** Switzerland
096, 150, 209, 228, 233, 248,
287, 310, 316, 379, 381, 382,
385
Pascal C. Baumann
pstar@mac.com
ww.pstar.ch,
ww.swissgraphicdesign.net

**PCT,** Germany
032
Peter Thaler
pct@punch-hole.de
ww.punch-hole.de

**Pfadfinderei,** Germany
148, 173, 208, 287, 390
critzla
critzla@pfadfinderei.com
ww.pfadfinderei.com

**phunk,** Singapore
031, 034, 036, 070, 080, 110,
111, 138, 144, 158, 175, 200,
222, 229, 230, 236, 284, 303,
323, 327, 335, 345, 346, 352,
353, 356, 360, 361, 366, 367,
370, 379, 380, 382
info@phunkstudio.com
ww.phunkstudio.com

**Pictomat,** Germany
144, 266
konstanze läufer
elaeufer@pictomat.de
ww.pictomat.de

**Planet Pixel,** Germany
245, 293, 298, 300, 318, 336,
353, 385
Planet Pixel - Funke Hiller
Wülfing GbR
mail@planetpixel.de
ww.planetpixel.de

**POSITRON CO., LTD.**
094, 109, 159, 228, 278, 281,
299, 374
ww.the-positron.com

**Power Graphixx,** Japan
032, 034, 042, 080, 083, 104,
107, 109, 129, 140, 164, 165,
194, 200, 206, 208, 210, 212,
214, 230, 232, 240, 245, 248,
252, 255, 270, 278, 279, 281,
285, 286, 288, 353, 361
support@power-graphixx.com
ww.power-graphixx.com

**PXPress,** Germany
070, 360
Kiendl-Müller, Krämer, Grunow
info@pxpress.com
ww.pxpress.com

**Q**

**QuickHoney,** USA
120, 325
Nana Rausch, Peter Stemmler
info@quickhoney.com
ww.quickhoney.com

**R**

**raum mannheim,** Germany
070, 084, 093, 097, 114, 119,
121, 183, 208, 249, 252, 265,
305, 377
info@raum-mannheim.com
ww.raum-mannheim.com

**re-p,** Austria
023, 037, 053, 206, 216, 258,
310
nt@re-p.org
ww.re-p.org

**Rinzen,** Australia
026, 104, 105, 111, 114, 131,
133, 137, 142, 143, 147, 148,
162, 165, 166, 167, 168, 169,
185, 186, 187, 236, 263, 308,
321, 329, 337, 338, 353, 361,
362
they@rinzen.com
ww.rinzen.com

**Rio Grafik,** Switzerland
104, 319, 336
info@riografik.ch
ww.riografik.ch

**CRAIG ROBINSON,** Germany
100, 101, 271
craig@flipflopflyin.com
ww.flipflopflyin.com

**RosendahlGrafik,** Germany
209, 244, 313, 319, 385
daten@rosendahlgrafik.de
ww.rosendahlgrafik.de

**Rot,** Switzerland
377
olivier houmard
ohoumard@bluewin.ch

**Dirk Rudolph,** Germany
052, 053, 054, 057, 059, 066,
289, 302, 303,
contact@dirkrudolph.de
ww.dirkrudolph.de

**S**

**SAKAMOTO,** Denmark
088, 105, 109, 233, 234, 252,
361
info@sakamoto.dk
ww.sakamoto.dk

Raoul SINIER, France
038, 304
raoul@noos.fr
ww.raspage.com,
ww.portfolio.raspage.com

Ana Starling, Brasil
218
anacstarling@hotmail.com
ww.sutura.org

STRADA, Germany
042, 080, 092, 144, 206, 248,
253, 312
strada@x3network.net

SuperHappyBunny Company, USA
059, 300, 324, 366
superhappylogos@superhappybun-
ny.com
ww.superhappybunny.com

Superpopstudio, Belgium
061, 125, 351, 354
Cesar Carrocera Giganto
superpopstudio@superpopstudio.com
ww.superpopstudio.com

Sweden, Sweden
034, 106, 122, 142, 252, 254,
281, 283, 285, 321, 380
hello@swedengraphics.com
ww.swedengraphics.com

Synchron, Switzerland
071
ralph steinbrüchel
steinbruchel@synchron.ch
ww.synchron.ch

Syrup Helsinki, Finland
052, 053, 110, 125, 130, 219,
248, 298, 332, 359, 341
office@syruphelsinki.com
ww.yruphelsinki.com

T

tankdesign, Switzerland
089, 097, 106, 148, 152, 153,
250, 258, 269, 299, 302, 309,
319, 357, 366, 380, 382
info@tankdesign.ch
ww.tankdesign.ch

Teamchman, France
328, 364, 374
rolito
rolito@teamchman.com
ww.teamchman.com
ww.rolitoland.com

tikkigirl, Germany
120, 342
isabell welz
isabell@tikkigirl.com
ww.tikkigirl.com

TOI Inc., Switzerland
133, 235, 386, 387
info@toi.ch
ww.ooze.ch

tokidoki, Italy
361
Simone Legno
simone@tokidoki.it
ww.tokidoki.it
ww.vianet.it

tomotomo.net, Japan
360
tomo@tomotomo.net
ww.tomotomo.net

tronics, Switzerland
034, 132, 253
Marco Fischer, Fabian Gasser
info@tronics.ch
ww.tronics.ch

Tycoon Graphics, Japan
104, 121, 208, 228, 243, 266,
276, 283, 286
mail@tyg.co.jp

typotherapy, Canada
022, 080, 081, 093, 094, 100,
104, 109, 209, 245, 253, 256,
311, 313
typotherapy+design
studio@typotherapy.com
ww.typotherapy.com

U

U.R.L., Austria
309
Tina Frank, Agentur für Informationsdesign GmbH
office@url.at
ww.url.at, ww.frank.at

Um|bruch Gestaltung, Germany
106, 110, 132, 246, 247
Ralf Strohmeier
ww.umbru.ch

unikum graphic design, Switzerland
152, 342
info@unikum.ch
ww.unikum.ch

V

vektor3, Switzerland
178, 231, 303
bureau@vektor3.com
ww.vektor3.com

Versus, Germany
049, 152, 309
Alexander Baumgardt
alex@abvk.de
ww.abvk.de

W

WG Berlin, Germany
028, 149, 283, 287, 385
livingroom@wg-berlin.com
ww.wg-berlin.com

Woodtli, Switzerland
022, 180, 181, 219, 299, 325
martin@woodt.li
ww.woodt.li

X

xonetik, USA
250, 268, 271, 343, 359
[mars] marcelo perez
mars@xonetik.net
ww.xonetik.net

Y

yippieyeah, UK
046, 179, 218, 381
Gunnar Bauer, Tina Borkowski
iLikeY!@yippieyeah.co.uk
ww.yippieyeah.co.uk

Yipyop, USA
359
Mike Langlie
mike@yipyop.com
ww.yipyop.com

Z

Judith Zaugg, Switzerland
341, 360
info@judithzaugg.ch
ww.judithzaugg.ch

Zinc, Argentina
342, 379
Cynthia Martinez
zinc@fibertel.com.ar
ww.zinc-design.com.ar

Zip Design, UK
154, 235, 278, 289, 291, 304,
316, 357, 366, 381, 384
charlie@zipdesign.co.uk
ww.zipdesign.co.uk

Zookeeper, France
255, 279, 284, 350, 359
dod@zookeeper
ww.zookeeper.fr

# WORK-INDEX

022.01 Luca Ionescu Design
o:   013
/:   ASAYAN, 2000
022.02 typotherapy+design
o:   Neksis Magazine
/:   Stephen Crowhurst, 2002
022.03 benjamin guedel
o:   beatle print
/:   benjamin guedel, 2000
022.04 Fourskin
022.05 Woodtli
o:   different strokes
/:   Martin Woodtli, 2001
022.06 FORMGEBER
o:   Ferrero
/:   Jochen Eeuwyk, 2001

023.01 Disco Döner
023.02 re-p

024.01 BlackDog
o:   Ed Caldwell Photography
/:   Mark Fox, 1997
024.02 IKU
o:   Decievers
/:   Ilan Katin, 1999
024.03 Chris Hutchinson
o:   thefinktank competition
/:   Chris Hutchinson, 2001
024.04 Electronic Curry Ltd.
o:   3*trees
/:   electronic curry, 1999

025.01 Electronic Curry Ltd.
o:   world council of church
/:   electronic curry, 2001

026.01 Chris Hutchinson
o:   thefinktank competition
/:   Chris Hutchinson, 2001
026.02 Luca Ionescu Design
026.03 Tsuyoshi Kusano
026.04 jum
o:   Fox, zumo.de
/:   jum, 2001

026.05 BlackDog
o:   Man Bites Dog
/:   Mark Fox, 1994
026.06 Rinzen
o:   Venom
/:   Rinzen, 2002
026.07 jum
o:   testbild.com
/:   Chris Glaubitz, 1998
026.08 nothing medialab
026.09 Guadamur
o:   ROCK SUCKS! magazine
/:   Miki Guadamur, 2002
026.10 Norm
ð:   Norm, 1999-2002
026.11 Guadamur
o:   White bread America
/:   Miki Guadamur, 2002
026.12 Guadamur
o:   Frootsie Collins
/:   Miki Guadamur, 2002
026.13 - .16 BlackDog
o:   The Buckeye Roadhouse
     (Real Restaurants)
/:   Mark Fox, 1991

027.01 hungryfordesign
o:   thewddg / devlab
/:   Nando Costa, 2001
027.02 hungryfordesign
o:   urban slut
/:   Nando Costa, 2000
027.03 Tsuyoshi Kusano
027.04 Tsuyoshi Kusano
027.05 forcefeed:swede
ð:   Oz Dean, 2000
027.06 benjamin guedel
o:   publicis
/:   benjamin guedel, 2001
027.07 moniteurs
o:   Gate 5,
     Navigationssysteme
/:   H. Specker, D. Simon, 2000
027.08 inTEAM Graphics

027.09 CODE
o:   worlds end switzerland
/:   daniel donati, 1998
027.10 jum
o:   Visual and manual
     awareness
/:   jum, 2000
027.11 IKU
o:   Oniko
/:   Ilan Katin, 2002
027.12 BlackDog
o:   SeeCommerce
/:   Mark Fox, 1997

028.01 WG Berlin
o:   network
/:   Andreas Wegner, 2002
028.02 MASA Colectivo Gráfico
o:   Ecologic Proyect
/:   Masa, 2002
028.03 Alphabetical Order
ð:   Alphabetical Order, 1998
028.04 Blammo
o:   Rockwell /
     Hand t-shirt logo
/:   parra, 2001

029.01 Gregory Gilbert-Lodge
o:   Die Weltwoche Zürich,
     Müller und Hess
/:   G. Gilbert-Lodge, 2002

030.01 New Future People
o:   Shin-Jinrui Corp
/:   New Future People, 2001

031.01 MASA Colectivo Gráfico
o:   Pirelli, Salón Pirelli
     de Jovenes Artistas
/:   Masa, 1997
031.02 phunk
o:   Judo
/:   Alvin Tan/phunk, 2001

032.01 Blammo
ð:   parra / idiot logo, 2000

032.02 Power Graphixx
o:   DLR Inc., printing logo
     for Trouper
/:   Power Graphixx, 2002
032.03 Niels Meulman
o:   Shoe seal
/:   Niels 'Shoe' Meulman,
     1993/2002
032.04 PCT
o:   Videoidyll
/:   pct, 2002

033.01 incorect
o:   WTC - Incorect logos
     for t-shirts
/:   incorect, 2001

034.01 phunk
o:   Infant games
/:   Melvin Chee/phunk, 2001
034.02 Tsuyoshi Kusano
034.03 phunk
o:   Kondense
/:   Melvin Chee/phunk, 2002
034.04 Power Graphixx
o:   IdN Magazine
/:   Power Graphixx, 2001
034.05 Tsuyoshi Kusano
034.06 jum
o:   fat cap
/:   jum, 2001
034.07 hungryfordesign
o:   coredump records
/:   Nando Costa, 2002
034.08 MASA Colectivo Gráfico
o:   Satelite
/:   Masa, 1999
034.09 tronics
034.10 Tsuyoshi Kusano
034.11 MASA Colectivo Gráfico
o:   Fantasma Productions
/:   Masa, 2000
034.12 Sweden
o:   Åbro, Ytterborn & Fuentes
/:   Sweden, 2000

**035.01 Tsuyoshi Kusano**

**036.01 Blammo**
o: Rockwell,
Paper Folding logo
/: parra, 2002
**036.02 - .03 onlab**
o: compad tools
/: onlab, 2002
**036.04 Finsta**
o: Las Palmas, Swedish
artist group
/: Finsta 2001
**036.05 phunk**
&: Melvin Chee/phunk, 2002
**036.06 phunk**
o: Flovor Inc.
/: Alvin Tan/phunk, 2002
**036.07 Markus Moström**
o: Johanna Lundell,
Massage therapist
/: Markus Moström, 2000
**036.08 Tsuyoshi Kusano**
**036.09 phunk**
o: How & Why Books
/: Alvin Tan/phunk, 2002
**036.10 Tim Jester**
o: the Edge
/: Tim Jester, 1996
**036.11 Deanne Cheuk**
**036.12 IKU**
o: Pleasure Dogs
/: Ilan Katin, 2001

**037.01 HandGun**
&: david zack custer, 2001
**037.02 re-p**
**037.03 Lobo**
o: Golden Shower
/: Carlos Bêla, 1999
**037.04 Norm**
&: Norm, 1999-2002

**038.01 Luca Ionescu Design**

**038.02 Norm**
&: Norm, 1999-2002
**038.03 Tsuyoshi Kusano**
**038.04 MASA Colectivo Gráfico**
o: Indigena, Personal Project
/: Masa, 2002
**038.05 MASA Colectivo Gráfico**
o: Marina del Rey,
Yacht club
/: Masa, 1997
**038.06 kong.gmbh**
o: Suisse Éole
/: kong, 1998
**038.07 Raoul SINIER**
&: Raoul Sinier, 1999
**038.08 nothing medialab**
**038.09 - .10 minigram**
o: system by minigram
/: minigram, 2002
**038.11 minigram**
o: evolution by minigram
/: minigram, 2002
**038.12 ghs web graphica**
o: A-SEVEN from DESCENTE
/: AKIHIRO IKEGOSHI, 2000

**039.01 New Future People**
o: Miscellaneous logos
/: New Future People,
1996-1999

**040.01 MASA Colectivo Gráfico**
o: loquesea network
/: Masá, 2000
**040.02 MASA Colectivo Gráfico**
&: Masa, 2002
**040.03 kong.gmbh**
&: kong.intern, 2001
**040.04 BlackDog**
o: PowerBar
/: Mark Fox, Matt Haligman,
1996

**041.01 MASA Colectivo Gráfico**
o: Ocho, Personal Project
/: Masa, 2002

**041.02 CISMA**
o: Andre's Tattoo
/: CISMA, 2001
**041.03 Tsuyoshi Kusano**
**041.04 Nendo Grafic Squad**
o: All Japan Records
/: Quentaro "Nendo ANI"
Fujimoto, 2001

**042.01 automatic art and design**
o: pier d'amico photography
/: charles wilkin, 1997
**042.02 BlackDog**
&: Architecture + Design
Forum
/: Mark Fox, 1998
**042.03 BlackDog**
o: Autodesk
/: Mark Fox, 1995
**042.04 BlackDog**
o: Tourneau
/: Mark Fox, 1999
**042.05 Dopepope**
&: Joe Lucchese, 2001-2002
**042.06 Power Graphixx**
&: Power Graphixx logo, 2001
**042.07 minigram**
o: compad.info
/: minigram, 2002
**042.08 FORMGEBER**
o: Massive Development, game
developer
/: Jochen Eeuwyk, 1999
**042.09 Ross Imms**
o: r-air recordings
/: Ross Imms, 2001
**042.10 STRADA**
o: US Forty GmbH -
Sportswear & Fashion Label
/: Stefan Rueckerl
**042.11 Tsuyoshi Kusano**
**042.12 Ben Mulkey**
o: Goldenboy
/: Ben Mulkey, 2001

**043.01 Little Eskimo**
o: Foji Electronic Toys
/: Jonas Loefgren, 2001
**043.02 Form**
o: 2WO THIRD3/Epic Records
/: Paul West, Paula Benson,
1994
**043.03 designershock/DSOS1**
**043.04 - .06 Lobo**
o: Golden Shower
/: C. Bêla, D. Kamioka, G.
Marcondes, M. Sader, M.
de Paula Santos, 2001
**043.07 Tsuyoshi Kusano**
**043.08 OCKTAK**
o: Hard
/: OCKTAK, 2002
**043.09 minigram**
**043.10 OCKTAK**
&: world council of church,
2001
**043.11 OCKTAK**
o: 310K - INSERT
/: 310K. Paul Rickus,
Ivo Schmetz, 2001
**043.12 New Future People**
o: Golden Joy Products
/: New Future People, 2002

**044.01 - .03 hungryfordesign**
o: the wddg
/: Nando Costa, 2000
**044.04 hungryfordesign**
o: derush
/: Nando Costa, 2002
**044.05 hungryfordesign**
o: hungryfordesign
/: Nando Costa, 2000
**044.06 hungryfordesign**
o: derush
/: Nando Costa, 2001
**044.07 - .10 hungryfordesign**
o: the wddg
/: Nando Costa, 2000

044.11 FORMGEBER
o:  Profashion, Fashion Label
/:  Siegmund Schlag, 1999
044.12 jum
o:  Digital Text
/:  jum, 1999

045.01 MK12
&:  molecule icon MK12, 2000
045.02 onlab
o:  onlab/chain.reaction
/:  onlab, 2002
045.03 FORMGEBER
o:  Profashion, Fashion Label
/:  Rolf Rinklin, 1999
045.04 FORMGEBER
o:  Profashion, Fashion Label
/:  Siegmund Schlag, 1999

046.01 yippieyeah
o:  Open
/:  Bauer / Borkowski, 1998

047.01 forcefeed:swede
o:  Zentronics
/:  Oz Dean, 2002

048.01 New Future People
o:  Join-Us Typeface
/:  New Future People, 1999

049.01 - .05 Versus
o:  visomat inc.
/:  Alexander Baumgardt, 1999

050.01 New Future People
o:  Ian Martin Assoc.
/:  New Future People, 1997
050.02 - .05 New Future People
o:  Lunatik video game,
    Pure Entertainments
/:  New Future People, 1996

051.01 New Future People
o:  M-74.com
/:  New Future People, 1999

052.01 augenbluten
o:  fantom
/:  IF, 2000
052.02 MASA Colectivo Gráfico
o:  Imposible, Proyect
/:  MASA, 2002
052.03 Luca Ionescu Design
052.04 Syrup Helsinki
o:  Lahti Mechanical
    Services Ltd.
/:  Teemu Suviala, 2000
052.05 Tsuyoshi Kusano
052.06 Machine
o:  exam project
    Rietveld Academy
/:  MACHINE, 1996
052.07 Luca Ionescu Design
052.08 Tsuyoshi Kusano
052.09 OCKTAK
o:  Fusion Inc.
/:  OCKTAK, 2000
052.10 OCKTAK
&:  OCKTAK, SNOW FLAKES, 1999
052.11 OCKTAK
o:  Waterg8 Europe
/:  OCKTAK, 2000
052.12 Dirk Rudolph
o:  Circle Music
/:  Dirk Rudolph, 2000

053.01 OCKTAK
o:  Sandokan - Vibration
/:  OCKTAK, 2001
053.02 Alphabetical Order
o:  Add Value Business
    Marketing Consultants
/:  Alphabetical Order, 2001
053.03 Dirk Rudolph
o:  Rammstein
/:  Dirk Rudolph, 2001
053.04 FORMGEBER
o:  Bassline Generation
/:  Heiko Ulrich, 1998
053.05 Alphabetical Order
o:  Unga Arkitekter
/:  Alphabetical Order, 2002

053.06 re-p
053.07 Tsuyoshi Kusano
053.08 minigram
o:  power by minigram
/:  minigram, 2002
053.09 Dirk Rudolph
o:  Beutler Rechtsanwälte
/:  Dirk Rudolph, 2000
053.10 Syrup Helsinki
o:  Koneisto Festival/Koneisto
    Production Oy
/:  Antti Hinkula & Teemu
    Suviala, 2000

054.01 IKU
&:  Ilan Katin, 1998
054.02 Tsuyoshi Kusano
054.03 Tsuyoshi Kusano
054.04 CISMA
&:  CISMA, 2001
054.05 HandGun
o:  Red Dragon
/:  david zack custer, 1999
054.06 Luca Ionescu Design
054.07 Dirk Rudolph
o:  WEA, DE/Vision Band Logo
/:  Dirk Rudolph, 1998
054.08 minigram
o:  evolution by minigram
/:  minigram, 2002
054.09 -.10 FORMGEBER
o:  Massive Development
/:  Jochen Eeuwyk, 1999
054.11 archetype:interactive
o:  sin / second line
/:  john wu, 2002
054.12 H617
o:  H
/:  Takeshi Hamada, 1999

055.01 kong.gmbh
&:  kong.intern, 2000
055.02 kong.gmbh
&:  kong.intern, 2001
055.03 OCKTAK
o:  Random
/:  OCKTA, 2000

055.04 Tim Jester
o:  Arcalux 1
/:  Tim Jester, 2002
055.05 -.08 Norm
&:  Norm, 1999-2002
055.09 Form
o:  Scritti Politti/
    Virgin Records
/:  Paul West, Paula Benson,
    Chris Hilton, 1999
055.10 nothing medialab
055.11 OCKTAK
o:  BULLIT.PROOF
/:  OCKTAK, 1999
055.12 Thorsten Geiger
o:  Brainbox/BerlinBETA,
/:  Thorsten Geiger/Rosendahl
    & Geiger, 1998

056.01 nothing medialab
056.02 FORMGEBER
o:  Massive Development
/:  Rolf Rinklin, 1999
056.03 nothing medialab
056.04 nothing medialab
056.05 hungryfordesign
o:  urban slut
/:  Nando Costa, 2000
056.06 FORMGEBER
o:  Massive Development
/:  Jochen Eeuwyk, 1999
056.07 Tim Jester
o:  Crucial Consulting
/:  Tim Jester, 2002
056.08 hausgrafik
o:  Nico Productions, Bern
/:  hausgrafik.ch, 2000

057.01 Alphabetical Order
o:  Cumulus
/:  Alphabetical Order, 2002
057.02 Marc Kappeler
o:  Down Town Tempo, bern
/:  Marc Kappeler, 1999
057.03 FORMGEBER
o:  Massive Development
/:  Jochen Eeuwyk, 1999

**057.04 Dirk Rudolph**
o:  SONO Band Logo, Polydor
√:  Dirk Rudolph, 2002

**058.01 Move Design**
o:  boomBang
√:  S. Lising, P. Spreenberg,
    C. Francis, 2001

**059.01 SuperHappyBunny Company**
o:  Yoga
√:  SuperHappyBunny
    Company, 2001
**059.02 Dirk Rudolph**
o:  Reamonn Band Logo/Circle
    Music
√:  Dirk Rudolph, 2001

**060.01 Tim Jester**
o:  SixSidesDesign 3
√:  Tim Jester, 1996
**060.02 augenbluten**
ℰ:  IF, 2002
**060.03 FORMGEBER**
o:  Massive Development
√:  Jochen Eeuwyk, 1999
**060.04 augenbluten**
o:  cyber hills golf fashion
√:  IF, 2000

**061.01 Superpopstudio**
ℰ:  Superpopstudio
    website, 2000

**062.01 New Future People**
ℰ:  New Future People
    webpage, 1998

**063.01 New Future People**
ℰ:  New Future People
    webpage, 1998

**064.01 Mission Design Agency**

**065.01 Tim Jester**
o:  SixSidesDesign 2
√:  Tim Jester, 1996
**065.02 Tim Jester**
o:  Origin Design
√:  Tim Jester, 1998
**065.03 Tim Jester**
o:  Misc. icons
√:  Tim Jester, 1998
**065.04 MASA Colectivo Gráfico**
o:  Caleidoscopio, Project
√:  Masa, 2001
**065.05 Tim Jester**
o:  Misc. icons
√:  Tim Jester, 1998
**065.06 Tim Jester**
o:  SixSidesDesign 1
√:  Tim Jester, 1996
**065.07 MASA Colectivo Gráfico**
ℰ:  MASA, 2002

**066.01 Luca Ionescu Design**
**066.02 Dirk Rudolph**
o:  Elektromotor, Motor Music
√:  Dirk Rudolph, 1996
**066.03 hungryfordesign**
ℰ:  Nando Costa, 1999

**067.01 Tsuyoshi Kusano**

**068.01 OCKTAK**
o:  BULLIT.PROOF
√:  OCKTAK, 1999
**068.02 OCKTAK**
o:  BULLIT.PROOF
√:  OCKTAK, PAUL RICKUS, 2002
**068.03 - .04 OCKTAK**
o:  BULLIT.PROOF
√:  OCKTAK, 2002
**068.05 - .08 OCKTAK**
o:  EYE-FI + SELF
√:  OCKTAK, 2002
**068.09 - .12 OCKTAK**
o:  Fullon
√:  OCKTAK, 2002

**069.01 - .04 OCKTAK**
ℰ:  OCKTAK, 2002
**069.05 - .09 OCKTAK**
ℰ:  OCKTAK, 1999
**069.10 OCKTAK**
ℰ:  OCKTAK, 2002
**069.11 OCKTAK**
ℰ:  OCKTAK, 2002
**069.12 OCKTAK**
ℰ:  OCKTAK, 1999

**070.01 Norm**
ℰ:  Norm, 1999-2002
**070.02 phunk**
o:  Shoppe SixteenluV
√:  Alvin Tan/phunk, 2001
**070.03 Bitsteam**
o:  Bitsteam, Personal CI
√:  Stephan Mathieu, 2000
**070.04 raum mannheim**
o:  artist ahead
√:  susann el salamoni, 1999
**070.05 Eboy**
**070.06 Norm**
ℰ:  Norm, 1999-2002
**070.07 kong.gmbh**
o:  Eidgenössisches
    Finanzdepartement, Bern
√:  kong., 2001
**070.08 PXPress**
**070.09 Chris Hutchinson**
o:  thefinktank competition
√:  Chris Hutchinson, 2001

**071.01 Synchron**
ℰ:  ralph steinbrüchel, 2000
**071.02 - .09 Synchron**

**072.01 Digitalultras**
ℰ:  Manuel Perfetto,
    Digitalultras, 2002

**073.01 - .05 minigram**
o:  expansion by minigram
√:  minigram, 2002

**074.01 e-Types**
o:  TDC - Internet
√:  Jonas Hecksher, 2001

**075.01 - .04 e-Types**
o:  TDC - Internet
√:  Jonas Hecksher, 2001

**076.01 e-Types**
o:  TDC - Internet
√:  Jonas Hecksher, 2001

**077.01 e-Types**
o:  TDC - Internet
√:  Jonas Hecksher, 2001

**080.01 e-Types**
o:  Euroman Publications
√:  Jonas Hecksher, 2000
**080.02 DSOS1**
o:  The APERTO AG
√:  Stefan Gandl, 1997
**080.03 Form**
o:  Staverton
√:  P. West, P. Benson, 1998
**080.04 FORMGEBER**
o:  Essence, Fashion Store
√:  Siegmund Schlag, 1999
**080.05 Mutabor**
o:  SinnerSchraderAG
√:  Mutabor, Carsten Raffel,
    2000
**080.06 CODE**
o:  condor- business of
    imagination, switzerland
√:  Reto Gehrig, 2000
**080.07 augenbluten**
o:  korridor textile design
√:  IF, 2001
**080.08 STRADA**
o:  Hirmer - Fashion Label
√:  Stefan Rueckerl
**080.09 typotherapy+design**
o:  Neksis Magazine
√:  Stephen Crowhurst, 2002

080.10 phunk
∂: William Chan/phunk, 2002
080.11 Défil Inc.
∂: dori dock, 1998
080.12 Blammo
o: Mr. Wix music /
   Chocolate party logo
/: parra, 2000
080.13 DSOS1
o: The ECONA AG, 1997
/: Stefan Gandl
080.14 Power Graphixx
o: Cleaning, logo
/: Power Graphixx, 2001
080.15 Method
o: Solid, Inc.
/: Mike Abbink, 2001
080.16 Power Graphixx
o: SELFISH, logo for artwork
   on SELFISH magazine
/: Power Graphixx, 2000

081.01 ghs web graphica
o: CIAOPANIC
/: AKIHIRO IKEGOSHI, 2001
081.02 B.ü.L.b grafix
081.03 Luca Ionescu Design
081.04 typotherapy+design
o: One / Fifteen
/: Noël Nanton , 2002
081.05 typotherapy+design
o: InBetweenDub
/: Noël Nanton, 2002
081.06 OCKTAK
o: Betamax Full Media Events
/: Paul Rickus, Ivo Schmetz,
   2001
081.07 ASYL DESIGN Inc.
o: Hougado Corp.
/: Naoki SATO, 1997

082.01 Tsuyoshi Kusano
082.02 Norm
∂: Norm, 1999-2002

082.03 ASYL DESIGN Inc.
o: Ohta Publishing Company
/: Naoki SATO, Kazuki
   Ohashi, 2001
082.04 BlackDog
o: Washoe Grill
/: Mark Fox, 2001
082.05 Norm
∂: Norm, 1999-2002
082.06 ASYL DESIGN Inc.
o: DesignExchange Co.,Ltd.
/: Naoki SATO, 2002
082.07 hausgrafik
o: Franticek Klossner
/: hausgrafik.ch, 2001
082.08 Eboy
∂: eBoy, 2000
082.09 augenbluten
o: annex
/: IF, 2000

083.01 Power Graphixx
o: Cleaning, logo
/: Power Graphixx, 2001
083.02 Luca Ionescu Design
083.03 Luca Ionescu Design
083.04 Luca Ionescu Design
083.05 Tsuyoshi Kusano
083.06 Luca Ionescu Design

084.01 Maniackers Design
o: FLOP DESIGN
/: Masashi Kato, 2002
084.02 augenbluten
o: the next level
/: IF, 2000
084.03 raum mannheim
o: rhein-neckar
/: susann el salamoni, 1999
084.04 augenbluten
∂: IF, 2001
084.05 OCKTAK
o: BULLIT.PROOF
/: OCKTAK, 1999

084.06 OCKTAK
o: BULLIT.PROOF
/: OCKTAK, 2001

085.01 augenbluten
∂: world council of church,
   2001
085.02 Niels Jansson
o: Sanana
/: Niels Jansson. 2001
085.03 Maniackers Design
085.04 Electronic Curry Ltd.
o: balibioskop, shadow
   theater event
/: electronic curry, 1999
085.05 ghs web graphica
o: MATSUSHITA ELECTRIC WORKS
/: AKIHIRO IKEGOSHI, 2002
085.06 ghs web graphica
o: MATSUSHITA ELECTRIC WORKS
/: AKIHIRO IKEGOSHI, 2002

086.01 OCKTAK
o: Fusion Inc.
/: OCKTAK, 2001
086.02 OCKTAK
o: Fusion Inc.
/: OCKTAK, 2000
086.03 OCKTAK
o: Fullon
/: OCKTAK, 2002
086.04 OCKTAK
o: Uphone
/: OCKTAK, 2001
086.05 OCKTAK
o: 310K - THING
/: Paul Rickus,
   Ivo Schmetz, 2001

087.01 OCKTAK
o: Time
/: OCKTAK, 2000

088.01 OCKTAK
o: EYE-FI + SELF
/: OCKTAK, 2002
088.02 Luca Ionescu Design
088.03 CODE
o: milk trend. Migros
   switzerland
/: reto gehrig, 1999
088.04 CODE
o: Muzo
/: Axel Pfänder, 2001
088.05 SAKAMOTO
o: Jan Buus Photographer
/: SAKAMOTO, 2002
088.06 CODE
o: tide clothes Morrows gmbh
/: reto gehrig, 2000

089.01 tankdesign
o: Tocco, Sascha Bachman,
   Maurice Zubler
/: Katarina Lang, Tina
   Leimbacher, 2002
089.02 Luca Ionescu Design

090.01 Tsuyoshi Kusano
090.02 Tsuyoshi Kusano
090.03 Disko Döner

091.01 ASYL DESIGN Inc.
o: Sony Music Entertainment
   (Japan) Inc.
/: Naoki SATO
091.02 Niels Jansson
o: Antikarma clothing
/: Niels Jansson, 2001
091.03 Tsuyoshi Kusano

092.01 STRADA
o: Scape - Electronic
   Music Label
/: S. Rueckerl, K. Höfling
092.02 STRADA
∂: Stefan Rueckerl, Andreas
   Doehring, STRADA

092.03 CODE
o:  pepper gmbh
/:  vera studhalter, 1999
092.04 OCKTAK
o:  Dance Valley - Hiquality
/:  OCKTAK, 1999
092.05 büro destruct
o:  Morris Audio
/:  Lopetz, 1999
092.06 Niels Jansson
o:  Kay-Kay inc.
/:  Niels Jansson, 2001

093.01 Kathrin Jachmann
o:  Karrierestrategien für die
    Onlinebranche
/:  Kathrin Jachmann, 2001
093.02 typotherapy+design
o:  typotherapy+design
/:  Stephen Crowhurst, 2002
093.03 raum mannheim
o:  planquadrat
/:  susann el salamoni, 2002

094.01 Alphabetical Order
o:  Sneaker Nation
/:  Alphabetical Order, 2002
094.02 Tsuyoshi Kusano
094.03 Tsuyoshi Kusano
094.04 Tsuyoshi Kusano
094.05 Tsuyoshi Kusano
094.06 DSOS1
o:  ONLINE OFFICE GMBH Berlin
/:  Stefan Gandl /DS, 1997
094.07 Designunion
o:  nurschrec!, Vienna
/:  Barbara Dechant, 2000
094.08 MAGNETOFONICA
o:  Babylon Motorhome,
/:  Dario Utreras, 2002
094.09 POSITRON CO.,LTD.
o:  THE MAD CAPSURE MARKETS
/:  Hiroaki Doi, 2001
094.10 Tsuyoshi Kusano
094.11 ASYL DESIGN Inc.
o:  Hougado Corp.
/:  Naoki SATO, 1999

094.12 typotherapy+design
o:  Spin Gallery
/:  Stephen Crowhurst, 2002

095.01 ASYL DESIGN Inc.
o:  Hougado Corp.
/:  Naoki SATO, 2000
095.02 ASYL DESIGN Inc.

096.01 DSOS1
o:  The DESIGNERDOCK
/:  Stefan Gandl /DS, 1997
096.02 kong.gmbh
o:  wahlirüefli, Architekten
    u. Raumplaner, Biel/Bienne
/:  kong., 2001
096.03 anja klausch
o:  Bluewin AG, Logoentwurf
/:  Anja Klausch bei
    MetaDesign AG, 2001
096.04 CODE
096.05 blindresearch
o:  dir.ecte
/:  sven zuege, 2002
096.06 p*star
o:  think software
/:  Pascal C. Baumann, 2002
096.07 OCKTAK
o:  BULLIT.PROOF
/:  OCKTAK, 1999
096.08 OCKTAK
o:  Shakedown - Player 1
/:  OCKTAK, 2002
096.09 OCKTAK
o:  Input Records
/:  OCKTAK, 1999
096.10 OCKTAK
o:  310K - THING
/:  Paul Rickus, Ivo Schmetz,
    2001
096.11 Form
o:  The Beat/Fuji
    International Productions
/:  Paul West, Paula Benson,
    Chris Hilton, 2002

096.12 Dopepope
o:  DOPEPOPE
/:  Joe Lucchese, 2001-2002
096.13 Marc Kappeler
o:  schmuckpreis schweiz
/:  Marc Kappeler, 2002
096.14 nothing medialab

097.01 CODE
o:  superkick switzerland
/:  daniel donati, 1999
097.02 raum mannheim
o:  spacetank
/:  susann el salamoni, 2000
097.03 Disko Döner
097.04 Tim Jester
o:  apex
/:  Tim Jester, 1999
097.05 ghs web graphica
o:  A-SEVEN from DESCENTE
/:  AKIHIRO IKEGOSHI, 2001
097.06 ghs web graphica
o:  CIAOPANIC
/:  AKIHIRO IKEGOSHI, 2002
097.07 tankdesign
o:  Tocco, Sascha Bachman,
    Maurice Zubler
/:  Katarina Lang / Tina
    Leimbacher, 2002
097.08 dubius?
o:  Cube science
/:  dubius?, 1998

098.01 Tina Backmann
o:  project St Martins college
    of art and design, London
/:  LJUVTUFF, T. Backman, 2001
098.02 Digitalultras
o:  Perfect Job,
    Digitalultras
/:  Manuel Perfetto, 2002

099.01 Luca Ionescu Design

100.01 typotherapy+design
o:  typotherapy+design
/:  Stephen Crowhurst, 2002

100.02 benjamin guedel
o:  soda magazin
/:  benjamin guedel, 2000
100.03 Jorge Alderete
o:  Guillen Publishing
/:  Jorge Alderete, 2002
100.04 dubius?
o:  Superfurniture Stores
/:  dubius?, 1999
100.05 CRAIG ROBINSON
∂:  CRAIG ROBINSON, 2001

101.01 Blammo
∂:  Parra / site logo, 2000
101.02 kong.gmbh
o:  MusiCalls, Biel/Bienne
/:  kong., 1999
101.03 Jorge Alderete
o:  Gratarola Jamas!
/:  Jorge Alderete, 1998
101.04 CRAIG ROBINSON
∂:  CRAIG ROBINSON, 2000

102.01 Artificial Environments
102.02 Artificial Environments
102.03 Artificial Environments

103.01 Finsta
o:  own project
/:  Killah, 2002

104.01 Rinzen
o:  Brisbane Marketing
/:  Rinzen, 2001
104.02 Bionic System
o:  Bionic-Systems.com
/:  Bionic Systems, 2001
104.03 MAGNETOFONICA
o:  SELL
/:  Dario Utreras
104.04 Tycoon Graphics
o:  FOR LIFE RECORDS
/:  tycoon graphics, 1996
104.05 CODE
o:  spider galaxy club
    switzerland
/:  Ryosuke Kawaguchi, 2002

104.06 Rinzen
o:  Smart
/:  Rinzen, 2001
104.07 typotherapy+design
o:  Sonic
/:  Stephen Crowhurst, 2002
104.08 Norm
∂:  Norm, 1999-2002
104.09 Power Graphixx
o:  SAL magazine,
/:  Power Graphixx, 2001
104.10 Niels Meulman
o:  advertising agency Nebok
/:  N. 'Shoe' Meulman, 1999
104.11 Power Graphixx
o:  DLR Inc., store logo for
    Building
/:  Power Graphixx, 2001
104.12 24HR
o:  Borneo Communication
/:  Ricky Tillblad, 2000
104.13 Power Graphixx
o:  SELFISH
/:  Power Graphixx, 2000
104.14 Rio Grafik
o:  forecast, magazine
/:  Rio Grafik, 1997
104.15 Rio Grafik
o:  trax@rohstofflager, club
/:  Rio Grafik, 1996

105.01 büro destruct
o:  Balduin
/:  Lopetz, 2000
105.02 büro destruct
o:  Phaeno
/:  Lopetz, 2001
105.03 SAKAMOTO
o:  coolburger.com
/:  SAKAMOTO, 2002
105.04 SAKAMOTO
o:  cocainelimointhehose.com
/:  SAKAMOTO, 2002
105.05 Move Design
o:  Xuny
/:  Samuel Lising, Peter
    Spreenberg, Richard
    Leighton, Kim West, 1999

105.06 Rinzen
o:  Slika
/:  Rinzen, 2001
105.07 Rinzen
o:  Glassworks
/:  Rinzen, 2001

106.01 LEVEL1
o:  kitchen
/:  Tsuyoshi Hirooka, 2001
106.02 Luca Ionescu Design
106.03 Um|bruch Gestaltung
o:  13th Street GmbH
/:  Um|bruch, 2000
106.04 Tsuyoshi Kusano
106.05 Luca Ionescu Design
106.06 balsi
o:  nothing medialab, bern
/:  balsi, 2001
106.07 Sweden
o:  NONS/Music Network
/:  Sweden, 1997
106.08 Norm
∂:  Norm, 1999-2002
106.09 Um|bruch Gestaltung
o:  Sun TV | Entertainment
    Factory
/:  Um|bruch, 2000
106.10 OCKTAK
o:  Random
/:  OCKTAK, 2000
106.11 tankdesign
o:  Tocco, Sascha Bachman,
    Maurice Zubler
/:  S. Lenggenhager, 2002
106.12 24HR
o:  Amen, Primal Music
/:  Ricky Tillblad, 1997
106.13 Markus Moström
o:  Docco. Blinkers,
    owner of commision
/:  Markus Moström, 2000
106.14 Finsta
∂:  Finsta, 2001
106.15 Deanne Cheuk

107.01 Niels Meulman
o:  Wave magazine
/:  N. 'Shoe' Meulman, 1996
107.02 Bionic System
107.03 ColdWater Graphiix
o:  ALSUR co.,ltd.
    EVOLVE Logo
/:  Tabito Mizuo , 2002
107.04 Luca Ionescu Design
107.05 Power Graphixx
o:  DLR Inc., logo for BQE
/:  Power Graphixx, 2001
107.06 Machine
o:  TRUE creative
    communication agency
/:  MACHINE, 2002
107.07 Power Graphixx
o:  Hakuhodo Inc.
/:  Power Graphixx, 2001
107.08 Machine
o:  showcase party by Barkers
    and others
/:  MACHINE, 2001

108.01 Tsuyoshi Kusano
108.02 FORMGEBER
o:  Paraglider Companies
/:  Rolf Rinklin, 1999
108.03 Disco Döner
108.04 FORMGEBER
o:  Paraglider Companies
/:  Rolf Rinklin, 1999
108.05 Dopepope
o:  DOPEPOPE
/:  Joe Lucchese, 2001-2002
108.06 FORMGEBER
o:  Paraglider Companies
/:  Rolf Rinklin, 1999
108.07 Hendrik Hellige
108.08 Form
o:  The Hospital
/:  Paul West, Paula Benson,
    1998

109.01 typotherapy+design
o:  typotherapy+design
/:  Noël Nanton, 2002

109.02 moniteurs
o:  Subotnic,
    Softwareentwickler
/:  H. Nehl, V. Schlecht, 2000
109.03 ASYL DESIGN Inc.
o:  Fuji Television
    Network Inc.
/:  Naoki SATO, 2001
109.04 Mutabor
o:  Mutabor 10
/:  Carsten Raffel, 2001
109.05 SAKAMOTO
109.06 Power Graphixx
o:  Cleaning
/:  Power Graphixx, 2001
109.07 minimise
o:  minimise
/:  Mark Clarke, 2002
109.08 Mutabor
o:  Cult Cars AG
/:  Mutabor, Axel Domke, 2001
109.09 POSITRON CO.,LTD.
o:  GEORGE'S FURNITURE,
    CIBONE
/:  Hiroaki Doi, 2001

110.01 büro destruct
∂:  Lopetz / MB, 2000
110.02 balsi
o:  linkup, webdesign, bern
/:  balsi, 1999
110.03 büro destruct
o:  Bigstar
/:  MB, 1998
110.04 Syrup Helsinki
/:  Antti Hinkula & Teemu
    Suviala
o:  Yakuta Ltd., 2001
110.05 Niels Meulman
o:  Future Card
/:  N. 'Shoe' Meulman, 1997
110.06 phunk
o:  phunk
/:  Alvin Tan/phunk, 2001
110.07 Electronic Curry Ltd.
∂:  electronic curry, 1999

110.08 Um|bruch Gestaltung
o:  Sun TV | Entertainment
    Factory
/:  Um|bruch, 2000
110.09 Tsuyoshi Kusano
110.10 Marc Kappeler
o:  schmuck galerie, jewellery
    galery, bern
/:  Marc Kappeler, 2001
110.11 ghs web graphica
o:  CIAOPANIC
/:  AKIHIRO IKEGOSHI, 2002
110.12 Luca Ionescu Design

111.01 Machine
♂:  MACHINE, TSHIRT, 2001
111.02 Tsuyoshi Kusano
111.03 Hendrik Hellige
111.04 büro destruct
o:  Brand New World
/:  Moritz, 2002
111.05 büro destruct
♂:  MB, 2002
111.06 phunk
o:  Guerilla Fonts
/:  Jackson Tan/phunk, 2002
111.07 Rinzen
o:  Brisbane Marketing
/:  Rinzen, 2001
111.08 Machine
♂:  DEPT, 1999
111.09 Hendrik Hellige
111.10 Maniackers Design
o:  desgin field G
/:  Masayuki Sato, 2001

112.01 büro destruct
o:  Echo Club / Kulturhallen
    Dampfzentrale
/:  Lopetz, 1999
112.02 Fourskin
112.03 Machine
o:  WWW.OURMACHINE.COM
/:  MACHINE, 2001
112.04 Deanne Cheuk
112.05 DED Associates
o:  Sauce
/:  DED, 2000

112.06 MASA Colectivo Gráfico
o:  Hip-Hop Inside,
    Trece Discos
/:  MASA, 2001
112.07 Machine
o:  Coffeeshop in Leiden
/:  ZEDZ&YALT, 1995
112.08 büro destruct
o:  boombox.net
/:  Lopetz, 2000
112.09 Maniackers Design
/:  Masayuki Sato
o:  NETON, Logo, 2000
112.10 Jorge Alderete
o:  Hula + Hula
/:  Jorge Alderete, 2002

113.01 344 Design
o:  Modernista!
    Sudden Industries
/:  Stefan G. Bucher, 2000
113.02 ColdWater Graphiix
o:  BEAMS-T, Dry Max 2 Logo
/:  Tabito Mizuo, 2001
113.03 balsi
o:  meienberg michael
    graphics, bern
/:  balsi, 2001
113.04 Machine
♂:  DEPT, 1998
113.05 Eboy

114.01 Luca Ionescu Design
114.02 Machine
o:  SERIAL DRILLERS PARTIES
/:  DEPT, 1998
114.03 Machine
o:  exam project at
    Rietveld Academy
/:  Machine, 1996
114.04 MAGNETOFONICA
114.05 Rinzen
o:  Empire
/:  Rinzen, 2001
114.06 raum mannheim
o:  sofabed
/:  susann el salamoni, 2001

114.07 Matthias Hübner
o:  bordfunk
/:  Matthias Hübner, 2002
114.08 raum mannheim
o:  heart
/:  frank hoffmann, 2001

115.01 Machine
o:  PROJECT 2000
/:  DEPT, 2000
115.02 Machine
♂:  MACHINE, TSHIRT, 2001

116.01 344 Design
o:  Interscope Geffen A&M
/:  Stefan G. Bucher, 2001
116.02 Bionic System
o:  Naga1, Belgium
/:  Bionic Systems, 2000
116.03 Niels Meulman
o:  clubnight Chemistry
/:  N. 'Shoe' Meulman, 1995

117.01 Gregory Gilbert-Lodge
o:  sidi blunt (café & tee)
    Zürich, Bruno Hiltebrand
/:  G. Gilbert-Lodge, 2002

118.01 OCKTAK
o:  Ascension
/:  OCKTAK, 2002
118.02 OCKTAK
o:  Sandokan
/:  OCKTAK, 2000
118.03 kong.gmbh
o:  Isotent, wärmegedämmtes
    Zeltsystem, Biel/Bienne
/:  kong., 1999
118.04 Hendrik Hellige
118.05 CODE
o:  Lovebugs, Warner Music,
    switzerland
/:  vera studhalter, 2001
118.06 CODE
o:  nevins. Bmg france
/:  Reto Gehrig / Ryosuke
    Kawaguchi, 2001

118.07 Kathrin Jachmann
o:  Pavillon am Weinbergsweg
/:  Kathrin Jachmann, 2000
118.08 344 Design
o:  Modernista!
/:  Stefan G. Bucher, 2000

119.01 CODE
o:  dj vitamin s. kaufleuten
    club. switzerland
/:  Ilana Aharon, 2001
119.02 CODE
o:  migros kulturprozent
/:  ilana aharon, 2001
119.03 Bionic System
o:  Bionic-Systems.com
/:  Bionic Systems, 2001
119.04 raum mannheim
o:  musikpark
/:  frank hoffmann, 2001
119.05 MIGUEL ANGEL LEYVA
♂:  MIGUEL ANGEL LEYVA, 2000
119.06 Bionic System
o:  Byron Peneranda, USA
/:  Bionic Systems, 2001
119.07 Bionic System
o:  Broken Beatz
    Entertainment, Germany
/:  Bionic Systems, 2000
119.08 Bionic System
o:  Naga1, Belgium
/:  Bionic Systems, 2000
119.09 CODE
o:  code in-house
/:  Ryosuke Kawaguchi, 2001
119.10 Bionic System
o:  Bionic-Systems.com
/:  Bionic Systems, 1999

120.01 Luca Ionescu Design
120.02 Cyclone Graphix
120.03 QuickHoney
o:  QuickHoney
/:  Nana Rausch, 2002
120.04 CODE
o:  migros kulturprozent
/:  ilana aharon, 2001

120.05 tikkigirl
o:   tikkigirl
/:   isabell welz, 2001
120.06 Bas Visual Concepts
120.07 Lindedesign
o:   mambo | schoolproject
/:   Christian Lindemann, 2002
120.08 HandGun
o:   Hong Kong Brand Action
     film festival
/:   david zack custer, 1998
120.09 büro destruct
o:   Kiff Kultur in der
     Futtermehl Fabrik
/:   Lopetz, 2000
120.10 inTEAM Graphics
120.11 OCKTAK
o:   OCKTAK - DZYN
/:   OCKTAK, 1998
120.12 nothing medialab

121.01 CODE
o:   flattrack band
     switzerland
/:   reto gehrig, 2002
121.02 raum mannheim
o:   lava
/:   martin keller, 2002
121.03 Finsta
o:   own project
/:   Finsta, 2001
121.04 Tycoon Graphics
o:   GRAPHICKERS
/:   tycoon g, 1996
121.05 Bas Visual Concepts
121.06 Fourskin
121.07 OCKTAK
o:   OCKTAK - LEUKNEUKEN
/:   OCKTAK, 2001

122.01 Sweden
o:   H&M / King
/:   Sweden, 2000
122.02 Niels Jansson
o:   Fokus Group.
/:   Niels Jansson, 2000

122.03 Luca Ionescu Design
122.04 kong.gmbh
o:   FUNIC, Standseilbahnen,
     Evilard
/:   kong., 2000

123.01 Bionic System
o:   F1rst Design, Germany
/:   Bionic Systems, 2000
123.02 Machine
o:   TRIPLE X EXPERIMENTAL
     MULTIMEDIA/Theaterfestival
/:   DEPT, 1999

124.01 Eboy
124.02 benjamin guedel
&:   benjamin guedel, 1999
124.03 benjamin guedel
&:   benjamin guedel, 1998
124.04 Machine
o:   Club RoXY Amsterdam
/:   DEPT, 1996
124.05 Luca Ionescu Design
124.06 benjamin guedel
o:   shaka hot shop
/:   benjamin guedel, 2001
124.07 benjamin guedel
o:   le stelle coiffure
/:   benjamin guedel, 2000
124.08 benjamin guedel
o:   indiana skateboards
/:   benjamin guedel, 2000
124.09 Machine
o:   Axion Software House
/:   DEPT, 1998
124.10 Machine
o:   Symbol Soup Book
/:   DEPT, 1998
124.11 Machine
&:   MACHINE, TSHIRT, 2002
124.12 Machine
o:   DEPT/Andre Plateel
/:   DEPT, 1998

125.01 benjamin guedel
o:   indiana skateboards
/:   benjamin guedel, 2001
125.02 Superpopstudio
&:   Superpopstudio, 2000
125.03 hausgrafik
o:   Reithalle Bern, Dachstock
/:   hausgrafik.ch, 2001
125.04 benjamin guedel
&:   benjamin guedel, 1999
125.05 archetype:interactive
o:   bubblegun / gary cheng
/:   stephen tsim, 2001
125.06 Syrup Helsinki
o:   Fast Sugar
/:   Teemu Suviala, 2001
125.07 Machine
o:   Praful, musician
/:   MACHINE, 2001
125.08 Norm
&:   Norm, 1999-2002
125.09 Hendrik Hellige
125.10 Eboy
&:   eBoy, 2002

126.01 - .02 Eboy
&:   eBoy, 2002
126.03 - .05 Eboy
&:   eBoy, 2000
126.06 Eboy
&:   eBoy, 2001

127.01 Mentary
o:   upperplayground
/:   gregory chapuisat, 2001
127.02 344 Design
o:   A&M Records
/:   Stefan G. Bucher, 2000
127.03 Eboy
&:   eBoy, 2002
127.04 344 Design
o:   A&M Records
/:   Stefan G. Bucher, 2000

128.01 Tsuyoshi Kusano
128.02 augenbluten
o:   nevins
/:   IF, 2002
128.03 augenbluten
o:   allmart
/:   IF, 2000
128.04 Hendrik Hellige

129.01 Power Graphixx
o:   Cleaning, printing logo
     for Cleaning
/:   Power Graphixx, 2001
129.02 OhioGirl
o:   Lakai Limited Footwear /
     Girl Skateboards
/:   Andy Mueller, 2002
129.03 Machine
o:   club: RoXY
/:   MACHINE, 1994

130.01 Tsuyoshi Kusano
130.02 Syrup Helsinki
o:   Xray magazine,
     Jim & Jill, Fashion Group
/:   Teemu Suviala, 2002

131.01 - 131.05 Rinzen
o:   Waikiki
/:   Rinzen, 2002

132.01 tronics
132.02 - .04 Um|bruch
o:   13th Street GmbH
/:   Um|bruch Gestaltung, 2000
132.05 tronics
132.06 - .08 Um|bruch
o:   Sun TV | Entertainment
     Factory
/:   Um|bruch Gestaltung, 2000
132.09 tronics
132.10 - .12 Um|bruch
o:   Sun TV | Entertainment
     Factory
/:   Um|bruch Gestaltung, 2000

**133.01 Rinzen**
o:  Brisbane Marketing
/:  Rinzen, 2001
**133.02 TOI Inc.**
o:  Liquid Sky, Ooze City.
/:  TOI, 1999

**134.01 123KLAN**
o:  UNIT 74
/:  123klan, 2000
**134.02 123KLAN**
o:  twenty five
/:  123klan, 1999
**134.03 - .04 123KLAN**
o:  drum n bass label
/:  123klan, 2002

**135.01 123KLAN**
o:  heavy.com
/:  123klan, 2001

**136.01 CODE**
o:  nevins. Bmg france
/:  Reto Gehrig / Ryosuke
    Kawaguchi, 2001
**136.02 CODE**
o:  dj vitamin s. kaufleuten
    club. switzerland
/:  Ryosuke Kawaguchi, 2001
**136.03 CISMA**
o:  A1 Club, switzerland
/:  Ryosuke Kawaguchi, 2002
**136.04 FORMGEBER**
o:  Universe, Artist Agency
/:  Siegmund Schlag, 1996
**136.05 OCKTAK**
o:  Flavorzone
/:  OCKTAK, 1999

**137.01 büro destruct**
o:  Olmo
/:  MB, 2001
**137.02 Jorge Alderete**
o:  Sitges, the International
    Film Festival of Catalonia
/:  Jorge Alderete, 2001

**137.03 Rinzen**
o:  Floor
/:  Rinzen, 2000
**137.04 Luca Ionescu Design**

**138.01 344 Design**
o:  Modernista!
/:  Stefan G. Bucher, 2000
**138.02 phunk**
o:  Temasek Design School
/:  William Chan, phunk, 2001
**138.03 hausgrafik**
o:  NABEL Advertainment, Bern
/:  hausgrafik.ch, 2002
**138.04 Luca Ionescu Design**

**139.01 Luca Ionescu Design**

**140.01 Power Graphixx**
o:  Mooks, printing logo for
    Mooks
/:  Power Graphixx, 2001
**140.02 Niels Meulman**
o:  hiphop group Dutch
    Masters
/:  N. 'Shoe' Meulman, 1995
**140.03 Machine**
♂:  MACHINE, TSHIRT, 2001
**140.04 Machine**
o:  Bezet Plastic Bag Project
/:  DEPT, 2000

**141.01 büro destruct**
o:  The Little Eagle
/:  Moritz, 1999
**141.02 michele del nobolo**
♂:  michele del nobolo/
    self promotion, 2002

**142.01 DSOS1**
♂:  Stefan Gandl /DS, 2001
**142.02 MASA Colectivo Gráfico**
o:  Los Amigos Invisibles,
    Warner Bros. Rec.
/:  MASA, 2002

**142.03 DSOS1**
o:  Nike Corp. USA
/:  Stefan Gandl /DS, 2002
**142.04 DED Associates**
o:  Kinky
/:  DED, 2001
**142.05 Machine**
o:  the mind, global
    creative network
/:  Machine, 2002
**142.06 Sweden**
o:  Happy Life Animation AB
/:  Sweden, 2001
**142.07 John J.Candy Design**
**142.08 büro destruct**
o:  Deka Dance
/:  H1, 2001
**142.09 Machine**
o:  BONOBO BAND
/:  DEPT, 1999
**142.10 büro destruct**
o:  Very Cherry,
    Exotic Dancers
/:  MB, 2001
**142.11 Niels Meulman**
o:  recordlabel Quaint
/:  N. 'Shoe' Meulman, 1997
**142.12 Rinzen**
o:  Mute
/:  Rinzen, 2000

**143.01 - .02 Rinzen**
o:  Empire
/:  Rinzen, 2001
**143.03 Rinzen**
o:  Brisbane Marketing
/:  Rinzen, 2001
**143.04 Rinzen**
o:  Family
/:  Rinzen, 2001

**144.01 - .04 Norm**
♂:  Norm, 1999-2002
**144.05 Sanjai Bhana**
o:  MindBENder
/:  Sanjai Bhana Illustration
    & Design, 2000

**144.06 Blammo**
♂:  Parra, logo, 2002
**144.07 phunk**
o:  FAKE Skates
/:  Melvin Chee/phunk, 2002
**144.08 benjamin guedel**
o:  seebad enge
/:  benjamin guedel, 2002
**144.09 dubius?**
o:  Futuresounds recordings
/:  dubius?, 2001
**144.10 Alphabetical Order**
o:  Åhlens
/:  Alphabetical Order, 1999
**144.11 Pictomat**
o:  jill 'jazz' levenberg
/:  konstanze läufer, 2001
**144.12 Electronic Curry Ltd.**
o:  töht bob, rock band
/:  electronic curry, 1998
**144.13 STRADA**
o:  Delirium - Record &
    Fashion Store
/:  S. Rueckerl, A. Doehring
**144.14 B.ü.L.b grafix**
**144.15 balsi**
o:  schulrestaurant
    la cultina
/:  balsi, 1998
**144.16 B.ü.L.b grafix**

**145.01 Luca Ionescu Design**
**145.02 Luca Ionescu Design**
**145.03 - .04 büro destruct**
o:  Sony Robotic
    Entertainment, Japan
/:  Lopetz, 2000

**146.01 - .04 DSOS1**
o:  Remote Productions Inc.
    New York
/:  Stefan Gandl /DS, 2002

**147.01 - .02 Rinzen**
o:  Brisbane Marketing
/:  Rinzen, 2001

Work index      o:clients      /:credits      422

148.01 Hendrik Hellige
148.02 Tsuyoshi Kusano
148.03 Pfadfinderei
♂: Critzla, 1995
148.04 tankdesign
o: Tocco, Sascha Bachman,
Maurice Zubler
/: Katarina Lang, 2002
148.05 Rinzen
o: Fabrique
/: Rinzen, 2001
148.06 Rinzen
o: Pure Pop
/: Rinzen, 2001

149.01 316tn
o: Swissrain, Bewässerungs-
technik für Golfplätze
/: Irene Filati, 2000
149.02 344 Design
o: MGS Productions,
/: Stefan G. Bucher, 2001
149.03 WG Berlin
o: SURF [Band Project]
/: Andreas Wegner, 1999
149.04 Hendrik Hellige
149.05 Form
o: Cherise/EastWest Records
/: Paula Benson, Tom
Crabtree, 2001
149.06 augenbluten
o: fantom
/: IF, 2000

150.01 Machine
o: PAKC
/: DEPT, 2000
150.02 p*star
o: Born Informatik and
Consulting
/: Pascal C. Baumann, 2002
150.03 archetype:interactive
o: cocoon (home decoration
company)
/: john wu, 2002

150.04 Hintze.gruppen
o: Lust Shop
/: Jesper Hintze Vildbrad,
2000/01

151.01 CODE
o: Lia-ne clothes.
/: Ilana Aharon, 2002
151.02 Form
o: Quilter
/: Paul West, 2000
151.03 e-Types
o: Munthe + Simonsen
/: Jonas Hecksher, 2000
152.01 - .02 tankdesign
o: Tocco, Sascha Bachman,
Maurice Zubler
/: Tina Leimbacher, 2002
152.03 Versus
o: automaten
/: Alexander Baumgardt, N/A
152.04 unikum graphic design
o: askforit gmbh, your muti-
media answers
/: Barbara Flueckiger, 2001
152.05 Eboy
o: Praxxis
/: eBoy, 2001
152.06 Mentary
o: nidecker
/: gregory chapuisat, 2001

153.01 tankdesign
o: Tocco, Sascha Bachman,
Maurice Zubler
/: Tina Leimbacher, 2002

154.01 Electronic Curry Ltd.
o: express, magazine
/: electronic curry, 1999
154.02 Zip Design
o: Urban Underground album
for Plump DJ's,
INCredible
/: Neil Bowen/Zip, 2001

154.03 HandGun
o: art city / minneapolis
/: david zack custer, 2001

155.01 LEVEL1
o: CEMENT PRODUCE DESIGN,
LIFE
/: Tsuyoshi Hirooka, 2001

156.01 MASA Colectivo Gráfico
♂: MASA, 2001
156.02 MASA Colectivo Gráfico
o: POW YV, POW Clothing
/: MASA, 2001
156.03 123KLAN
o: scien klor
/: 123klan, 2001
156.04 123KLAN
♂: 123klan, 2001

157.01 123KLAN
o: klor
/: 123klan, 2002

158.01 phunk
♂: Alvin Tan/phunk, 2002
158.02 phunk
♂: Alvin Tan/phunk, 2001
158.03 phunk
o: 2k tees
/: Melvin Chee/phunk, 2002
158.04 Tim Jester
o: 2AM
/: Tim Jester, 1996
158.05 forcefeed:swede
158.06 123KLAN
♂: 123klan, 2000
158.07 123KLAN
o: miss klor tag
/: 123klan, 1999
158.08 dubius?
o: Beatmaster
/: dubius?, 2001
158.09 Tim Jester
o: MOAS
/: Tim Jester, 1998

158.10 Tim Jester
o: JESTER
/: Tim Jester, 1996

159.01 POSITRON CO.,LTD.
♂: Hiroaki Doi/POSITRON
(T-shirts logo),1998

160.01 jutojo
o: 12" cover for Jazzanova:
"Soon Part Two"/Jazzanova
Compost Records
/: jutojo, 2002

161.01 jutojo
o: logo for Jazzanova
/: jutojo, 2001

162.01 Marc Kappeler
o: syndrome shirts, chicago,
unreleased
/: Marc Kappeler, 2002
162.02 Machine
o: Katinka Collee
/: MACHINE, 2001
162.03 Rinzen
o: Empire
/: Rinzen, 2001
162.04 blindresearch
o: elements
/: sven zuege, 2000
162.05 Rinzen
o: Family
/: Rinzen, 2001
162.06 ASYL DESIGN Inc.
o: DesignExchange Co.,Ltd.
/: Naoki SATO, 2001

163.01 augenbluten
o: bausparer
/: IF, 2001
163.02 augenbluten
♂: IF (self-promo), 1998
163.03 augenbluten
o: suffer
/: IF, 2001

Work index          o:clients          /:credits

163.04 augenbluten
o:  magic vinyl
/:  IF, 2000
163.05 grasp at the air Co.
o:  CLUB KING Co.
/:  grasp at the air Co.,LTD,
    1999

164.01 Luca Ionescu Design
164.02 Luca Ionescu Design
164.03 Luca Ionescu Design
164.04 Power Graphixx
o:  Sample Design Works
/:  Power Graphixx, 2001
164.05 Machine
o:  Branding Radicals Company
/:  MACHINE, 2002
164.06 grasp at the air Co.
o:  Electrock
/:  grasp at the air Co.,LTD,
    1999
164.07 Tsuyoshi Kusano
164.08 Luca Ionescu Design
164.09 Machine
o:  Symbol Soup book
/:  DEPT, 1998

165.01 Rinzen
o:  Family
/:  Rinzen, 2001
165.02 Luca Ionescu Design
165.03 ghs web graphica
o:  CLUB DAWN
/:  AKIHIRO IKEGOSHI, 2001
165.04 Power Graphixx
o:  Phunk Studio, printing
    logo for Transmission 02
/:  Power Graphixx, 2002
165.05 Matthias Hübner
o:  HEFTIG
    (techno music fanzine)
/:  Matthias Hübner, 2001
165.06 Luca Ionescu Design
165.07 Bionic System
o:  Similis Game Development,
    Germany
/:  Bionic Systems, 2001

165.08 Power Graphixx
/:  Hiroaki Doi, logo, 1998
165.09 Luca Ionescu Design
165.10 Luca Ionescu Design
165.11 LEVEL1
o:  CEMENT PRODUCE DESIGN
/:  Tsuyoshi Hirooka, 2001
165.12 onlab
o:  urban
/:  onlab, 2002

166.01 Luca Ionescu Design
166.02 Rinzen
o:  Family
/:  Rinzen, 2001

167.01 - .02 Rinzen
o:  Family
/:  Rinzen, 2001

168.01 - .02 Rinzen
o:  Family
/:  Rinzen, 2001

169.01 - .02 Rinzen
o:  Family
/:  Rinzen, 2001

170.01 Blammo
o:  Rockwell / Sixties rock
    t-shirt logo
/:  parra, 2001
170.02 - .03 Machine
o:  exam project at
    Rietveld Academy
/:  MACHINE, 1996
170.04 hausgrafik
/:  hausgrafik.ch, 2001
170.05 hausgrafik
o:  www.heidicolor.ch
/:  hausgrafik.ch, 2001
170.06 Blammo
o:  Paradiso Amsterdam /
    Bassline party logo
/:  parra, 2002

170.07 Niels Meulman
o:  Shoe seal
/:  N. Meulman, 1993/2002

171.01 Blammo
o:  Rednose Distrikt / HumHum
    records logo
/:  parra, 2002
171.02 Blammo
o:  Somethin' else / dj Clyde
    mixtape cover
/:  parra, 2002

172.01 Blammo
o:  de Melkweg Amsterdam /
    Exhale party logo
/:  parra, 2002
172.02 Marc Kappeler
o:  zines bouquet, rockband
/:  Marc Kappeler, 1999
172.03 LEVEL1
o:  BEAMS, UMA never die
/:  Tsuyoshi Hirooka, 2001
172.04 Tsuyoshi Kusano
172.05 Blammo
o:  Fatbeats Amsterdam / dj
    SP mixtape design
/:  parra, 2002
172.06 Tsuyoshi Kusano

173.01 Pfadfinderei
o:  Lab.style
/:  Critzla, 1999
173.02 Pfadfinderei
o:  Lab.land (club WMF)
/:  Critzla, 2001
173.03 OCKTAK
/:  OCKTAK, 1999
173.04 OCKTAK
o:  OCKTAK - A QUESTION
    OF STYLE
/:  OCKTAK, 1999
173.05 forcefeed:swede
o:  spek design
/:  Oz Dean, Amber Dean,
    Terry Ponsillo, 1999

173.06 Machine
o:  RoXY
/:  DEPT, 1998

174.01 LEVEL1
o:  LEVEL1
/:  Tsuyoshi Hirooka, 2002
174.02 augenbluten
o:  lock up computergame
/:  IF, 2000
174.03 Tsuyoshi Kusano
174.04 Norm
/:  Norm, 1999-2002
174.05 Tsuyoshi Kusano
174.06 Tsuyoshi Kusano
174.07 Tsuyoshi Kusano
174.08 Tsuyoshi Kusano
174.09 Tsuyoshi Kusano

175.01 Tsuyoshi Kusano
175.02 phunk
/:  Alvin Tan/phunk, 2001
175.03 GRIFF
175.04 phunk
o:  phunk
/:  William Chanv, 2002

176.01 A'
/:  Clarissa Tossin, 2002

177.01 A'
/:  Clarissa Tossin, 2002

178.01 - .04 vektor3
o:  private work, stofflager
/:  vektor3, 2002

179.01 yippieyeah
o:  Open
/:  Bauer / Borkowski, 1998

180.01 - .08 Woodtli
o:  onthespot
/:  Martin Woodtli, 2000

**181.01 - .03 Woodtli**
o: onthespot
/: Martin Woodtli, 2000

**182.01 augenbluten**
o: cyber hills golf fashion
/: IF, 2000
**182.02 jutojo**
o: logo for Aspekte Schall-
    platten / Sonarkollektiv
/: jutojo, 1998
**182.03 augenbluten**
o: cyber hills golf fashion
/: IF, 2000
**182.04 MAGNETOFONICA**
o: Hamburguefonstiv
/: Dario Utreras, 2001-2002

**183.01 gottfolk /fiskar**
o: Fridrik Karlsson
/: Dagur Hilmarsson, 2001
**183.02 HandGun**
o: positive negative
/: david zack custer, 1998
**183.03 Matthias Hübner**
∅: knaartz tm, 2001
**183.04 raum mannheim**
o: spacetank
/: susann el salamoni,2000
**183.05 raum mannheim**
/: susann el salamoni
    membran,1998
**183.06 Tina Backmann**
o: project at St Martins
    college of art and
    design, London
/: LJUVTUFF, T. Backman, 2001
**183.07 Tsuyoshi Kusano**
**183.08 Hendrik Hellige**
**183.09 Alphabetical Order**
o: B***k
/: Alphabetical Order, 2002

**184.01 Norm**
∅: Norm, 1999-2002
**184.02 hausgrafik**
∅: QUER Werbefabrik, 1998

**184.03 Machine**
o: Bezet Plastic Bag Project
/: DEPT, 2000
**184.04 Luca Ionescu Design**
**184.05 Machine**
o: ESCAPE
/: DEPT, 1998
**184.06 augenbluten**
o: alpha, www.augenbluten.de
/: IF, 2001
**184.07 Machine**
o: Barkers DJ Booking Agency
/: MACHINE, 2001

**185.01 Rinzen**
o: Empire
/: Rinzen, 2001
**185.02 Rinzen**
o: Supafun
/: Rinzen, 2001
**185.03 Rinzen**

**186.01 Machine**
o: Arling&Cameron, Music
    for Imaginary Films
/: DEPT, 2001
**186.02 Rinzen**
o: Lychee Lounge
/: Rinzen, 2000

**187.01 Rinzen**
o: Lychee Lounge
/: Rinzen, 2000
**187.02 Rinzen**
o: Carbon
/: Rinzen, 2001
**187.03 Form**
o: Form Hommage to Freia
/: Paul West, Tom Crabtree,
    2002
**187.04 Luca Ionescu Design**

**188.01 - .04 e-Types**
o: Danish Film Institute, CI
/: R. Koch, J. Hecksher, A.
    Täckmann, Leo Scherfig, 1998

**189.01 - .06 Trixi Barmettler**

**190.01 LEVEL1**
o: Electric SAL, SAL YOGAKU
    MANIA prototype 1
/: Tsuyoshi Hirooka, 2002
**190.02 LEVEL1**
o: Electric SAL, SAL YOGAKU
    MANIA prototype 2
/: Tsuyoshi Hirooka, 2002
**190.03 Nendo Grafic Squad**
∅: Quentaro "Nendo ANI"
    Fujimoto, 2000
**190.04 Nendo Grafic Squad**
o: ASCII
/: Quentaro "Nendo ANI"
    Fujimoto,1999
**190.05 Nendo Grafic Squad**
o: Poster Exhibition "Nisen
    (N.Y.C.)"
/: Quentaro "Nendo ANI"
    Fujimoto, 2000
**190.06 Nendo Grafic Squad**
∅: Quentaro "Nendo ANI"
    Fujimoto, 1998

**191.01 LEVEL1**
o: Hakuhodo, First thing
    first
/: Tsuyoshi Hirooka, 2001
**191.02 LEVEL1**
o: Happy New
/: Tsuyoshi Hirooka, 2001

**192.01 Nendo Grafic Squad**
o: Poster Exhibition "Nisen
    Osaka"
/: "Nendo ANI" Fujimoto,
    2000
**192.02 Nendo Grafic Squad**
o: INOZO
/: Quentaro "Nendo ANI"
    Fujimoto, 2000
**192.03 Nendo Grafic Squad**
∅: Quentaro "Nendo ANI"
    Fujimoto, 2001

**192.04 Nendo Grafic Squad**
o: Castro
/: Quentaro "Nendo ANI"
    Fujimoto, 1999
**192.05 OCKTAK**
o: OCKTAK - WICKED
/: OCKTAK, 2000
**192.06 LEVEL1**
o: enterbrain, mou hito
    hineri
/: Tsuyoshi Hirooka,2001

**193.01 Nendo Grafic Squad**
∅: Quentaro "Nendo ANI"
    Fujimoto, 1998
**193.02 Nendo Grafic Squad**
o: Poster Exhibition "Nisen
    Tokyo"
/: Quentaro "Nendo ANI"
    Fujimoto,2000
**193.03 Maniackers Design**
o: Shinko Music Pub.Co.,LTD.
/: Masayuki Sato, 2001

**194.01 Nendo Grafic Squad**
∅: Quentaro "Nendo ANI"
    Fujimoto, 1997
**194.02 Nendo Grafic Squad**
o: Clubking
/: Quentaro "Nendo ANI"
    Fujimoto, 2001
**194.03 LEVEL1**
o: BNN, design flex
/: Tsuyoshi Hirooka, 2001
**194.04 Power Graphixx**
o: SELFISH
/: Power Graphixx, 2000
**194.05 Nendo Grafic Squad**
o: Drill Schaft Records
/: Quentaro "Nendo ANI"
    Fujimoto, 1999
**194.06 Nendo Grafic Squad**
o: psycho horror novel
/: Quentaro "Nendo ANI"
    Fujimoto, 2002

**195.01 Tsuyoshi Kusano**

**195.02 Nendo Grafic Squad**
&: Quentaro "Nendo ANI"
 Fujimoto,2000

**196.01 Nendo Grafic Squad**
&: Quentaro "Nendo ANI"
 Fujimoto, 1997
**196.02 Nendo Grafic Squad**
o: Yoshimoto Shin Kigeki
/: Quentaro "Nendo ANI"
 Fujimoto, 2000
**196.03 Nendo Grafic Squad**
o: Drill Schaft Records
/: Quentaro "Nendo ANI"
 Fujimoto, 1999

**197.01 LEVEL1**
o: private, ICBM
/: Tsuyoshi Hirooka, 2000

**198.01 Maniackers Design**
o: Shinko Music Pub.Co.,LTD.
/: Masayuki Sato, 2001
**198.02 Maniackers Design**
o: Shogakukan Co.,LTD.
/: Masayuki Sato, 2001
**198.03 Maniackers Design**
o: Yoko Nihonbashi
/: Masayuki Sato, 2001
**198.04 Tsuyoshi Kusano**

**199.01 Nendo Grafic Squad**
o: Santa Inoue Sho-den sha
/: Quentaro "Nendo ANI"
 Fujimoto, 2000
**199.02 Nendo Grafic Squad**
&: Quentaro "Nendo ANI"
 Fujimoto, 2001
**199.03 Maniackers Design**
o: holiday keikaku.
/: Masayuki Sato & Hiroko
 Takiguchi, 2000

**200.01 Tsuyoshi Kusano**
**200.02 Power Graphixx**
o: ghs web graphica
/: logo remix for ghs web
 graphica exhibition, 2001

**200.03 phunk**
&: Jackson Tan, phunk, 2002
**200.04 Nendo Grafic Squad**
o: Harada Senmonka
/: Quentaro "Nendo ANI"
 Fujimoto, 2000

**201.01 LEVEL 1**
o: minimum vibration
/: Tsuyoshi Hirooka, 2000

**202.01 Maniackers Design**
o: CYBIRD Co.,LTD.
/: Masayuki Sato, 2002
**202.02 Nendo Grafic Squad**
o: MTV Japan
/: Quentaro "Nendo ANI"
 Fujimoto, 1999
**202.03 Tsuyoshi Kusano**
**202.04 LEVEL 1**
o: private, chibaragi
/: Tsuyoshi Hirooka, 2000
**202.05 grasp at the air Co.**
o: NHK
/: SHINKEN JYUDAI SHABERIBA,
 2000
**202.06 Maniackers Design**
o: CYBIRD Co.,LTD.
/: Masayuki Sato, 2002

**203.01 ghs web design**
o: NINTENDO
/: AKIHIRO IKEGOSHI, 2001
**203.02 OCKTAK**
&: OCKTAK - WICKED, 2000
**203.03 Tsuyoshi Kusano**
**203.04 Tsuyoshi Kusano**

**206.01 Power Graphixx**
o: SELFISH, logo for movie
 "PRJ17" on SELFISH
/: Power Graphixx, 2000
**206.02 123KLAN**
&: 123klan, 1992
**206.03 Power Graphixx**
o: DLR Inc.,logo for BQE
/: Power Graphixx, 2000

**206.04 Power Graphixx**
o: Space Shower Network Inc.,
 logo for TV program
/: Power Graphixx, 2002
**206.05 Tsuyoshi Kusano**
**206.06 Dopepope**
o: DOPEPOPE
/: Joe Lucchese, 2001-2002
**206.07 re-p**
**206.08 STRADA**
o: US Forty GmbH -
 Sportswear & Fashion Label
/: Stefan Rueckerl
**206.09 Ben Mulkey**
o: Red Establishment
/: Ben Mulkey, 2002
**206.10 Dopepope**
&: Joe Lucchese, 2001-2002
**206.11 FORMGEBER**
o: Pornobass, Music Label
/: Robin Pastyr, 1998
**206.12 Blammo**
o: Rockwell, t-shirt logo
/: parra, 2002

**207.01 Tsuyoshi Kusano**
**207.02 CODE**
o: nds bags, switzerland
/: reto gehrig, 1999
**207.03 Tsuyoshi Kusano**
**207.04 kong.gmbh**
o: mlzd architekten
/: kong, 2000
**207.05 123KLAN**
o: 20/20
/: 123klan, 2002
**207.06 B.ü.L.b grafix**
**207.07 Alphabetical Order**
/: Alphabetical Order
o: N/A, 2000

**208.01 Maniackers Design**
o: NETON Logo
/: Masayuki Sato, 2000
**208.02 Tycoon Graphics**
&: Tycoon Graphics, 1996
**208.03 Power Graphixx**
o: DLR Inc.,logo for Trouper
/: Power Graphixx, 2002

**208.04 Sanjai Bhana**
o: RISS, 2001
/: Sanjai Bhana Illustration
 & Design, 2001
**208.05 Power Graphixx**
&: Power Graphixx, 2002
**208.06 Tsuyoshi Kusano**
**208.07 Dopepope**
o: DOPEPOPE
/: Joe Lucchese, 2001-2002
**208.08 Norm**
&: Norm, 1999-2002
**208.09 Pfadfinderei**
o: Mia. (Elektropunk Band)
/: Critzla, 1999
**208.10 Pfadfinderei**
o: EPIC/SonyMusic. SONNIT
/: Martin Aleith, Critzla,
 2002
**208.11 raum mannheim**
o: rhein-neckar
/: alexandra wagner, 2001
**208.12 Bionic System**
&: Bionic-Systems.com, 1998

**209.01 FORMGEBER**
o: Profashion, Fashion Label
/: Rolf Rinklin, 1999
**209.02 typotherapy+design**
o: Instant Coffee
/: Stephen Crowhurst, 2002
**209.03 RosendahlGrafik**
&: Lars Borngräber, 1998
**209.04 Dopepope**
&: Joe Lucchese, 2001-200
**209.05 p*star**
o: cpk, Pensionskasse
 Automobilgewerbe
/: Pascal C. Baumann, 2001
**209.06 Form**
o: Darkside FX
/: P. West, C. Hilton, 2001
**209.07 Form**
o: Caro Communications
/: Paula Benson, Paul West,
 Rob Gaitt, 1999
**209.08 Luca Ionescu Design**
**209.09 jum**

209.10 jum
209.11 - .12 New Future People
o:   Jeff&Joyce Material Goods
/:   New Future People, 2001

210.01 Tsuyoshi Kusano
210.02 Maniackers Design
210.03 Luca Ionescu Design
210.04 Power Graphixx
o:   NISEN TOKYO exhibition,
     logo for NISEN TOKYO
/:   Power Graphixx, 2000
210.05 Markus Moström
o:   Private/Wedding between
     Christian & Angelique
/:   Markus Moström, 2001
210.06 augenbluten
♂:   IF self-promotional, 1999
210.07 DED Associates
o:   UNIT
/:   DED, 1999
210.08 Ross Imms
o:   www.fortyeightk.com
/:   Ross Imms, 2000

211.01 24HR
o:   Eclectic Bob, Logo
/:   Ricky Tillblad, 2000

212.01 B.ü.L.b grafix
212.02 Fourskin
212.03 Power Graphixx
♂:   Power Graphixx, 1997
212.04 Gregory Gilbert-Lodge
o:   Craig Tilford
     (Deliciae Vitae), London
/:   G. Gilbert-Lodge, 2002
212.05 123KLAN
♂:   123klan, 2000
212.06 Machine
o:   Bezet Plastic Bag Project
/:   DEPT, 1998
212.07 Tsuyoshi Kusano
212.08 Matthias Hübner
o:   dejavu deluxe (programm)
/:   Matthias Hübner, 2000

213.01 dubius?
♂:   dubius?, 2000
213.02 dubius?
o:   Nice Designers
/:   dubius?, 1999

214.01 Maniackers Design
214.02 123KLAN
o:   tm
/:   123klan, 2000
214.03 Power Graphixx
o:   DLR Inc.,logo for Trouper
/:   Power Graphixx, 2001
214.04 Luca Ionescu Design
214.05 Power Graphixx
o:   SAL Magazine, logo
/:   Power Graphixx, 2001
214.06 DED Associates
o:   OLI
/:   DED, 2001
214.07 büro destruct
o:   Popcorn Store 2
/:   Moritz, 2002
214.08 Power Graphixx
o:   flightlab, logo for
     artwork on G20 books
/:   Power Graphixx, 2002
214.09 designershock/DSOS1
o:   DS, DSOS1
/:   Stefan Gandl/DS, 2001
214.10 Tsuyoshi Kusano
214.11 Power Graphixx
o:   DLR Inc., logo for Trouper
/:   Power Graphixx, 1999
214.12 Power Graphixx
o:   DLR Inc.,logo for Trouper
/:   Power Graphixx, 2002

215.01 balsi
o:   universität bern
/:   balsi, 1999
215.02 Luca Ionescu Design
215.03 Ben Mulkey
o:   Red Establishment
/:   Ben Mulkey, 2002
215.04 Tsuyoshi Kusano

216.01 Dopepope
♂:   Joe Lucchese, 2001-2002
216.02 jum
o:   agentworx brand
/:   jum, 2000
216.03 Form
o:   The Darling Department
/:   P. West, P. Benson, 1995
216.04 Tsuyoshi Kusano
216.05 Chris Hutchinson
o:   submission to thefinktank
     logo competition
/:   Chris Hutchinson, 2001
216.06 Form
o:   Grace/Perfecto
/:   Paul West, Paula Benson,
     Lisa Lee, 1997
216.07 344 Design
o:   344 Design
/:   Stefan G. Bucher, 1999
216.08 re-p
o:   austrian film archive
/:   nik thoenen, 1999
216.09 BlackDog
o:   Will Mosgrove Photography
/:   Mark Fox, 1992
216.10 archetype:interactive
o:   sin (garment)
/:   john wu, 2002
216.11 kong.gmbh
o:   deux mille et deux
     émotions, Kulturprojekt
     von Biel/Bienne
/:   kong, 2002
216.12 BlackDog
o:   EMusic, Scheyer/SF
/:   Mark Fox, 1999

217.01 LEVEL1
o:   all japan records
/:   Tsuyoshi Hirooka, 2001
217.02 Lobo
o:   website uia.com.br
/:   Carlos Bêla, 1998
217.03 nothing medialab
217.04 Form
o:   Tall Paul/ VC Recordings
/:   Paul West,
     Malcolm Buick, 1997

217.05 archetype:interactive
o:   nu (fashion)
/:   john wu, 2002
217.06 archetype:interactive
♂:   john wu, 1999
217.07 BlackDog
217.08 MIGUEL ANGEL LEYVA
o:   CN, Mexico
/:   MIGUEL ANGEL LEYVA, 2000
217.09 anja klausch
o:   DMC, Logoentwurf
/:   Anja Klausch bei
     MetaDesign AG, 2001
217.10 Norm
♂:   Norm, 1999-2002
217.11 jum
o:   Gaming Company Logo 02
/:   jum, 2000
217.12 Form
o:   BBC TV
/:   P. West, P. Benson, 1996

218.01 yippieyeah
♂:   Bauer, Borkowski, 2001
218.02 OhioGirl
o:   Supersphere.com
/:   Andy Mueller, 1999
218.03 Ana Starling
o:   Trama Produções
     Artisticas, Circuito
     Universitário
/:   Ana Starling, 2001
218.04 Dopepope
♂:   Joe Lucchese, 2001-2002

219.01 - .07 Woodtli
o:   GrosseHalle
/:   Andrea Dreier and
     Martin Woodtli, 1996
219.08 Syrup Helsinki
o:   Loisto
/:   Antti Hinkula & Teemu
     Suviala, 2002
219.09 hungryfordesign
o:   Halo
/:   Nando Costa, 1999
219.10 New Future People
o:   Daniel + Donna, Logos
/:   New Future People, 2002

**220.01 123KLAN**
♂: 123klan, 2002
**220.02 Tsuyoshi Kusano**
**220.03 Blammo**
o: Rockwell, rwell logo
/: parra, 2002
**220.04 123KLAN**
o: 3hc
/: 123klan, 2001
**220.05 123KLAN**
o: pixel fury.com
/: 123klan, 2000
**220.06 123KLAN**
o: sc winter vectorial
   collection
/: 123klan, 2000

**221.01 Blammo**
o: KO party / poster
/: parra, 2002

**222.01 jum**
o: macrotypography.com
   Logotype
/: jum, 2002
**222.02 Blammo**
o: KO party,
   dj Shadow poster
/: parra, 2002
**222.03 Blammo**
o: Rockwell, the 'R' logo
/: parra, 2002
**222.04 jum**
**222.05 phunk**
o: Kondense
/: Melvin Chee/phunk, 2001
**222.06 Niels Meulman**
o: clubnight Chemistry 3,s
/: N. 'Shoe' Meulman, 1998
**222.07 Blammo**
o: KO party / poster
/: parra, 2002
**222.08 Move Design**
o: Adventure Zone Network
/: Samuel Lising, Peter
   Spreenberg, Richard
   Leighton, 1999

**223.01 Tsuyoshi Kusano**
**223.02 büro destruct**
o: Delan Records
/: H1, 1999

**224.01 Luca Ionescu Design**
**224.02 Luca Ionescu Design**
**224.03 Luca Ionescu Design**
**224.04 Luca Ionescu Design**

**225.01 Finsta**
**225.02 Taylor Deupree**
o: Line Logo
/: Richard Chartier

**226.01 büro destruct**
o: Visual Interesting Thing/
   Mouthwatering
/: Lopetz, 2000
**226.02 Machine**
o: C72
/: Machine, 2001
**226.03 CODE**
o: drive by shooting. Oliver
   nanzig, photographer
/: Reto Gehrig, 2001
**226.04 Machine**
o: Bezet Plastic Bag Project
/: DEPT, 2000

**227.01 CODE**
o: A1 Club, switzerland
/: Ryosuke Kawaguchi, 2002
**227.02 Sanjai Bhana**
♂: Sanjai Bhana Illustration
   & Design, 2001
**227.03 Machine**
o: High Tech Soul Movement
   Club Night
/: DEPT, 2000
**227.04 büro destruct**
o: Büro Discotec
/: Lopetz / MB, 2000

**228.01 Dopepope**
♂: Joe Lucchese, 2001-2002
**228.02 Dopepope**
o: Tim Saccenti Photography
/: Joe Lucchese, 2001-2002

**228.03 POSITRON CO.,LTD.**
o: Mixed-up Confusion,
   FFF logo
/: Hiroaki Doi, 2000
**228.04 Sanjai Bhan**
o: MindBENder
/: Sanjai Bhana Illustration
   & Design, 2000
**228.05 Dopepope**
♂: Joe Lucchese, 2001-2002
**228.06 Dopepope**
o: Tim Saccenti Photography
/: Joe Lucchese, 2001-2002
**228.07 MASA Colectivo Gráfico**
o: Five Times Loco,
   Trece Discos
/: MASA, 2001
**228.08 Tycoon Graphics**
o: RECRUIT
/: tycoon g, 1995
**228.09 Dopepope**
♂: Joe Lucchese, 2001-2002
**228.10 p*star**
o: Frehner Finanzberatung
/: Pascal C. Baumann, 2002

**229.01 phunk**
♂: William Chan/phunk, 2002

**230.01 Tsuyoshi Kusano**
**230.02 Tsuyoshi Kusano**
**230.03 Tsuyoshi Kusano**
**230.04 Tsuyoshi Kusano**
**230.05 augenbluten**
♂: IF (self promo), 1998
**230.06 phunk**
o: AM7
/: Melvin Chee/phunk, 2001
**230.07 Tsuyoshi Kusano**
**230.08 Power Graphixx**
o: SELFISH, logo for movie
   "PRJ17" on SELFISH
/: Power Graphixx, 2000
**230.09 augenbluten**
♂: IF (self promo), 2000
**230.10 Machine**
♂: DEPT, 1998
**230.11 Tsuyoshi Kusano**

**230.12 Niels Jansson**
o: Antikarma clothing
/: Niels Jansson, 2001

**231.01 vektor3**
o: private work, stofflager
/: vektor3, 2002

**232.01 Power Graphixx**
o: DLR Inc.,
   logo for Trouper
/: Power Graphixx, 2001
**232.02 Luca Ionescu Design**
**232.03 Tsuyoshi Kusano**

**233.01 DED Associates**
o: F.UK
/: DED, 2000
**233.02 p*star**
o: Farner Computing
/: Pascal C. Baumann, 2002
**233.03 SAKAMOTO**
o: WAMMELFISSE
/: SAKAMOTO, 2002

**234.01 Hendrik Hellige**
**234.02 Hendrik Hellige**
**234.03 FORMGEBER**
o: MCC, Music Label
/: Heiko Ulrich, 1998
**234.04 Tsuyoshi Kusano**
**234.05 kong.gmbh**
♂: kong., 2001
**234.06 SAKAMOTO**
o: SKVULP.DK
/: SAKAMOTO, 2002
**234.07 Form**
o: Online Music Awards/
   Music Week
/: Paul West, Paula Benson,
   Chris Hilton, 2000

**235.01 Zip Design**
o: Artful Dodger, London
   Records
/: Neil Bowen/Zip, 2000
**235.02 TOI Inc.**
♂: TOI Inc., 1999

**236.01 Alphabetical Order**
o:  Sneaker Nation
/:  Alphabetical Order, 1997
**236.02 phunk**
o:  AM7
/:  Alvin Tan, 2001
**236.03 Luca Ionescu Design**
**236.04 Lobo**
&:  C. Bêla, D. Kamioka, G.
    Marcondes, M. Sader, M.
    de Paula Santos, 2001
**236.05 Rinzen**
&:  Rinzen, 2001
**236.06 Rinzen**
o:  Venom
/:  Rinzen, 2001
**236.07 Digitalultras**
o:  Perfect Job,
    Digitalultras
/:  Manuel Perfetto, 2002
**236.08 Rinzen**
o:  Empire
/:  Rinzen, 2001

**237.01 Luca Ionescu Design**

**238.01 buffet für gestaltung**
o:  HTA, Hochschule für
    Technik und Architektur
/:  buffet f. gestaltung, 1999

**239.01 buffet für gestaltung**
o:  HTA, Hochschule für
    Technik und Architektur
/:  buffet f. gestaltung, 1999

**240.01 ghs web graphica**
o:  NINTENDO
/:  AKIHIRO IKEGOSHI, 2002
**240.02 ghs web graphica**
&:  AKIHIRO IKEGOSHI, 1998
**240.03 Sanjai Bhana**
o:  J.L. Acupuncture
/:  Sanjai Bhana Illustration
    & Design, 2002
**240.04 archetype:interact ve**
o:  ann siu
    (silk product shop)
/:  john wu, 2002

**240.05 ghs web graphica**
o:  MAEKAWA san
/:  AKIHIRO IKEGOSHI, 2002
**240.06 LEVEL1**
o:  BEAMS
/:  Tsuyoshi Hirooka, 2002
**240.07 Sanjai Bhana**
o:  Chieko
/:  Sanjai Bhana Illustration
    & Design, 2002
**240.08 Power Graphixx**
o:  Hakuhodo Inc., logo for
    Kohkoku magazine
/:  Power Graphixx, 2001

**241.01 Tsuyoshi Kusano**
**241.02 ghs web graphica**
o:  A-SEVEN from DESCENTE
/:  AKIHIRO IKEGOSHI, 2001
**241.03 LEVEL1**
o:  Honda lady
/:  Tsuyoshi Hirooka, 2001
**241.04 Nendo Grafic Squad**
&:  Quentaro "Nendo ANI"
    Fujimoto, 2000

**242.01 Cyclone Graphix**
**242.02 Cyclone Graphix**
**242.03 123KLAN**
o:  scien & klor
    japan version
/:  123klan, 2000
**242.04 Disco Döner**

**243.01 LEVEL1**
o:  BEAMS, Re:
/:  Tsuyoshi Hirooka, 2002
**243.02 Tycoon Graphics**
o:  NTV
/:  tycoon g, 2001
**243.03 ASYL DESIGN Inc.**
o:  OP-TRANCE!/logo / Kirin
    Plaza Osaka
/:  Naoki SATO, 2001

**244.01 blindresearch**
o:  kontrast
/:  sven zuege, 2001

**244.02 - .03 Mutabor**
&:  Carsten Raffel, 2001
**244.04 nothing medialab**
**244.05 dubius?**
o:  Ouagadougou
/:  dubius?, 2001
**244.06 RosendahlGrafik**
&:  Lars Borngräber, 1998

**245.01 Planet Pixel**
**245.02 Planet Pixel**
**245.03 Bionic System**
o:  Nagal, Belgium
/:  Bionic Systems, 2000
**245.04 Power Graphixx**
o:  Hakuhodo Inc., logo
    for Kohkoku magazine
/:  Power Graphixx, 2001
**245.05 typotherapy+design**
o:  Expansions
/:  Noël Nanton, 2002
**245.06 büro destruct**
o:  Rainbow
/:  MB, 2000

**246.01 - .06 Um|bruch**
o:  Protective
/:  Um|bruch Gestaltung, 2001

**247.01 - .02 Um|bruch**
o:  Protective
/:  Um|bruch Gestaltung, 2001
**247.03 CODE**
o:  stuck switzerland
/:  daniel donati, 1999
**247.04 blindresearch**
o:  qute
/:  sven zuege, 2002
**247.05 moniteurs**
o:  General Magic, Music Label
/:  Heike Nehl, 1997
**247.06 B.ü.L.b grafix**

**248.01 Syrup Helsinki**
o:  Tabloidtryck i Norden AB
/:  Teemu Suviala, 2002

**248.02 ColdWater Graphiix**
o:  ORATOK Intern.mtsd Logo
/:  Tabito Mizuo, 2000
**248.03 STRADA**
o:  BMC - Event Agency
/:  Stefan Rueckerl
**248.04 p*star**
o:  Pure Instant Water
/:  Pascal C. Baumann, 2000
**248.05 Todd Hansson**
o:  Gasket
/:  Todd Hansson, Michael
    Christoffel, 2000
**248.06 BlackDog**
o:  Toolwire
/:  Mark Fox, 2000
**248.07 ColdWater Graphiix**
o:  ALSUR co.,ltd.
    VESPUCCI Logo
/:  Tabito Mizuo, 1998
**248.08 B.ü.L.b grafix**
**248.09 Power Graphixx**
o:  flightlab, logo for
    artwork on G20 books
/:  Power Graphixx, 2002
**248.10 BlackDog**
o:  Egreetings
/:  Mark Fox, 1998
**248.11 forcefeed:swede**
o:  LMH Property Services,
/:  Oz Dean, 2000
**248.12 Thorsten Geiger**
o:  theCo.de
/:  Thorsten Geiger, 1999

**249.01 Move Design**
o:  Intel Student Design
    Competition
/:  S. Lising, P. Spreenberg,
    Chris Fracis, 2001
**249.02 raum mannheim**
o:  camelot, filmproductions
/:  frank hoffmann, 2000
**249.03 Mutabor**
&:  Carsten Raffel, 2000

**249.04 Taylor Deupree**
o: 12K
/: Taylor Deupree, 2000
**249.05 Machine**
o: Clubnight
/: MACHINE, 2001
**249.06 nothing medialab**

**250.01 Bionic System**
**250.02 augenbluten**
o: essence / tablewater
/: IF, 2000
**250.03 CODE**
o: kubik. switzerland
/: Ryosuke Kawaguchi, 2001
**250.04 jutojo**
∅: jutojo, logo, 1999
**250.05 New Future People**
o: World Masters Logo
/: New Future People, 2002
**250.06 Form**
o: Fabulous Films
/: P. West, M. Buick, 1997
**250.07 büro destruct**
o: Inventar der Fündmünzen
der Schweiz
/: MB, 2001
**250.08 DED Associates**
o: Sonic 360
/: DED, 2000
**250.09 xonetik**
o: 3LOBYTE ResearchLab
/: [mars] marcelo perez,
2001
**250.10 xonetik**
o: 3CEL
/: [mars] marcelo perez,
2001
**250.11 Fourskin**
**250.12 tankdesign**
o: Tocco, Sascha Bachman,
Maurice Zubler
/: S. Lenggenhager, 2002

**251.01 anja klausch**
o: Gut Boltenhof
/: Anja Klausch, 2001

**251.02 kong.gmbh**
o: Bike Station
/: kong., 2000
**251.03 Ben Mulkey**
∅: Ben Mulkey, 2001
**251.04 Thorsten Geiger**
o: Partner für Berlin
/: Thorsten Geiger,
Die Gestalten, 2000
**251.05 FORMGEBER**
o: DJ SeeBase, Club Projekt
/: Heiko Ulrich, 1996
**251.06 AREADESIGN**
o: LAKE PARADE, Techno Music
Parade, Geneva
/: Alberto Russo, 2001

**252.01 CODE**
o: drive by shooting. Oliver
nanzig, photographer
/: Reto Gehrig, 2001
**252.02 Bionic System**
o: One Industries, USA
/: Bionic Systems, 2001
**252.03 SAKAMOTO**
o: Brøndby IF
/: SAKAMOTO, 2002
**252.04 Maniackers Design**
**252.05 Maniackers Design**
o: DIGITAL STUDIO Co.,LTD.
TV Game Production
/: Masayuki Sato, 2001
**252.06 Bionic System**
o: Bionic-Systems.com
/: Bionic Systems, 2000
**252.07 - .08 Power Graphixx**
o: flightlab, logo for
artwork on G20 books
/: Power Graphixx, 2002
**252.09 raum mannheim**
o: lava
/: martin keller, 2002
**252.10 Sweden**
o: Fieldwork
/: Sweden, 1997
**252.11 nothing medialab**
**252.12 nothing medialab**

**253.01 tronics**
o: tronics
/: Marco Fischer, Fabian
Gasser, 2001
**253.02 Mutabor**
o: s. Oliver
/: Silke Eggers, 2001
**253.03 FORMGEBER**
o: "Sabotage" - Profashion,
Fashion Label
/: Jochen Eeuwyk, 1992
**253.04 STRADA**
o: Guls - Sublabel US Forty
/: Stefan Rueckerl
**253.05 Sanjai Bhana**
∅: Sanjai Bhana Illustration
& Design, 2001
**253.06 344 Design**
o: bossa:nova
/: Stefan G. Bucher, 2001
**253.07 typotherapy+design**
o: Jay Manuel
/: Noël Nanton, 2002
**253.08 Designunion**
o: Keuledruck, Berlin
/: Barbara Dechant, 2001
**253.09 büro destruct**
o: Arnold Meyer
/: H1, 2000
**253.10 Mutabor**
∅: Axel Domke, 2001
**253.11 DED Associates**
o: Birmingham Media Centre
/: DED, 1997
**253.12 jutojo**
o: logo for No Zession Rec./
Sonarkollektiv
/: jutojo, 1998

**254.01 Sweden**
o: NONS / Music Network
/: Sweden, 2000
**254.02 123KLAN**
o: event
/: 123klan, 2002
**254.03 123KLAN**
o: smoke that shit
/: 123klan, 2000

**255.01 Zookeeper**
∅: dod (olivier
ducuing), 2001
**255.02 Power Graphixx**
o: GASBOOK, logo for movie
"Q&A" on GASBOOK
/: Power Graphixx, 2002

**256.01 typotherapy+design**
o: Workplace Gallery
/: Stephen Crowhurst, 2002
**256.02 Mutabor**
∅: Carsten Raffel, 2001
**256.03 Mutabor**
∅: Carsten Raffel, 2001
**256.04 Mutabor**
o: Rotring
/: Johannes Plass, 1999
**256.05 Lindedesign**
o: lindedesign
/: Christian Lindemann, 2001

**257.01 - .04 Mutabor**
o: Classen Papier
/: Carsten Raffel, 2001
**257.05 Mutabor**
∅: Carsten Raffel, 2001

**258.01 re-p**
**258.02 Luca Ionescu Design**
**258.03 CODE**
o: merz & partner, events
/: Daniel Donati, 1998
**258.04 gottfolk /fiskar**
o: Argus, advertising agency
/: Dagur Hilmarsson, 1994
**258.05 tankdesign**

**259.01 24HR**
o: Joia Music, Logo
/: Ricky Tillblad, 2002
**259.02 anja klausch**
o: Cusa, ein Produkt der
HDP GmbH
/: Anja Klausch für
outermedia, 2000

**259.03 John J.Candy Design**
o:  Yeti (Interior and
    furniture designers)
/:  David Kandell, 2000
**259.04 anja klausch**
o:  Baubedarf Gütersloh,
    Wettbewerbsentwurf
/:  Anja Klausch, 1997

**260.01 e-Types**
o:  Framfab AB
/:  Jens Kajus, Jonas
    Hecksher, 2000
**260.02 e-Types**
o:  Energi E2
/:  Jens Kajus, 2000
**260.03 e-Types**
o:  Framfab AB
/:  Jens Kajus, Jonas
    Hecksher, 2000
**260.04 e-Types**
o:  Energi E2
/:  Jens Kajus, 2000

**261.01 e-Types**
o:  Energi E2
/:  Jens Kajus, 2000

**262.01 OCKTAK**
o:  Sandokan - Vibration
/:  OCKTAK, 2001
**262.02 OCKTAK**
o:  DJN - LOVE2001
/:  OCKTAK, 2001
**262.03 OCKTAK**
o:  Waterg8 Europe
/:  OCKTAK, 2000
**262.04 OCKTAK**
o:  Fusion Inc.
/:  OCKTAK, 2001

**263.01 24HR**
o:  24HR International AB
/:  Ricky Tillblad, 1999
**263.02 OCKTAK**
o:  45Degree
/:  OCKTAK, 2002

**263.03 OCKTAK**
♂:  OCKTAK, 2001
**263.04 Rinzen**
o:  Loft
/:  Rinzen, 2000
**263.05 OCKTAK**
o:  OCKTAK - BUGS N DROIDS
/:  OCKTAK, 1999

**264.01 Electronic Curry Ltd.**
o:  tricot de luxe
/:  electronic curry, 2001
**264.02 Electronic Curry Ltd.**
o:  gallery edouardo
    mitterand
/:  electronic curry, 2000

**265.01 Alphabetical Order**
o:  Cumulus
/:  Alphabetical Order, 2002
**265.02 Lobo**
o:  website rraurl.com
/:  Carlos Bêla, 2001
**265.03 CODE**
o:  x-rei, switzerland
/:  Ryosuke Kawaguchi, 2001
**265.04 CODE**
o:  Migros kulturprozent
/:  reto gehrig, 2001
**265.05 raum mannheim**
o:  schönhauser
/:  el salamoni, 2000
**265.06 Move Design**
♂:  Peter Spreenberg, Samuel
    Lising, Move Design, 2000

**266.01 ghs web graphica**
o:  LINECOM
/:  AKIHIRO IKEGOSHI, 2001
**266.02 Mutabor**
o:  ISNM, International
    School of New Media
/:  Solke Eggers, Christian
    Dworak, 2001
**266.03 Tycoon Graphics**
o:  TOY'S FACTORY
/:  tycoon g, 1994

**266.04 forcefeed:swede**
o:  design for chunks
/:  Oz Dean, 2001
**266.05 Pictomat**
o:  jan-christoph bruhnke
/:  konstanze läufer, 2001
**266.06 Mutabor**
o:  Mutabor 10
/:  Carsten Raffel, 2001

**267.01 Luca Ionescu Design**
**267.02 Luca Ionescu Design**
**267.03 Dopepope**
o:  Tim Saccenti Photography
/:  Joe Lucchese, 2001-2002
**267.04 Sanjai Bhana**
o:  delta force
/:  Sanjai Bhana Illustration
    & Design, 2001.
**267.05 balsi**
o:  urban sound, bern
/:  balsi, 1999
**267.06 Luca Ionescu Design**

**268.01 Lobo**
o:  MTV Brasil
/:  Carlos Bêla, 2000
**268.02 xonetik**
o:  xonetik
/:  [mars] marcelo perez, 2001
**268.03 anja klausch**
o:  AUDI AG
/:  Anja Klausch bei
    MetaDesign AG, 2000

**269.01 tankdesign**
♂:  Katarina Lang, Tina
    Leimbacher, Sebastian
    Lenggenhager, 2001
**269.02 Mutabor**
o:  Mutabor 10
/:  H. Paravincini, 2001
**269.03 Mutabor**
o:  Theater 3000
/:  H. Paravincini, 2000

**270.01 dubius?**
♂:  dubius?, 1998

**270.02 augenbluten**
o:  bee cube
/:  IF, 2002
**270.03 Mutabor**
o:  Mutabor 10
/:  Carsten Raffel, 2001
**270.04 Power Graphixx**
o:  SELFISH, logo for "PRJ17"
/:  Power Graphixx, 2000

**271.01 xonetik**
o:  Nautan Publishing
/:  [mars] marcelo perez, 2002
**271.02 DED Associates**
o:  Hydrogen Dukebox
/:  DED, 1998
**271.03 nothing medialab**
**271.04 CRAIG ROBINSON**
♂:  CRAIG ROBINSON, 1999
**271.05 grasp at the air Co.**
o:  CLUB KING Co.
/:  grasp at the air
    Co.Ltd., 2000
**271.06 123KLAN**
♂:  123klan, 2000

**272.01 dubius?**
o:  P5 productions
/:  dubius?, 1998
**272.02 BlackDog**
o:  Embarko
/:  Mark Fox, 1989
**272.03 Tsuyoshi Kusano**
**272.04 Mentary**
♂:  gregory chapuisat, 2001
**272.05 Chris Hutchinson**
o:  Gracy, Hair Stylist
/:  Chris Hutchinson, 2000
**272.06 Blammo**
o:  Rockwell, Sign logo
/:  parra, 2002

**273.01 New Future People**
o:  Leederville Skate Park
/:  New Future People,
    1998/99

274.01 e-Types

275.01 Cyclone Graphix

276.01 Nendo Grafic Squad
∂: Quentaro "Nendo ANI"
   Fujimoto, 1999
276.02 Tycoon Graphics
∂: TYCOONGRAPHICS, 1997

277.01 Tina Backmann
o: proposals for Kemab,
   Sweden Karlskoga energy
   and enviromental issues
∕: LJUVTUFF, 2000

278.01 büro destruct
o: Realizers
∕: MB, 2002
278.02 Bionic System
o: Bionic-Systems.com
∕: Bionic Systems, 1999
278.03 blindresearch
o: nightcrawler, party logo
∕: sven zuege, 2000
278.04 blindresearch
o: antitainment,
   record label
∕: sven zuege, 2002
278.05 Nendo Grafic Squad
o: IMAGICA
∕: Quentaro "Nendo ANI"
   Fujimoto, 2000
278.06 24HR
o: Primal Music
∕: Ricky Tillblad, 1997
278.07 ghs web graphica
o: CIAOPANIC
∕: AKIHIRO IKEGOSHI, 2002
278.08 POSITRON CO.,LTD.
o: Beach House
∕: Hiroaki Doi, 2000
278.09 ghs web graphica
o: MATSUSHITA ELECTRIC WORKS
∕: AKIHIRO IKEGOSHI, 2000
278.10 Zip Design
o: Offspring, PR company
∕: Neil Bowen/Zip, 2001

278.11 Power Graphixx
o: flightlab, G20 books
∕: Power Graphixx, 2002
278.12 Nendo Grafic Squad
∂: Quentaro "Nendo ANI"
   Fujimoto, 2000
278.13 Tsuyoshi Kusano
278.14 LEVEL1
o: Kamon of LEVEL1
∕: Tsuyoshi Hirooka, 2000
278.15 ghs web graphica
o: IKEGOSHI GYOKUDOSHA
∕: AKIHIRO IKEGOSHI, 2001
278.16 archetype:interactive
o: boombeat music,
   keith wong
∕: john wu, 2002

279.01 - .03 Chris Hutchinson
∂: Chris Hutchinson, 2002
279.04 Chris Hutchinson
o: Visoda
∕: Chris Hutchinson, 2001
279.05 archetype:interactive
o: ezine
∕: john wu, 2000
279.06 CODE
o: chocolate films
   switzerland
∕: Ryosuke Kawaguchi, 2001
279.07 Artificial Environments
279.08 Matthias Hübner
o: wildwild.web
∕: Matthias Hübner, 2001
279.09 gottfolk /fiskar
∂: Dagur Hilmarsson, 2000
279.10 Tsuyoshi Kusano
279.11 Zookeeper
o: IGNITE
∕: dod (olivier ducuing), 2001
279.12 artetic
o: Destination Paradise GbR
∕: Irene Marx, 2001
279.13 BlackDog
o: David Breskin
∕: Mark Fox,
   Scott Gagner, 2000

279.14 CODE
o: spider galaxy club
∕: Daniel Donati, 1999
279.15 Power Graphixx
o: DLR Inc., logo for BQE
∕: Power Graphixx, 2000
279.16 büro destruct
o: Kulturhallen
   Dampfzentrale
∕: MB, 2000

280.01 MASA Colectivo Gráfico
o: Simbiosis, Proyect
∕: MASA, 2002
280.02 büro destruct
∕: MB, 2002
280.03 Form
∂: Form, Paul West, Paula
   Benson, 1997
280.04 archetype:interactive
o: code cafe
∕: john wu, 2001
280.05 MAGNETOFONICA
o: Salon de acuarelistas de
   Venezuela
∕: Dario Utreras, 2001
280.06 MASA Colectivo Gráfico
o: Rexim, Proyect
∕: MASA, 2002

281.01 POSITRON CO.,LTD.
o: LOTUS (cafe logo)
∕: Hiroaki Doi, 1999
281.02 ColdWaterGraphiix
o: Saws Company ltd. Bomboo
   Shoots Logo
∕: Tabito Mizuo, 1999
281.03 Sweden
o: Fox Sports, Cliff Freeman
   & Partners, Traktor Film
∕: Sweden
281.04 John J.Candy Design
o: High
∕: John Esberg, 2001
281.05 Power Graphixx
o: SELFISH, logo for artwork
   on SELFISH magazine
∕: Power Graphixx, 2000

281.06 Luca Ionescu Design
281.07 o-matic corp.
o: Razorfish Subnetwork
∕: Marina Zurkow, 1999

282.01 Method
o: Atom Films
∕: Bob Connelly, 2000
282.02 FORMGEBER
o: Blitztrade,
   Trading Software
∕: Siegmund Schlag, 1999
282.03 Lobo
o: Upload
∕: C. Bêla, D. Kamioka, G.
   Marcondes, M. Sader, M.
   dc Paula Santos, 2001
282.04 John J.Candy Design
o: Science fiction bokhandeln
∕: John Esberg, 2001
282.05 Tsuyoshi Kusano
282.06 Luca Ionescu Design
282.07 DED Associates
o: DP Leisure
∕: DED, 2000
282.08 archetype:interactive
o: phoenix & dragon trust
∕: john wu
282.09 Hirschindustries
282.10 dubius?
o: Organic
∕: dubius?, 2000
282.11 Niels Meulman
o: TBWA/e-company
∕: N.'Shoe' Meulman, 1997
282.12 Deanne Cheuk

283.01 jutojo
o: Recreation Rec., Sonarkollektiv (record label)
∕: jutojo, 1998
283.02 Bionic System
o: Similis Game Development
∕: Bionic Systems, 2001
283.03 WG Berlin
o: Network
∕: Andreas Wegner, 1996/2001

**283.04 Electronic Curry Ltd.**
o:  real tempo,
    record company
/:  electronic curry, 2001
**283.05 Machine**
o:  New Frontier Festival
/:  DEPT, 1999
**283.06 Tsuyoshi Kusano**
**283.07 LEVEL1**
o:  Hitmaker, CRAZY TAXI CAB
    COMPANY
/:  Tsuyoshi Hirooka, 2001
**283.08 Sweden**
o:  Pocky
/:  Sweden, 2000
**283.09 Tycoon Graphics**
o:  MOTION ELEMENT
/:  tycoon g, 2001
**283.10 AREADESIGN**
o:  FIDUCIAIRE V. HUMBERSET
/:  Alberto Russo, 2002

**284.01 HandGun**
o:  active
/:  david zack custer, 1997
**284.02 hungryfordesign**
o:  gategate
/:  Nando Costa, 1999
**284.03 Zookeeper**
o:  les ACP
/:  dod (olivier ducuing), 1999
**284.04 Zookeeper**
o:  ZINK family artist
    groupement
/:  dod (olivier ducuing), 2000
**284.05 MASA Colectivo Gráfico**
o:  South Point Surfboards
/:  MASA, 2001
**284.06 phunk**
o:  Milk Co.
/:  Melvin Chee/phunk, 2000

**285.01 Sweden**
o:  H&M,
    Hollingworth-Mehrotra
/:  Sweden, 1998
**285.02 ala webstatt**
o:  digitalhome
/:  ala & rek, 2001

**285.03 Sweden**
o:  Dramalabbet
/:  Sweden, 2000
**285.04 Power Graphixx**
o:  Hakuhodo inc., logo for
    Koukoku Magazine
/:  Power Graphixx, 2001

**286.01 Power Graphixx**
o:  SELFISH, logo
/:  Power Graphixx, 2000
**286.02 augenbluten**
o:  rewind allstars
/:  IF, 2000
**286.03 augenbluten**
o:  roboleague
/:  IF, 2000
**286.04 Ross Imms**
o:  r-air recordings
/:  Ross Imms, 2001
**286.05 büro destruct**
o:  ESPN
/:  MB, 2000
**286.06 Luca Ionescu Design**
**286.07 Luca Ionescu Design**
**286.08 büro destruct**
o:  X-Ray Consulting AG
/:  MB, 2001
**286.09 Tsuyoshi Kusano**
**286.10 augenbluten**
o:  chiba hilton hotel
/:  IF, 2000
**286.11 büro destruct**
o:  MTV USA
/:  MB, 2001
**286.12 büro destruct**
o:  Die Gestalten Verlag
/:  Lopetz, 2001
**286.13 Ross Imms**
o:  UK Records LTD
/:  Ross Imms, 2001
**286.14 Tsuyoshi Kusano**
**286.15 Power Graphixx**
o:  SELFISH, logo
/:  Power Graphixx, 2000
**286.16 Tycoon Graphics**
o:  INTENTIONALLIES
/:  tycoon g, 1996

**287.01 Pfadfinderei**
o:  Brainbox
/:  Critzla, 1995
**287.02 p*star**
o:  EVO Records
/:  Pascal C. Baumann, 1999
**287.03 WG Berlin**
o:  High Times/Technik Raves
/:  Andreas Wegner, 1997
**287.04 archetype:interactive**
o:  fuse / eddie liu
/:  john wu, 2000
**287.05 archetype:interactive**
o:  purpleblue
/:  john wu, 2002
**287.06 archetype:interactive**
o:  ewedding.com.hk/david lui
/:  john wu
**287.07 DED Associates**
o:  Sonic 360
/:  DED, 2000

**288.01 Tsuyoshi Kusano**
**288.02 LEVEL1**
o:  BEAMS, GAME OVER
/:  Tsuyoshi Hirooka, 2002
**288.03 OhioGirl**
o:  The Quiet Life
/:  Andy Mueller, 1998
**288.04 Power Graphixx**
o:  Hakuhodo inc.,logo for
    Koukoku Magazine
/:  Power Graphixx, 2001
**288.05 Power Graphixx**
o:  Club King, logo for movie
/:  Power Graphixx, 2001
**288.06 Deanne Cheuk**
**288.07 Luca Ionescu Design**
**288.08 OhioGirl**
o:  Ohio Gold Records
/:  Andy Mueller, 1996
**288.09 büro destruct**
o:  Büro Discotec
/:  Lopetz, 1999
**288.10 augenbluten**
o:  abstract asylum
/:  IF, 2000

**289.01 Dirk Rudolph**
o:  Fridge Records
/:  Dirk Rudolph, 2001
**289.02 Move Design**
o:  Big Design
/:  P. Spreenberg, S. Lising,
    D. Blodorn, 2001
**289.03 DED Associates**
o:  Green Recordings
/:  DED, 2001
**289.04 Zip Design**
o:  Organised Kaos,
    record label
/:  Neil Bowen/Zip, 2001
**289.05 DED Associates**
o:  Foundation
/:  DED, 1999
**289.06 balsi**
o:  piabanderini
    kommunikation
/:  balsi, 2002
**289.07 grasp at the air Co.**
o:  ORIGINAL
/:  grasp at the air
    Co.Ltd, 2000
**289.08 Hirschindustries**
o:  DJ-Sets Multimedia AG
/:  Ollie Peters, 2001

**290.01 DED Associates**
∅:  DED, 1999
**290.02 New Future People**
**290.03 grasp at the air Co.**
o:  sl@ck mute video, LOGO
/:  grasp at the air
    Co. Ltd, 2000
**290.04 minimise**
∅:  Kenny Leigh/Lizzy Healy,
    minimise, 2001
**290.05 Luca Ionescu Design**
**290.06 Luca Ionescu Design**
**290.07 John J.Candy Design**
o:  Eu-upplysningen
    (Eu information centre)
/:  John Esberg, 2000
**290.08 MASA Colectivo Gráfico**
o:  Elevega, Elevega
    Electricity company
/:  MASA, 2001

290.09 Luca Ionescu Design
290.10 Norm
⌀: Norm, 1999-2002
290.11 Artificial Environments
290.12 Hirschindustries
o: Telemetric/mfs Berlin
/: Ollie Peters, 2000

291.01 Tsuyoshi Kusano
291.02 Zip Design
o: DJ Scissorkicks, Fuised
   and Bruised
/: Neil Bowen/Zip, 1999
291.03 Luca Ionescu Design
291.04 MASA Colectivo Gráfico
o: Flontek, Project
/: MASA, 2002
291.05 HandGun
⌀: handgun, david zack
   custer, 2001
291.06 büro destruct
o: Berner Ensemble
/: H1, 2000
291.07 büro destruct
o: ESPN
/: MB, 2000
291.08 MIGUEL ANGEL LEYVA
o: FAKEFUNK
/: MIGUEL ANGEL LEYVA, 1998
291.09 LEVEL1
o: BEAMS, Recycled
/: Tsuyoshi Hirooka, 2002
291.10 büro destruct
o: Evil Production
/: Moritz, 1999
291.11 DED Associates
o: Sonic 360
/: DED, 2000
291.12 balsi
o: gafferfilm, franz martig
/: balsi, 2001

292.01 MAGNETOFONICA
o: Salon de acuarelistas de
   Venezuela
/: Dario Utreras, 2001

292.02 Dopepope
o: West London Deep
/: Joe Lucchese, 2001
292.03 benjamin guedel
o: stereo psycho team
/: benjamin guedel ,1999

293.01 Luca Ionescu Design
293.02 Planet Pixel
293.03 ghs web graphica
o: CAZICAZI magazine
/: AKIHIRO IKEGOSHI, 1998
293.04 ghs web graphica
⌀: AKIHIRO IKEGOSHI, 2000
293.05 Luca Ionescu Design

294.01 büro destruct
o: Mas Yendo, New York
   City/Springer Verlag
/: H1, 1999

295.01 - .02 Move Design
o: Cosmic Music Network
/: Samuel Lising, Peter
   Spreenberg, Richard
   Leighton, 1999

296.01 - .11 nothing medialab
296.12 Eboy
⌀: eBoy, 2001

297.01 nothing medialab
297.02 MELON DEZIGN
o: THE FALTO SHOW logo
/: MELON DEZIGN, 2000
297.03 nothing medialab
297.04 MASA Colectivo Gráfico
o: South Orinoco, Sawmill
   Corporation, Yekuana
   Films
/: MASA, 1996
297.05 nothing medialab
297.06 Electronic Curry Ltd.
o: out soon, events agency
/: electronic curry, 2002

298.01 Syrup Helsinki
o: Enala//Hyysalo
/: Teemu Suviala, 2001
298.02 Move Design
o: Site Solutions
/: Peter Spreenberg, Samuel
   Lising, 2000
298.03 Matthias Hübner
o: wildwild.web
/: Matthias Hübner, 2001
298.04 nothing medialab
298.05 Planet Pixel
298.06 CODE
o: riva com, switzerland
/: daniel donati, 1998
298.07 e-Types
298.08 Hendrik Hellige

299.01 Woodtli
o: Kiosk
/: Martin Woodtli, 1995-1998
299.02 büro destruct
⌀: MB, 1999
299.03 POSITRON CO.,LTD.
o: TABLE MODERN SERVICE
/: Hiroaki Doi, 2001
299.04 Luca Ionescu Design
299.05 Sanjai Bhana
o: jess-O
/: Sanjai Bhana Illustration
   & Design, 2001
299.06 - .07 Form
o: Ultra/EastWest Records
/: Paul West, Paula Benson,
   John Siddle, 1998
299.08 HandGun
o: czr
/: david zack custer, 1998
299.09 - .11 Form
o: Ultra/EastWest Records
/: Paul West, Paula Benson,
   John Siddle, 1998
299.12 balsi
o: vintage textile gmbh
/: balsi, 1999

299.13 tankdesign
o: The Hair Lounge, M. Suter
/: Katarina Lang, 2001
299.14 Todd Hansson
⌀: Todd Hansson, 1999
299.15 Alphabetical Order
o: Sneaker Nation
/: Alphabetical Order, 1997
299.16 Form
o: Ultra/EastWest Records
/: Paul West, Paula Benson,
   John Siddle, 1998

300.01 Gobler Toys
o: Gobler Toys
/: Steve Casino, 2002
300.02 Planet Pixel
300.03 grasp at the air Co.
o: ASAYAN
/: grasp at the air
   Co. Ltd, 2001
300.04 CODE
o: m for music festival.
/: reto gehrig, 2000
300.05 jum
o: E-Logotype
/: jum, 1999
300.06 GRIFF
300.07 Nendo Grafic Squad
o: Bar "Den"
/: Quentaro "Nendo ANI"
   Fujimoto, 2002
300.08 büro destruct
o: Bundlebit B&B
/: Lopetz, 2001
300.09 büro destruct
o: Reitschule Bern
/: MB, 1999
300.10 24HR
o: PSD
/: Ricky Tillblad, 1998
300.11 hausgrafik
o: ISC Club, Bern
/: hausgrafik.ch, 2000
300.12 Niels Meulman
o: Amsterdam Dance Event
/: N. 'Shoe' Meulman, 1997

Work index          o:clients          /:credits          434

300.13 Cyclone Graphix
300.14 SuperHappyBunny Company
o: Art In Motion Festival
/: SuperHappyBunny Company,
   2002
300.15 24HR
o: VS market
/: Ricky Tillblad, 2001
300.16 Disco Döner

301.01 John J.Candy Design
o: Led recordings
/: David Kandell, 2000
301.02 Form
o: Gourmet Organix
/: Paul West, Paula Benson,
   Chris Hilton, 1999
301.03 Alphabetical Order
o: MacFilm
/: Alphabetical Order, 2001
301.04 DSOS1
o: Frontal Studios GmbH.
/: Stefan Gandl /DS, 1999

302.01 Form
o: UniForm
/: P. West, P. Benson, 1997
302.02 büro destruct
o: Coffee Records
/: Lopetz, 1998
302.03 Sanjai Bhana
&: Sanjai Bhana Illustration
   & Design, 2001.
302.04 Bas Visual Concepts
302.05 ghs web graphica
o: A-SEVEN from DESCENTE
/: AKIHIRO IKEGOSHI, 2001
302.06 Dirk Rudolph
o: Motor Music
/: Dirk Rudolph, 1995
302.07 123 KLAN
o: first class graffix
/: 123klan, 2001
302.08 Tim Jester
o: SuperDome
/: Tim Jester, 2002

302.09 tankdesign
o: Tocco, Sascha Bachman,
   Maurice Zubler
/: Katarina Lang, 2002
302.10 büro destruct
o: Hotel Fashion
/: MB, 1998
302.11 Sanjai Bhana
&: Sanjai Bhana Illustration
   & Design, 2001
302.12 Tim Jester
o: ShovelHead
/: Tim Jester, 2000

303.01 Dirk Rudolph
o: Circle Music
/: Dirk Rudolph, 2001
303.02 phunk
&: William Chan/phunk, 2002
303.03 Mutabor
o: Rotring
/: Johannes Plass, 1999
303.04 vektor3
o: private work, stofflager
/: vektor3, 2002
303.05 Dopepope
o: DOPEPOPE
/: Joe Lucchese, 2001-2002
303.06 Niels Meulman
o: clubnight Chemistry
/: N. 'Shoe' Meulman, 1995
303.07 benjamin guedel
o: TA-media
/: benjamin guedel, 1999
303.08 Tim Jester
o: Ronin Dojo
/: Tim Jester, 1997

304.01 Zip Design
o: flyer, The Scala
/: Caroline Moorhouse,
   Neil Bowen, 2000
304.02 Zip Design
304.03 Raoul SINIER

304.04 moniteurs
o: Transmediale,
   Medienfestival
/: Heidi Specker,
   Ivo Gadea, 2001

305.01 raum mannheim
o: projekt über die
   diffenébrücke, friesen
   heimer insel
/: frank hoffmann, 2002

306.01 - .03 e-Types
o: Munthe + Simonsen
/: Jonas Hecksher, 2000

307.01 e-Types
o: Astion A/S
/: Jens Kajus, Marie
   Lübecher, 2000

308.01 Rinzen
o: Smile Dental
/: Rinzen, 1998
308.02 kong.gmbh
&: kong., 2001
308.03 Method
o: fusionOne
/: Olivier Chetelat, 1999
308.04 Method
o: Verb
/: Bethany Koby, Olivier
   Chetelat, Mike Abbink,
   2001

309.01 Versus
o: visomat inc.
/: Alexander Baumgardt, 2000
309.02 U.R.L.
309.03 tankdesign
o: Tocco, Sascha Bachman,
   Maurice Zubler
/: S. Lenggenhager, 2002
309.04 kong.gmbh
o: fff, fotografie franziska
   frutiger, Nidau
/: kong., 1999

309.05 U.R.L.

310.01 MASA Colectivo Gráfico
o: Suministros industriales,
   Lemos C.A.
/: MASA, 2001
310.02 p*star
o: Frehner Consulting
/: Pascal C. Baumann, 2002
310.03 24HR
o: Double-n
/: Ricky Tillblad, 2001
310.04 re-p
310.05 blindresearch
o: blindresearch
/: sven zuege, 2001
310.06 balsi
o: marcel studer, bern
/: balsi, 2002
310.07 balsi
o: ununima, basel
/: balsi, 2001
310.08 büro destruct
o: Deka Dance
/: H1, 2001
310.09 Electronic Curry Ltd.
o: formica, design shop
/: electronic curry, 2002

311.01 DED Associates
o: Sonic 360
/: DED, 1999
311.02 DED Associates
o: WRDC
/: DED, 2001
311.03 Form
o: Wasted Talent
/: Paul West, Paula Benson,
   2000
311.04 typotherapy+design
o: Bug Eyed Records
/: Stephen Crowhurst, 2002
311.05 Luca Ionescu Design
311.06 FORMGEBER
o: Vitamun, Energie Drink
/: Robin Pastyr, 1998

**311.07 CISMA**
**311.08 Bionic System**
o:  Precision Breakbeat
    Research, Germany
✓:  Bionic Systems, 2001
**311.09 FORMGEBER**
o:  Centurion, Real Estade
✓:  Heiko Ulrich, 1996

**312.01 Bionic System**
o:  Bionic-Systems.com
✓:  Bionic Systems, 2000
**312.02 STRADA**
o:  NGN - Fashion Label
✓:  Stefan Rueckerl, Eugen
    Taran, Karin Höfling
**312.03 123KLAN**
∅:  123klan, 1999
**312.04 316tn**
o:  Wettbewerbskommission,
    Firma Bidule
✓:  Irene Filati, 1999

**313.01 Electronic Curry Ltd.**
o:  golden victor, record
    company
✓:  electronic curry, 2000
**313.02 DED Associates**
o:  Crucible
✓:  DED, 2001
**313.03 typotherapy+design**
o:  typotherapy+design
✓:  Stephen Crowhurst, 2002
**313.04 New Future People**
o:  Surf City, Melbourne
✓:  New Future People, 2001
**313.05 MASA Colectivo Gráfico**
o:  Digital 33,
✓:  MASA, 2002
**313.06 dubius?**
o:  5 magazine
✓:  dubius?, 2000
**313.07 jutojo**
o:  logo for Sonarkollektiv
✓:  jutojo, 1998

**313.08 24HR**
o:  Bozooka.com, Logo
✓:  Ricky Tillblad, 2000
**313.09 RosendahlGrafik**
o:  Studio Babelsberg Motion
    Präsentationsentwurf
✓:  Anja Rosendahl, 2001
**313.10 Bionic System**
o:  Bionic-Systems.com
✓:  Bionic Systems, 1999
**313.11 OCKTAK**
o:  Sandokan
✓:  OCKTAK, 2001
**313.12 Disco Döner**

**314.01 Luca Ionescu Design**
**314.02 Luca Ionescu Dcoign**
**314.03 Luca Ionescu Design**
**314.04 inTEAM Graphics**

**315.01 Luca Ionescu Design**
**315.02 Luca Ionescu Design**

**316.01 Eboy**
∅:  eBoy, 2002
**316.02 Zip Design**
o:  Enter, ID for Press
    company
✓:  Neil Bowen and Peter
    Chadwick/Zip, 2000
**316.03 p*star**
o:  Blow Job Jazz Band
✓:  Pascal C. Baumann, 2001

**317.01 Eboy**
∅:  eBoy, 2002

**318.01 Planet Pixel**
**318.02 jum**
o:  Hemisphere
✓:  jum, 2001
**318.03 kong.gmbh**
o:  Postkartenlabel, kong.
    Biel/Bienne
✓:  kong., 1996
**318.04 Disco Döner**

**318.05 BlackDog**
o:  Red Herring
    (Real Restaurants)
✓:  Mark Fox, 1999
**318.06 Eboy**
∅:  eBoy, 1998
**318.07 Form**
o:  CHAPS
✓:  P. West, P. Benson, 1995
**318.08 GRIFF**
**318.09 büro destruct**
∅:  H1 / Lopetz, 2001
**318.10 Eboy**
∅:  eBoy, 2001
**318.11 Tim Jester**
o:  Troop 11
✓:  Tim Joctor, 1999
**318.12 büro destruct**
∅:  Lopetz, 2002

**319.01 anja klausch**
o:  Reinaldo Coddou H.,
    Fotograf
✓:  Anja Klausch, 1998
**319.02 Disco Döner**
**319.03 Tsuyoshi Kusano**
**319.04 Chris Hutchinson**
∅:  Chris Hutchinson, 2002
**319.05 RosendahlGrafik**
o:  Studio Babelsberg Motion
    Präsentationsentwurf
✓:  Anja Rosendahl,
    Lars Borngäber, 2001
**319.06 tankdesign**
o:  Art Affair, Jörg Magener
✓:  Tina Leimbacher, 2000
**319.07 buka grafik**
o:  Kobal Kanapathypillai
✓:  buka, 2001/2002
**319.08 BlackDog**
o:  San Francisco Museum
    of Modern Art
✓:  Mark Fox, 1997
**319.09 GRIFF**
**319.10 nothing medialab**

**319.11 Rio Grafik**
o:  Barbara Rusterholz
✓:  Rio Grafik, 1996
**319.12 Mutabor**
o:  Mutabor 10
✓:  Axel Domke, 2001

**320.01 Eboy**
∅:  eBoy, 2000
**320.02 Eboy**
∅:  eBoy, 2000
**320.03 123KLAN**
∅:  123klan, 2001
**320.04 ghs web graphico**
∅:  AKIHIRO IKEGOSHI, 1999

**321.01 Rinzen**
o:  Venom
✓:  Rinzen, 2002
**321.02 Mutabor**
o:  Beisner Druck
✓:  Simone Campe, Jessica
    Hoppe, 2001
**321.03 Rinzen**
∅:  Rinzen, 2001
**321.04 Sweden**
o:  Dagens Nyheter
✓:  Sweden, 2001

**322.01 BlackDog**
o:  Bianchi USA
✓:  Mark Fox, 1989
**322.02 24HR**
o:  GreanTeam
✓:  Ricky Tillblad, 1996
**322.03 Lobo**
o:  MTV Brasil
✓:  C. Bêla, D. Kamioka, G.
    Marcondes, M. Sader, M.
    de Paula Santos, 2002
**322.04 Gregory Gilbert-Lodge**
∅:  G. Gilbert-Lodge, 1999

**323.01 Bionic System**
o:  Disloc, Germany
✓:  Bionic Systems, 2001

323.02 Luca Ionescu Design
323.03 24HR
o: Baxter, Primal Music
√: Ricky Tillblad, 1998
323.04 phunk
o: Kondense
√: Melvin Chee/phunk, 2001

324.01 - .02 Eboy
∂: eBoy, 2001
324.03 SuperHappyBunny Company
o: Sawdust
√: SuperHappyBunny Company,
1999
324.04 nothing medialab

325.01 lasercade
o: Lasercade
√: Michael Murphy, 2001
325.02 QuickHoney
325.03 Nendo Grafic Squad
∂: Quentaro "Nendo ANI"
Fujimoto, 2000
325.04 Woodtli
o: onthespot
√: Martin Woodtli, 2000

326.01 Finsta
∂: Finsta, 2001
326.02 grasp at the air Co.
o: CLUB KING Co.
√: grasp at the air
Co.,LTD, 2000

327.01 Niels Meulman
o: Caulfield & Tensing
√: N. 'Shoe' Meulman, 1992
327.02 Blammo
o: KO party / poster
√: parra, 2002
327.03 phunk
o: MixPress Inc
√: Melvin Chee/phunk, 2002
327.04 OhioGirl
o: Lakai Limited Footwear /
Girl Skateboards
√: Andy Mueller, 2002

328.01 GRIFF
328.02 Disco Döner
328.03 jum
o: Gaming Company Logo 03
√: jum, 2000
328.04 jum
o: Gaming Company Logo 01
√: jum, 2000
328.05 GRIFF
328.06 jum
o: a paper-sign
√: jum, 2000
328.07 jum
o: chatbook 14
√: jum, 2000
328.08 Form
o: UniForm
√: Paul West, Paula Benson,
Lisa Lee Nick Hard, 1997
328.09 Teamchman
328.10 Maniackers Design
o: Shoeisha Co.,LTD.BOOK &
CD-ROM, Sample Logo.
√: Masayuki Sato, 2000
328.11 GRIFF
328.12 michele del nobolo
∂: michele del nobolo, 2001

329.01 Rinzen
o: Kitten
√: Rinzen, 2001
329.02 Sanjai Bhana
∂: Sanjai Bhana Illustration
& Design, 2001
329.03 MAGNETOFONICA
o: Salon de acuarelistas de
Venezuela
√: Dario Utreras, 2001
329.04 Luca Ionescu Design

332.01 Syrup Helsinki
o: Soumi Design
√: Teemu Suviala, 2001
332.02 MASA Colectivo Gráfico
o: La Leche
√: MASA, 2000

333.01 Luca Ionescu Design
333.02 Luca Ionescu Design

334.01 benjamin guedel
∂: benjamin guedel, 1999
334.02 OhioGirl
o: Shiner / O&O Recordsings
√: Andy Mueller, 2001
334.03 Tsuyoshi Kusano
334.04 Fourskin

335.01 Norm
∂: Norm, 1999-2002
335.02 Die Gestalten
o: Chased by Cowboys
√: Birga Meyer, 2002
335.03 Norm
∂: Norm, 1999-2002
335.04 Tod Hansson
o: Map Magazine
√: Todd Hansson, 2001
335.05 phunk
o: Judo
√: William Chan/phunk, 2001

336.01 Dopepope
o: 33 degrees
√: Joe Lucchese, 2000
336.02 Planet Pixel
336.03 ColdWater Graphiix
o: UPU ltd. Mister
Hollywood Logo
√: Tabito Mizuo, 2000
336.04 Rio Grafik
o: Fucking Beautiful, punk
rock band
√: Rio Grafik, 2001

337.01 Rinzen
o: Venom
√: Rinzen, 2002
337.02 Luca Ionescu Design
337.03 CODE
o: id event ag, switzerland
√: daniel donati, 1998

337.04 Rinzen
o: Venom
√: Rinzen, 2002

338.01 - .03 Rinzen
o: Venom
√: Rinzen, 2002
338.04 jum
o: 1001 Nights
√: jum, 2001
338.05 - .06 incorect
o: Handic Corporation
Women and broken knee
√: incorect, 2002
338.07 incorect
o: incorect logotype
Spank me
√: incorect, 2002
338.08 Dopepope
o: Tim Saccenti Photography
√: Joe Lucchese, 2001-2002

339.01 jum
o: Surfine for
Brett-Magazine
√: jum, 2001
339.02 jum
o: form-one, deviline
√: jum, 2001
339.03 jum
o: Playmate
√: jum, 2001
339.04 jum
o: form-one company launch
√: jum, 1999
339.05 jum
o: Omegaman
√: jum, 1999
339.06 jum
o: form-one man
√: jum, 1999

340.01 Gregory Gilbert-Lodge
o: Riff Raff Bar Zürich,
Andrea Bürgi
√: G. Gilbert-Lodge, 1999

340.02 Luca Ionescu Design
340.03 Fourskin
340.04 Blammo
o: Somethin' else / dj Clyde
   CD cover
/: parra, 2002
340.05 Blammo
o: Rockwell / tweaked horse
   t-shirt logo
/: parra, 2001
340.06 jum
o: Diving
/: jum, 1998
340.07 Blammo
o: KO party / poster
/: parra, 2001
340.08 123KLAN
ȸ: 123klan, 2000

341.01 jum
o: GUM 5 Sinne
/: jum, 1999
341.02 Syryp Helsinki
o: City of Turku
/: Teemu Suviala, 2002
341.03 jum
o: Eliteforce Mascot
/: jum, 2001
341.04 Judith Zaugg
o: Open
/: Bauer / Borkowski, 1998
341.05 hungryfordesign
o: hungryfordesign
/: Nando Costa, 2000

342.01 jum
o: Meermaid for
   Brett-Magazine
/: jum, 2001
342.02 jum
o: Schiffe versenken
/: jum, 2001
342.03 jum
o: Nur für Dich
/: jum, 1999
342.04 tikkigirl
o: tikkigirl
/: isabell welz, 2001

342.05 nothing medialab
342.06 LEVEL1
o: Sorry, Now under
   construction
/: Tsuyoshi Hirooka, 2001
342.07 designershock/DSOS1
o: Babuschka Logo und
   T-Shirt print
/: Birte Ludwig, 2001
342.08 unikum graphic design
ȸ: unikum graphic design,
   S. Ringgenberg,
   B. Flueckiger, 2002
342.09 - .10 Zinc
o: survive
   (flyercenter.cccb.org)
/: Cynthia Martinez, 2000
342.11 - .12 Form
o: The Beat/Fuji
   International Productions
/: Paul West, Paula Benson,
   Chris Hilton, 2002

343.01 xonetik
ȸ: [mars] marcelo perez,
   xonetik, 1999
343.02 BlackDog
o: Amyx Foto
/: Mark Fox, 1990
343.03 John J.Candy Design
o: Homokalas (Gay club
   promotors)
/: David Kandell, 2001
343.04 MASA Colectivo Gráfico
o: Genetica,
   Genetica Records
/: MASA, 2002
343.05 LEVEL1
o: Recycle me
/: Tsuyoshi Hirooka, 2000
343.06 Gregory Gilbert-Lodge
343.07 jum
o: Surprise!
/: jum, 1999
343.08 Gregory Gilbert-Lodge
o: Gobler Toys
/: Steve Casino, 2000

343.09 MK12
o: A symbol to warn folks if
   there is an antiquated
   and stupid looking Olde
   Tyme Ghost about.
/: MK12, 1911
343.10 MK12
o: Burt Chan is a Chiro-
   practor for those posture
   slackers in the Graphic
   Design field.
/: MK12, 2000
343.11 nothing medialab
343.12 Move Design
o: Bridge Design
/: Samuel Lising, Peter
   Spreenberg, Richard
   Leighton, 2000

344.01 LEVEL1
o: clubking, LOVE & HATE
/: Tsuyoshi Hirooka, 2001
344.02 LEVEL1
o: clubking, snakeman show
/: Tsuyoshi Hirooka, 2001
344.03 incorect
o: Hurry up!
/: incorect, 2002
344.04 Chris Hutchinson
ȸ: Chris Hutchinson, 2002

345.01 phunk
o: Hotel Love
/: Melvin Chee/phunk, 2002

346.01 jum
o: Tiki-Surf
/: jum, 2001
346.02 Ross Imms
o: www.fortyeightk.com
/: Ross Imms, 2001
346.03 phunk
ȸ: Melvin Chee/phunk, 2001

347.01 - .03 Derrick Hodgson
o: MDRL creative
/: Derrick Hodgson, 2001/2002

348.01 Dopepope
o: DOPEPOPE
/: Joe Lucchese, 2001-2002
348.02 Dopepope
o: DOPEPOPE, 33 degrees
/: Joe Lucchese, 2000-2002

349.01 Dopepope
o: DOPEPOPE
/: Joe Lucchese, 2001-2002

350.01 OhioGirl
o: Lakai Limited Footwear /
   Girl Skateboards
/: Andy Mueller, 2002
350.02 bigsexyland
o: bigsexyland.de, design
   mag
/: Björn Hansen, 2002
350.03 Zookeeper
o: IGNITE (zookeeper ltd UK)
/: dod (olivier ducuing),
   2001
350.04 michele de nobolo
ȸ: michele del nobolo
   self promotion, 2001
350.05 inTEAM Graphics
350.06 Zookeeper
o: ORANGE MILK Power
   popband
/: dod (olivier ducuing),
   2001

351.01 incorect
ȸ: incorect, 2002
351.02 Superpopstudio
o: Superpopstudio website
/: Superpopstudio, 2002

352.01 MAGNETOFONICA
o: Hermanas Trapenses.
   (Charity food -artesanal
   pasta made by nuns-)
/: Dario Utreras, 2001
352.02 Tsuyoshi Kusano

**352.03 phunk**
o:  Judo
/:  Melvin Chee/phunk, 2001
**352.04 BlackDog**
o:  Jesus Christ Superstar
    (Landmark Entertainment)
/:  Mark Fox, 1992
**352.05 Disco Döner**

**353.01 phunk**
o:  Judo
/:  Melvin Chee/phunk, 2001
**353.02 Hellgolfers**
**353.03 dubius?**
o:  Testosterone records
/:  dubius?, 1999
**353.04 Power Graphixx**
o:  Cleaning, printing logo
    for Cleaning
/:  Power Graphixx, 2001
**353.05 Planet Pixel**
**353.06 Planet Pixel**
**353.07 Rinzen**
o:  Kitten
/:  Rinzen, 2001

**354.01 ghs web graphica**
&#11088;:  AKIHIRO IKEGOSHI, 2002
**354.02 Blammo**
o:  Rockwell / rocky
    t-shirt logo
/:  parra, 2002
**354.03 Fourskin**
o:  Fourskin
/:  Patrick Tan, 2001/2002
**354.04 Superpopstudio**
o:  Superpopstudio website
/:  Superpopstudio, 2002
**354.05 Dopepope**
o:  DOPEPOPE
/:  Joe Lucchese, 2001-2002
**354.06 Fourskin**
**354.07 Blammo**
o:  Rockwell / Jimmy
    t-shirt logo
/:  parra, 2001

**354.08 Nendo Grafic Squad**
o:  KIRIN BEER, AOI promotion
/:  Quentaro "Nendo ANI"
    Fujimoto, 2001

**355.01 Fourskin**
**355.02 Luca Ionescu Design**
**355.03 Luca Ionescu Design**
**355.04 Cyclone Graphix**
**355.05 Gregory Gilbert-Lodge**
o:  james blunt growshop
    Zürich, Bruno Hiltebrand
/:  G. Gilbert-Lodge, 1998
**355.06 incorect**
o:  Razor - Be Beautifull
/:  incorect, 2002
**355.07 Luca Ionescu Design**
**355.08 Nendo Grafic Squad**
&#11088;:  Quentaro "Nendo ANI"
    Fujimoto, 2000

**356.01 Blammo**
o:  Somethin' else / mixtape
    cover logo
/:  parra, 2001
**356.02 Blammo**
o:  Mojo Concerts / Busta
    Rhymes flyer
/:  parra, 2002
**356.03 phunk**
o:  Judo
/:  Alvin Tan/phunk, 2001
**356.04 Blammo**
o:  Rockwell / Monk
    t-shirt logo
/:  parra, 2002
**356.05 Blammo**
o:  Virgin records / Extince
/:  parra, 2001
**356.06 Blammo**
o:  my friend Guillaume
/:  parra, 2001
**356.07 Blammo**
o:  Jazzcrimes magazine
    amsterdam
/:  parra, 2001

**356.08 Fourskin**

**357.01 - .02 tankdesign**
o:  The Hair Lounge,
    Michaela Suter
/:  Katarina Lang, 2001
**357.03 Blammo**
o:  Somethin' else / dj Clyde
    CD cover
/:  parra, 2002
**357.04 Zip Design**
o:  Zip Self promotion
/:  Ruby Lee, Malcolm Buick,
    Peter Chadwick, 1999
**357.05 hungryfordesign**
o:  Burt Reynolds
/:  Nando Costa, 2001
**357.06 Alphabetical Order**
o:  N/A
/:  Alphabetical Order, 1996
**357.07 incorect**
o:  Two CORRECT Business
    company logos
/:  incorect, 2002
**357.08 incorect**
o:  Incorect Food Company
/:  incorect, 2002

**358.01 Mutabor**
o:  Mutabor 10
/:  Carsten Raffel, 2001
**358.02 jum**
o:  Gorilla Events
/:  jum, 2002
**358.03 Cyclone Graphix**
**358.04 Mutabor**
o:  Mutabor 10
/:  Carsten Raffel, 2001
**358.05 MK12**
o:  La Fábrica del Mannequin
/:  MK12, 1984
**358.06 Dopepope**
o:  Joe Lucchese, DOPEPOPE,
    2001-2002
**358.07 Electronic Curry Ltd.**
o:  formica, special use
/:  electronic curry, 2002

**358.08 24HR**
o:  Dixie
/:  Ricky Tillblad, 2001
**358.09 Luca Ionescu Design**
**358.10 Hirschindustries**
o:  The Hirschpeople
/:  Ollie Peters, 2000-01

**359.01 AREADESIGN**
o:  BOLTON GROOVE, House
    Music DJ's
/:  Alberto Russo, 2002
**359.02 Jorge Alderete**
&#11088;:  Jorge Alderete, 2000
**359.03 Yipyop**
**359.04 MASA Colectivo Gráfico**
o:  La Cocina Records,
    Trece Discos
/:  MASA, 2001
**359.05 Niels Jansson**
o:  Coconut surf gear
/:  Niels Jansson, 2001
**359.06 Luca Ionescu Design**
**359.07 Blammo**
o:  KO party / logo + ROCK
    WELL clothing Logo
/:  parra, 2001
**359.08 123KLAN**
&#11088;:  123klan, 2002
**359.09 Mutabor**
o:  Mutabor 10
/:  Carsten Raffel, 2001
**359.10 Syrup Helsinki**
o:  Soundfreak Oy
/:  Teemu Suviala, 2001
**359.11 xonetik**
o:  xonetik
/:  [mars] marcelo perez, 2000
**359.12 Zookeeper**
o:  Mosaika, voix
    de femmes festival
/:  dod(olivier ducuing), 2001

**360.01 automatic art + design**
o:  c'est susan hair care
/:  charles wilkin, 2000

360.02 phunk
o: phunk
/: Jackson Tan/phunk, 2001
360.03 Artificial Environments
360.04 MASA Colectivo Gráfico
o: Repuestos Urbe clothing,
  Urbe Inc.
/: MASA, 1997
360.05 New Future People
o: Golden Joy Products
/: New Future People, 2002
360.06 PXPress
360.07 büro destruct
o: Evil Production
/: Moritz, 2000
360.08 MIGUEL ANGEL LEYVA
ø: MIGUEL ANGEL LEYVA, 1998
360.09 Fourskin
360.10 Chris Hutchinson
o: submission to thefinktank
  logo competition
/: Chris Hutchinson, 2001
360.11 OCKTAK
o: OCKTAK - SIMPLEFOLK
/: OCKTAK, 1999
360.12 New Future People
o: Golden Joy Products
/: New Future People, 2002
360.13 Judith Zaugg
o: Kornhausbibliotheken
/: Judith Zaugg, 2001
360.14 tomotomo.net
o: VIA:
/: tomoko takeue, 1999
360.15 Luca Ionescu Design
360.16 Alphabetical Order
o: N/A
/: Alphabetical Order, 1998

361.01 tokidoki
361.02 New Future People
o: Golden Joy Products
/: New Future People, 2002
361.03 balsi
o: dead but holy
  productions, bern
/: balsi, 2001

361.04 Hendrik Hellige
361.05 jum
o: Headhunting Tribe
/: jum, 2001
361.06 Power Graphixx
o: DLR Inc., printing logo
  for Trouper
/: Power Graphixx, 2000
361.07 Thomas Mischler
ø: Thomas Mischler,2002
361.08 SAKAMOTO
o: me-anti-me.com
/: SAKAMOTO, 2001
361.09 jum
o: R-Flaming
/: jum, 2002
361.10 Thomas Mischler
ø: Thomas Mischler, 2001
361.11 Rinzen
o: Venom
/: Rinzen, 2002
361.12 Eboy
ø: eBoy, 1999
361.13 Gobler Toys
o: Gobler Toys
/: Steve Casino and Jen
  Cooper, 2002
361.14 augenbluten
o: cyber hills fashion
/: IF, 2000
361.15 phunk
o: Judo
/: Jackson Tan/phunk, 2000

362.01 Rinzen
o: Venom
/: Rinzen, 2002
362.02 - .03 Mirko Borsche
o: Tiger magazine/jetzt
  Magazin
/: Mirko Borsche, 2002

363.01 Gregory Gilbert-Lodge
o: The Face London, Craig
  Tilford
/: G. Gilbert-Lodge, 2000

364.01 Teamchman
364.02 Teamchman
364.03 Teamchman
364.04 moniteurs
o: a.k.t. Informations-
  systeme
/: Heidi Specker, Volker
  Schlecht, 2000
364.05 Artificial Environments
364.06 Artificial Environments
364.07 Artificial Environments
364.08 Artificial Environments
364.09 AREADESIGN
o: BIFF2000 & BILLY BEAR,
  Rap Music Group
/: Alberto Russo, 2002
364.10 büro destruct
o: Barry
/: MB, 2000
364.11 jum
o: Bullroarer
/: jum, 2000
364.12 AREADESIGN
o: BLUEWIN,(Moskito Logo,
  Bluewin web animation)
/: Alberto Russo, 2001

365.01 BlackDog
ø: Mark Fox, 1985
365.02 BlackDog
o: Eveready Battery Co.
/: Mark Fox,
  Jeff Carino, 1999
365.03 Norm
ø: Norm, 1999-2002
365.04 Blammo
ø: parra / logo, 2001
365.05 automatic art + design
o: urban outfitters
/: charles wilkin, 1997
365.06 Form
o: Atomic Kitten/Innocent
  Records
/: Paul West, Paula Benson,
  John Siddle, 1999
365.07 DED Associates
o: BUYDED.COM
/: DED, 2002

365.08 incorect
o: Dog cleaner system, Issue
  from "user's guide manual"
/: incorect, 2002
365.09 DED Associates
o: La Leche
/: ED, 2001
365.10 DSOS1
o: DS, DSOS1
/: Stefan Gandl /DS, 2001

366.01 - .02 tankdesign
o: Refental Ranch, Erika
  Meyer-Burkard
/: Tina Leimbacher, 2002
366.03 Zip Design
o: Orang Utan,
  photography agency
/: Neil Bowen, Peter
  Chadwick, 2000
366.04 Mutabor
o: Cult Cars AG
/: Mutabor, Axel Domke, 2001
366.05 phunk
o: Electric Gorilla
/: William Chan/phunk, 2001
366.06 123KLAN
o: event organisation
/: 123klan, 2000
366.07 GRIFF
366.08 Bionic System
o: Disloc, Germany
/: Bionic Systems, 2001
366.09 Alphabetical Order
o: Koala Press
/: Alphabetical Order, 2002
366.10 Luca Ionescu Design
366.11 Luca Ionescu Design
366.12 SuperHappyBunny Company
ø: SuperHappyBunny Company
  2001
366.13 phunk
o: Dead Inc
/: Melvin Chee/phunk, 2001

367.01 Luca Ionescu Design
367.02 Disco Döner

**367.03 e-Types**
o:  Gyldendal
/:  Marie Lübecher, Rasmus
    Koch, Jonas Hecksher,2000
**367.04 blindresearch**
o:  burt
/:  sven zuege, 2002
**367.05 Blammo**
o:  www.Blammo.nl,
    sticker logo
/:  parra, 2001
**367.06 Blammo**
o:  Rockwell / Sir Robin
    t-shirt logo
/:  parra, 2001
**367.07 Luca Ionescu Design**
**367.08 Luca Ionescu Design**
**367.09 phunk**
o:  2k tees
/:  Alvin Tan/phunk, 2002
**367.10 New Future People**
o:  Golden Joy Products
/:  New Future People, 2002
**367.11 Maniackers Design**
o:  holiday keikaku, Design
    Company Logo.
/:  Masayuki Sato, 2000
**367.12 Tim Jester**
o:  International Aikido
    Association
/:  Tim Jester, 1997
**367.13 blindresearch**
∅:  sven zuege, 2000

**368.01 Gregory Gilbert-Lodge**
o:  Rote Fabrik Zürich, Mischa
    Sutter
/:  G. Gilbert-Lodge, 2001
**368.02 minigram**
o:  minitrophy
/:  minigram, 2002
**368.03 Hirschindustries**
o:  The Hirschpeople
/:  Ollie Peters, 2000-01

**369.01 Blammo**
o:  Stichting Inzet /
    BaoBab Logo
/:  parra, 2001

**370.01 Mentary**
o:  mentary
/:  gregory chapuisat, 2001
**370.02 CODE**
o:  617 club, switzerland
/:  vera studhalter, 2001
**370.03 phunk**
o:  2k tees
/:  Melvin Chee/phunk, 2002
**370.04 incorect**
o:  Cancer Numérique; logo
/:  incorect. 2002
**370.05 Blammo**
o:  Blammo.nl / logo
/:  parra, 2002
**370.06 Blammo**
o:  Saiko / animal
    t-shirt logo
/:  parra, 2000
**370.07 phunk**
∅:  William Chan/phunk, 2002
**370.08 jum**
o:  Stuck on Design
/:  jum, 1999
**370.09 Luca Ionescu Design**
**370.10 Blammo**
**370.11 Blammo**
o:  Rockwell / cowboy
    t-shirt logo
/:  parra, 2001
**370.12 Blammo**
o:  Rednose Distrikt / HumHum
    records & Rednose
    distrikt logo
/:  parra, 2002
**370.13 minigram**
o:  play by minigram
/:  minigram, 2002
**370.14 automatic art + design**
o:  capricorn records
/:  charles wilkin, 1999

**370.15 - .16 Blammo**
o:  Saiko / animal
    t-shirt logo
/:  parra, 2000

**371.01 HandGun**
o:  art city / city of
    minneapolis
/:  david zack custer, 2001
**371.02 Mika Mischler**
**371.03 Deanne Cheuk**
**371.04 designiskinky**
o:  Design is Kinky
/:  Andrew Johnstone, 2000

**372.01 minigram**
o:  2mg
/:  minigram, 2002

**373.01 minigram**
o:  2mg
/:  minigram, 2002

**374.01 - .02 lasercade**
o:  Lasercade
/:  Michael Murphy, 2001
**374.03 Mentary**
o:  mentary
/:  gregory chapuisat, 2001
**374.04 POSITRON CO.,LTD.**
o:  DESTROYDER, THE MAD
    CAPSURE MARKETS
/:  Hiroaki Doi, 2000
**374.05 Tsuyoshi Kusano**
**374.06 Teamchman**
**374.07 Mentary**
o:  upperplayground
/:  gregory chapuisat, 2001
**374.08 Dopepope**
o:  33 degrees
/:  Joe Lucchese, 2000
**374.09 hungryfordesign**
o:  hungryfordesign
/:  Nando Costa, 1999
**374.10 Apakstudio**
o:  Apakstudio
/:  Aaron Piland, 2002

**375.01 Luca Ionescu Design**
**375.02 123KLAN**
o:  electro music label
/:  123klan, 1999
**375.03 Bionic System**
o:  Bionic-Systems.com
/:  Bionic Systems, 1998
**375.04 Sanjai Bhana**
∅:  Sanjai Bhana Illustration
    & Design, 2001
**375.05 Bionic System**
o:  Bionic-Systems.com
/:  Bionic Systems, 2001

**376.01 CODE**
o:  gerling racing
    switzerland
/:  Ryosuke Kawaguchi, 2001
**376.02 grasp at the air Co.**
o:  Higashinakano Film
    festival of ATSUSHI(Event
    LOGO for a TV program
/:  grasp at the air
    Co.,LTD, 2000
**376.03 Hirschindustries**
o:  Burner Prod.
/:  Ollie Peters, 2001
**376.04 Mutabor**
o:  Lüneburg Haus
/:  H. Paravincini, 1999
**376.05 HandGun**
o:  Soo Visual Arts Center
/:  david zack custer, 2001
**376.06 moniteurs**
o:  Filmgalerie 451,
    Videothek
/:  Sibylle Schlaich, 1995
**376.07 incorect**
o:  INFIRE Corp. -
    Childrens in fire
/:  incorect, 2002
**376.08 123KLAN**
∅:  123klan, 1999
**376.09 büro destruct**
o:  Stuntwear
/:  Moritz, 2002

**376.10 Alphabetical Order**
o: N/A
/: Alphabetical Order, 1998
**376.11 BlackDog**
o: Café Speed, Chip Ganassi
Racing Team (Target)
/: M. Fox, M. Lidke, 1998
**376.12 BlackDog**
o: Dallas Burn, Major League
Soccer (Nike)
/: Mark Fox, 1995
**376.13 Luca Ionescu Design**
**376.14 Bionic System**
o: Rotweiss, Germany
/: Bionic Systems, 2001

**377.01 raum mannheim**
o: kulturzentrum alte
feuerwache mannheim
/: frank hoffmann, 1999
**377.02 Rot**
**377.03 344 Design**
o: Modernista!
/: Stefan G. Bucher, 2000
**377.04 Fernando Leal**
o: Trama
/: Fernando Leal, 2002
**377.05 HandGun**
o: dairy council
/: david zack custer, 1997
**377.06 Form**
o: Ultra/EastWest Records
/: Paul West, Paula Benson,
John Siddle, 1998

**378.01 HandGun**
o: handgun
/: david zack custer, 2001
**378.02 benjamin guedel**
o: indiana skateboards
/: benjamin guedel, 2001
**378.03 HandGun**
o: handgun
/: david zack custer, 2001
**378.04 Blammo**
o: Saiko / Un t-shirt logo
/: parra, 2000

**378.05 HandGun**
o: handgun
/: david zack custer, 2002
**378.06 123KLAN**
⌀: 123klan, 2002
**378.07 jum**
o: Armed Animals
/: jum, 2000
**378.08 Chris Hutchinson**
o: spec for Handgun Control
/: Chris Hutchinson, 1999
**378.09 Blammo**
o: Stricly magazine,
gun logo
/: parra, 2002
**378.10 hungryfordesign**
o: aquababy
/: Nando Costa, 2000

**379.01 nothing medialab**
**379.02 John J.Candy Design**
o: John J. Candy design
(for love symbol)
/: John Esberg, 2001
**379.03 Trixi Barmettler**
**379.04 phunk**
o: Shoppe SixteenluV
/: Alvin Tan/phunk, 2001
**379.05 DED Associates**
o: Gash
/: DED, 2000
**379.06 Tsuyoshi Kusano**
**379.07 Zinc**
o: chicoflama
/: Cynthia martinez, 1999
**379.08 p*star**
o: UK Love, Tribute
to the Queen
/: Pascal C. Baumann, 2002
**379.09 New Future People**
o: Golden Joy Products
/: New Future People, 2002

**380.01 123KLAN**
**380.02 FORMGEBER**
o: Profashion, Fashion Label
/: Rolf Rinklin, 1999

**380.03 Tim Jester**
o: 6-spot
/: Tim Jester, 1998
**380.04 Sweden**
o: Fox Sports, Cliff Freeman
& Partners, Traktor Film
/: Sweden
**380.05 Nendo Grafic Squad**
⌀: Quentaro "Nendo ANI"
Fujimoto, 2001
**380.06 nothing medialab**
**380.07 Thomas Mischler**
⌀: Thomas Mischler, 2002
**380.08 Blammo**
o: Rockwell (t-shirt logo)
/: parra, 2001
**380.09 tankdesign**
o: Tank
/: Katarina Lang, 2001
**380.10 CODE**
o: atlantis club,
switzerland
/: Ryosuke Kawaguchi, 2002
**380.11 phunk**
o: Judo
/: Melvin Chee/phunk, 2001
**380.12 Tsuyoshi Kusano**

**381.01 Machine**
o: Sporkcreative Agency
/: DEPT, 2000
**381.02 Cyclone Graphix**
**381.03 Luca Ionescu Design**
**381.04 Zip Design**
o: Nebula Records
/: Chris Harrison and Peter
Chadwick/Zip, 2000
**381.05 p*star**
o: P* Urban Design
/: Pascal C. Baumann, 2001
**381.06 MASA Colectivo Gráfico**
o: 13, Trece discos
/: MASA, 2001
**381.07 Zip Design**
o: Groove Armada,
Jive/Pepper Records
/: Malcolm Buick and Peter
Chadwick/Zip, 1999

**381.08 123KLAN**
⌀: 123klan, 2000
**381.09 yippieyeah**
o: Ultrafunky Media
/: Bauer / Borkowski, 2001
**381.10 nothing medialab**
**381.11 FORMGEBER**
o: Massive Development, game
developer
/: Jochen Eeuwyk, 1999

**382.01 tankdesign**
o: Art Affair, Jörg Magener
/: Katarina Lang / Tina
Leimbacher, 2000
**382.02 büro destruct**
o: Flaregun, America
/: MB, 1999
**382.03 Bionic System**
o: F1rst Design, Germany
/: Bionic Systems, 2000
**382.04 augenbluten**
o: reason
/: IF, 2000
**382.05 Form**
o: Five/RCA
/: P. West, P. Benson, 1999
**382.06 ColdWater Graphiix**
o: Glide
/: Tabito Mizuo , 2001
**382.07 phunk**
o: Judo
/: William Chan/phunk, 2000
**382.08 p*star**
o: p*star
/: Pascal C. Baumann, 2002
**382.09 tankdesign**
o: Tank
/: Katarina Lang, 2001
**382.10 büro destruct**
o: World of Venus
/: Moritz, 2001

**383.01 Blammo**
o: Last Chance shop in the
jungle of suriname
/: parra, 2001

**383.02 Form**
o: Ultra/EastWest Records
/: Paul West, Paula Benson,
  John Siddle, 1998
**383.03 Blammo**
o: Rockwell / star&
  t-shirt logo
/: parra, 2001
**383.04 minigram**
o: ninja star
/: minigram, 2002
**383.05 Mentary**
o: upperplayground
/: gregory chapuisat, 2001

**384.01 Hirschindustries**
o: The Studio Bakers, Delhi
/: Ollie Peters, 2000
**384.02 Blammo**
o: Rockwell (t-shirt logo)
/: parra, 2001
**384.03 Zip Design**
o: Mob Records
/: Mr Jago/Zip, 2001
**384.04 Finsta**
o: El Sheriffo, rap producer
/: Finsta, 2001
**384.05 Finsta**
&#8499;: Finsta, t-shirt, 2001
**384.06 Finsta**
o: Fuck Ya'll productions,
  record label
/: Finsta, 2001
**384.07 FORMGEBER**
o: Loft, Music Club Redesign
/: Siegmund Schlag, 1996
**384.08 Deanne Cheuk**
**384.09 Luca Ionescu Design**
**384.10 Sanjai Bhana**
o: AUX
/: Sanjai Bhana Illustration
  & Design, 2000.
**384.11 Disco Döner**

**385.01 RosendahlGrafik**
o: Babelsberg Motion
  Pictures
/: Lars Borngräber, 2001

**385.02 p*star**
o: Kulturzentrum
  Stufenbau Ittigen
/: Pascal C. Baumann , 1998
**385.03 Planet Pixel**
**385.04 Deanne Cheuk**
**385.05 John J.Candy Design**
o: Urban deli (Information
  regarding metropolitan
  cities)
/: David Kandell, 2000
**385.06 WG Berlin**
o: Solid Ground Events
/: Andreas Wegner, 2001

**386.01 TOI Inc.**
o: TOI, logo application,
  the streets of Ooze City
/: TOI, 2002
**386.02 TOI Inc.**
o: Ooze project
/: TOI, 1999 - 2002

**387.01 - .02 TOI Inc.**
o: Ooze project
/: TOI, 1999 - 2002

**388.01 - .02 Mirko Borsche**
o: Tiger Magazine/
  jetzt Magazin
/: Mirko Borsche, 2002

**389.01 - .04 Mirko Borsche**
o: Tiger Magazine/
  jetzt Magazin
/: Mirko Borsche, 2002

**390.01 Pfadfinderei**

**391.01 Tsuyoshi Kusano**
**391.02 Tsuyoshi Kusano**

A Selected Logo Collection

Edited by R. Klanten, M. Mischler, N. Bourquin
Layout and Design by N. Bourquin
Fontdesign T-Star Mono Rounded by M. Mischler, Font:
Cover Design by Lopetz/Büro Destruct
LosLogos is a trademark of Büro Destruct, Berne

Prologue:"The logo: taking stock" by Roland Müller
Preface:  "What is a logo?" by Manuel Krebs, Dimitri Bruni/Norm
Translated by Michael Robinson
Proof-Reading by Sonja Commentz

Production management by Janni Milstrey
Production assistance by Katja Haub, Birga Meyer, Kathrin Jachmann

Editorial support Japan by Junko Tozaki

Published by Die Gestalten Verlag, Berlin
Made in Germany

Check out: www.loslogos.org

Bibliographic information published by the Deutsche Nationalbibliothek
The  Deutsche Nationalbibliothek lists this publication in the Deutsche
Nationalbibliografie; detailed bibliographic data are available in the Internet
at http://dnb.d-nb.de.

ISBN 978-3-931126-92-6

For your local dgv distributor please check out:
www.die-gestalten.de